WHITE FLAG

Putz Thun

PAMPAM

Women with cameras. Pictures of you=us

by

Luca Lo Pinto

At the start of the 1970s the Austrian photographer and filmmaker Friedl Kubelka made a series of self-portraits entitled Pin-Ups, photographing herself in seductive poses in front of a mirror. In response to a question about this work, in a recent interview Kubelka said: "I was such a nice-looking young girl and I was so unhappy... I wanted to be the object of desire. I wanted somebody. But I wanted to also be the person that renders the object of desire... There's a tension between voyeurism and exhibitionism. You think of the model as the exhibitionist and the photographer as the voyeur. In fact, the voyeur has to decide his desire in a split second, using the shutter of the camera. You can hear his desire. Good photographers always reveal themselves somehow more than the model."

Perhaps because, in artistic terms, they too grew up in Vienna, Hanna Putz and Sophie Thun seem to have absorbed Kubelka's words: they have found a way of revealing themselves while performing simultaneously as both subject and object.

White Flag is a duo work that was conceived to be organised in the pages of a book. It is the result of a close dialogue between two young women, two photographers, two friends, developed in a frenetic, engaged, lively ping pong of images.

Over the course of two years, Hanna and Sophie have photographed each other in a constant reversal of roles, poses, gazes and spaces; in doing so, the boundaries between mutual portraiture and self-portraiture have been blurred.

In the collective imagination, especially in that of fashion, women have always been the object of a male gaze, the object of desire par excellence. In this perspective, Jo Spence, Francesca Woodman and Vivian Maier were among the first photographers to overturn the stereotype of the woman as muse/object, through self-portraits that challenged traditional gender roles. Their photographs are statements about the power of the subjective gaze: they express the urgent need, on the part of their makers, to choose for themselves their mode of representation. They somehow anticipated the question posed later by feminist culture: "where do women stand in relation to the subjective experience of looking and making meaning of images of women?"

Hanna and Sophie answer this question with a visual notebook that lends itself to a wide range of interpretations.

They photograph each other in the widest range of settings: the open countryside, a train, offices, a studio. All the photographs are edited in keeping with a precise composition, faithfully reporting on the experience as it transpired. Diptychs in which from time to time they appear in the act of taking the picture, or of its preparation. Each diptych registers a dual gaze inside a shared zone, where the space of the images is brought alive by the bodies of Hanna and Sophie, their cameras and the places in which they move.

Having set the rules of the game, they interpret them with absolute freedom, giving rise to a lively, carefree reflection on the act of making photographs itself.

Ansel Adams asserted that there are always two people in any photograph: the photographer and the viewer. In this case there are three, and the viewer is put in the position of being simultaneously participant and voyeur, inside and outside.

It is a dualism of roles similar to that of the protagonists, who alternate between being the prey and the huntress in a vortex of shots. A physical and metaphorical duel in an utterly feminine key that erases the vertical photographer/model relationship; they wield the camera like a weapon with which to capture and take possession of the other. The device takes on the semblance of an optical prosthesis, an extension of the body and the gaze, to take part in a struggle where the roles of the "dominant" and the "dominated" are subjected to constant slippage.

Though photography is generally considered a means of capturing reality and is connected to an idea of voyeurism, here both subjects have the awareness of being caught on film. Nevertheless, this happens inside an improvised choreography where control seems to be threatened by the fact that the photographs are taken in an almost synchronistic way, making it hard to precisely govern the composition of the image, as demonstrated by the off-focus shots. If on the one hand the analog camera implies more time for the shot and the impossibility of seeing a preview, the photographs of Hanna and Sophie suggest an immediacy typical of a digital device. In White Flag the camera, besides being a tool, is the protagonist, reaching the point of often covering the faces of the artists, transforming them into hybrid creatures.

The dual movement between surrender to the unconscious and the fully intentional shot resembles zooming in and out, plunging in and then retaking one's distance. While on the one hand this mechanism ensures maximum heterogeneity, on the other it lays the groundwork for a precise, strategic strike, deprived of any factor of chance. The process is like a game of cat and mouse: the cat pretends to let the mouse escape, only to grab it again, taking back control before letting it go once more, ready for the next assault.

If taking a person's picture usually means transforming them into an object that can be symbolically possessed, here the equality of forces and the complicity shared by Hanna and Sophie subvert this interpretation, transforming the battle into a declaration of love.

IMPRINT

Edited by Hanna Putz and Sophie Thun
Design by Ismini Adami
Text by Luca Lo Pinto

Translation by Stephen V. Piccolo
Proof Reading by Sarah Thomas

Printed by Holzhausen Druck GmbH

Edition 500
Published by PAMPAM Publishing
Nollendorfstraße 11
10777 Berlin
Germany

pampampublishing.com
info@pampampublishing.com

All photographs by
Hanna Putz and Sophie Thun 2019

Printed in Austria

PAMPAM Publishing: ISBN 978-3-9820480-1-7

THANK YOU:

Amaryllis Sommerer, Rupert Putz,
Róża & Franz Thun, Daniel Richter,
Ismini Adami, Luca Lo Pinto,
Barbara Putz-Plecko, Mima Schwahn,
Sarah Thomas, Pascal Petignat.

Distributed by VfmK
Verlag für moderne Kunst GmbH

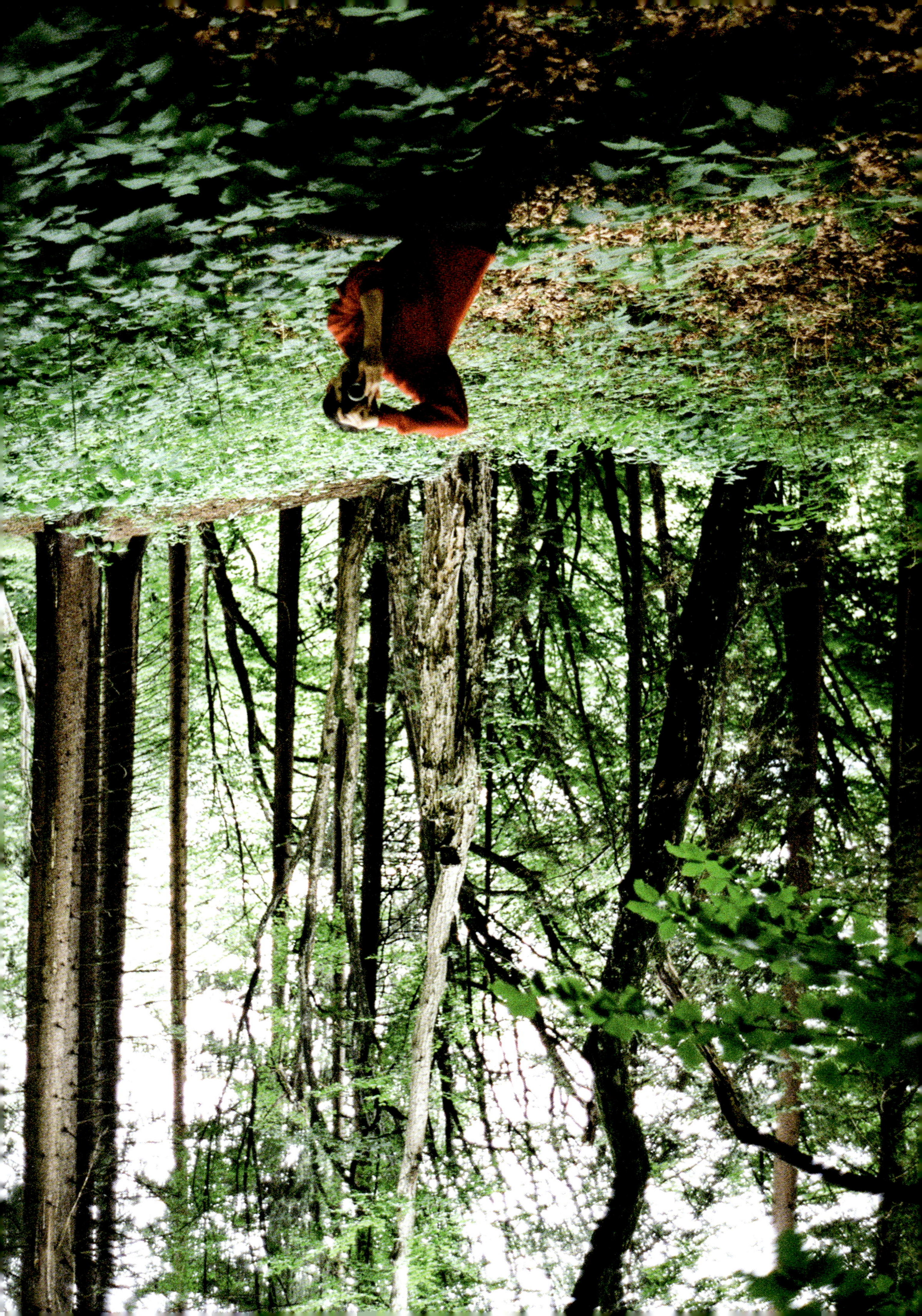

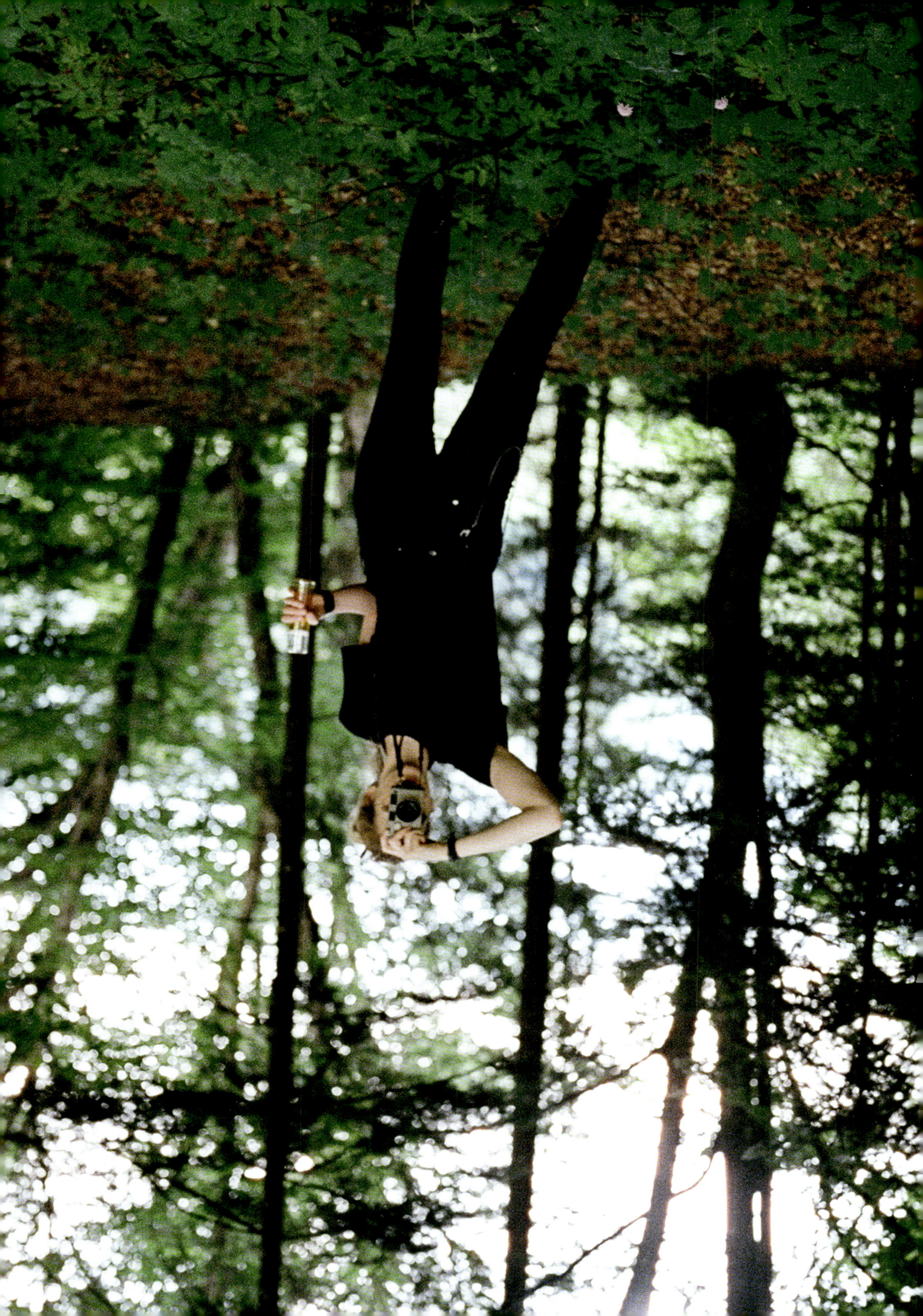

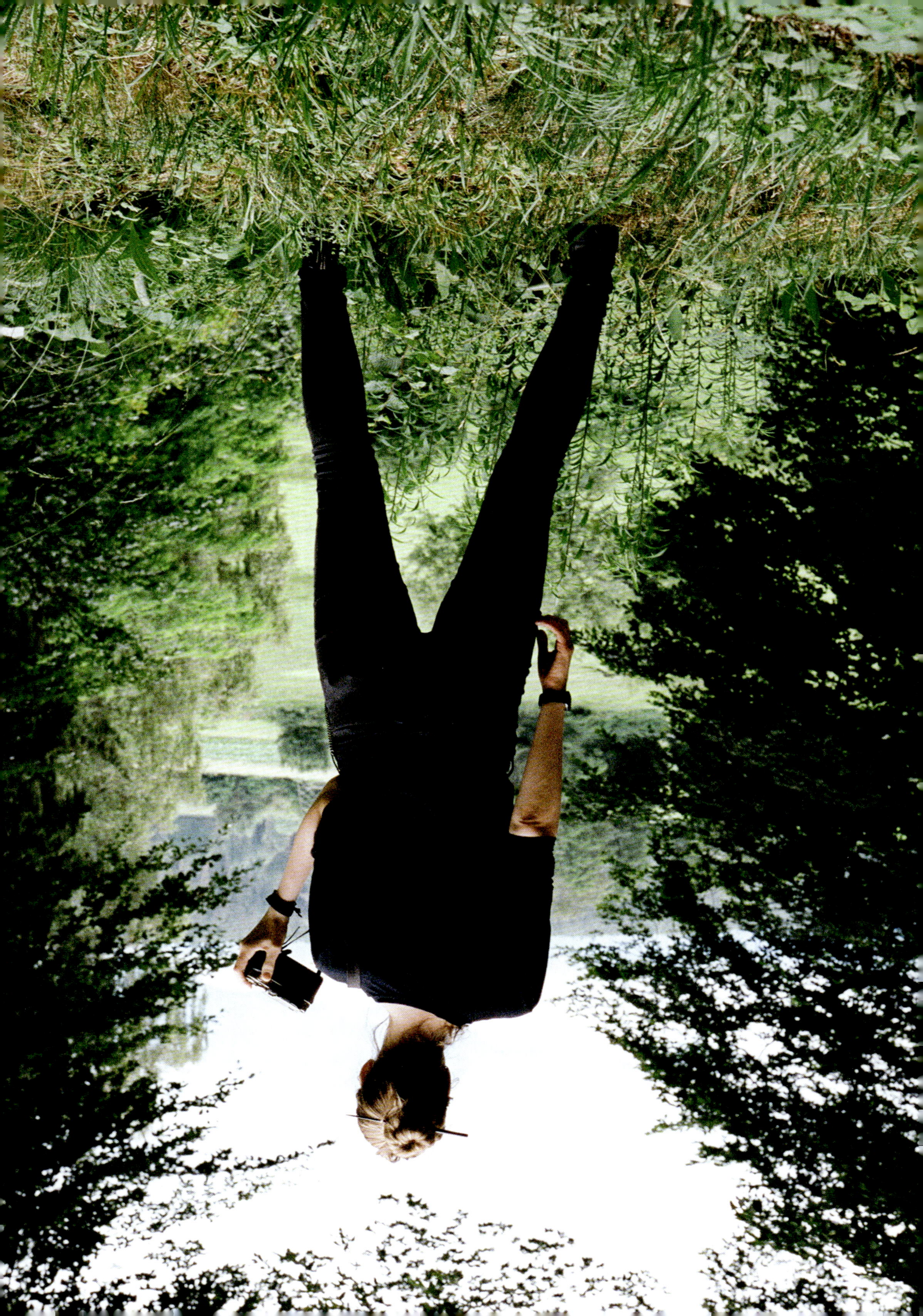

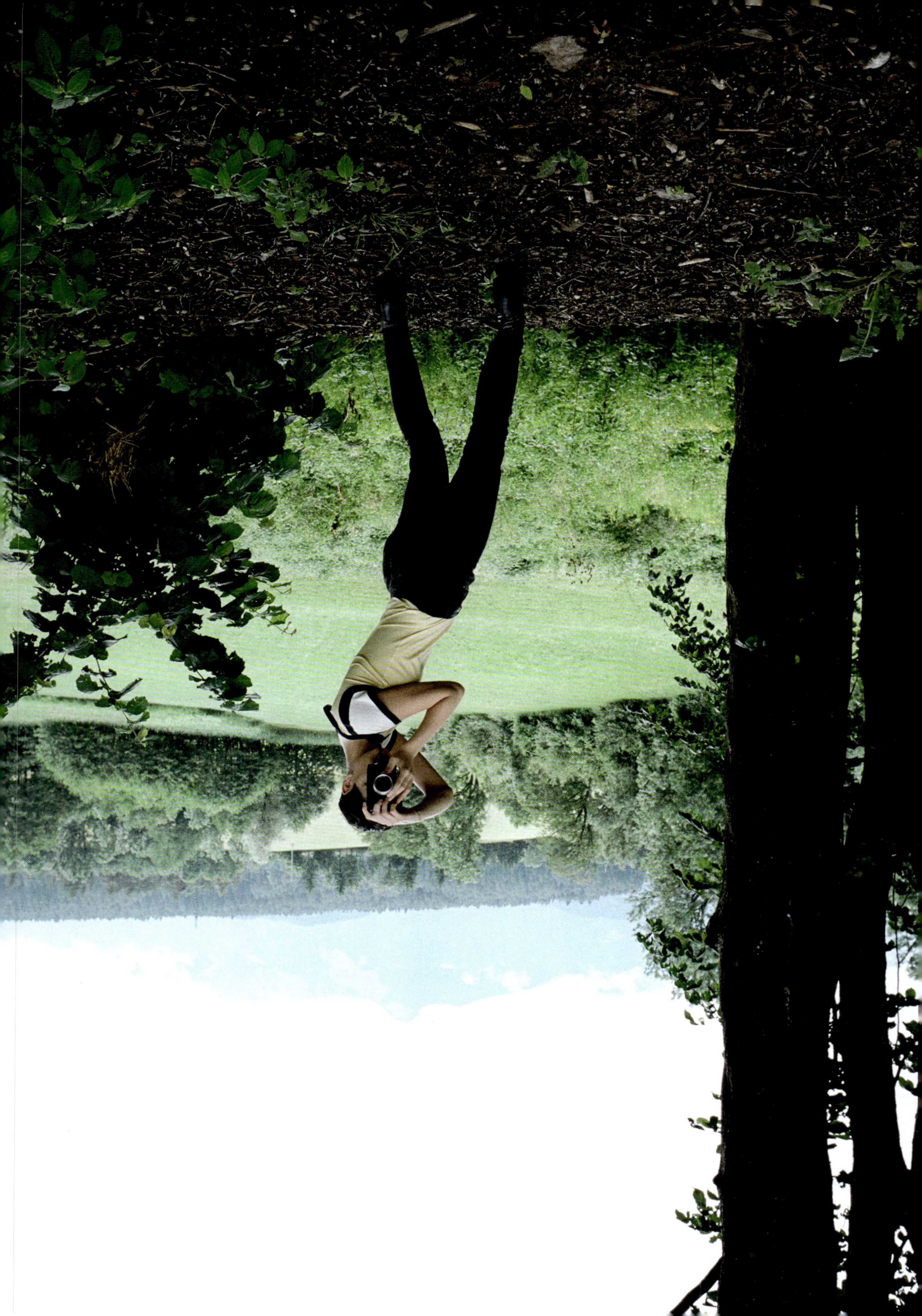

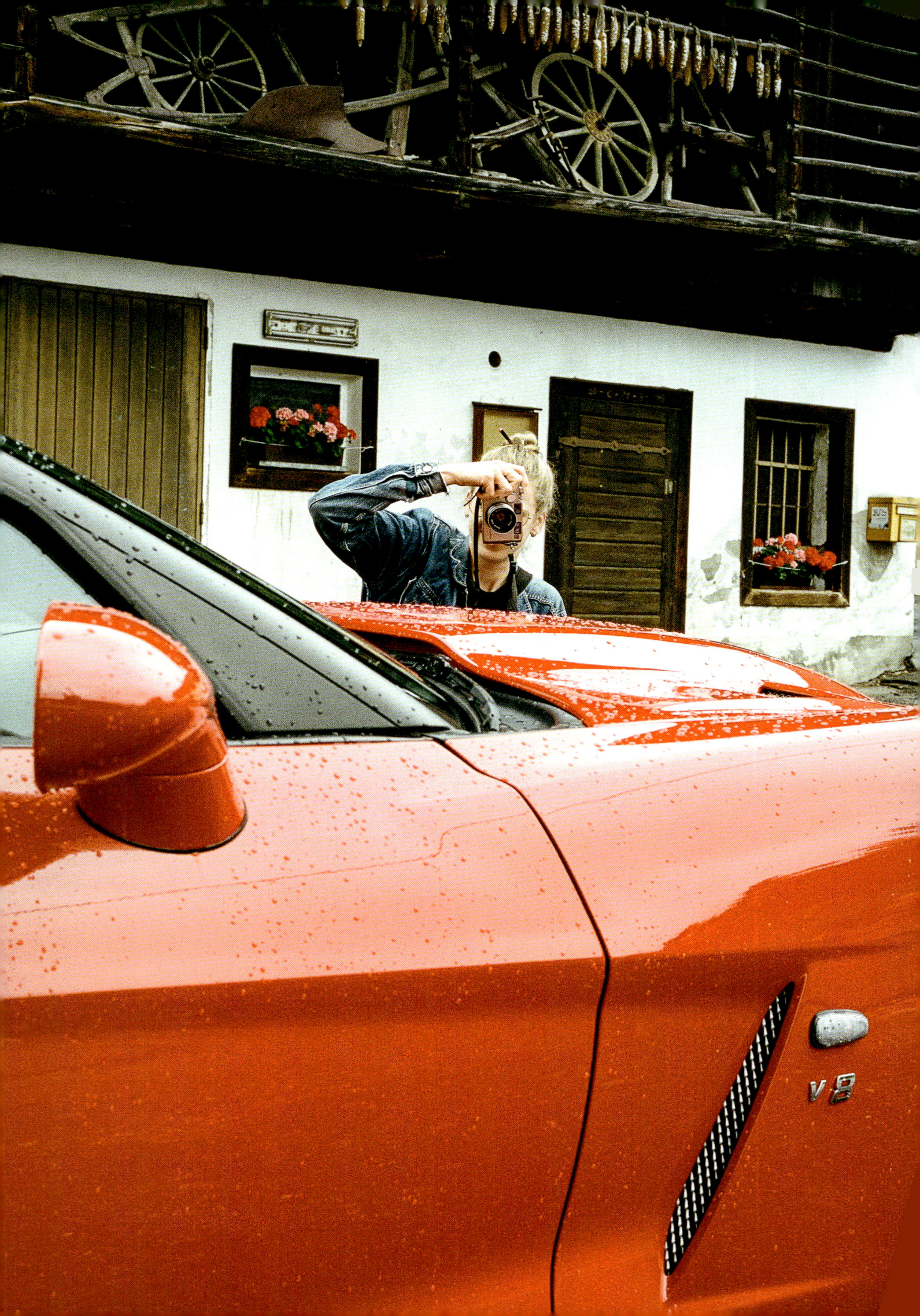
V8

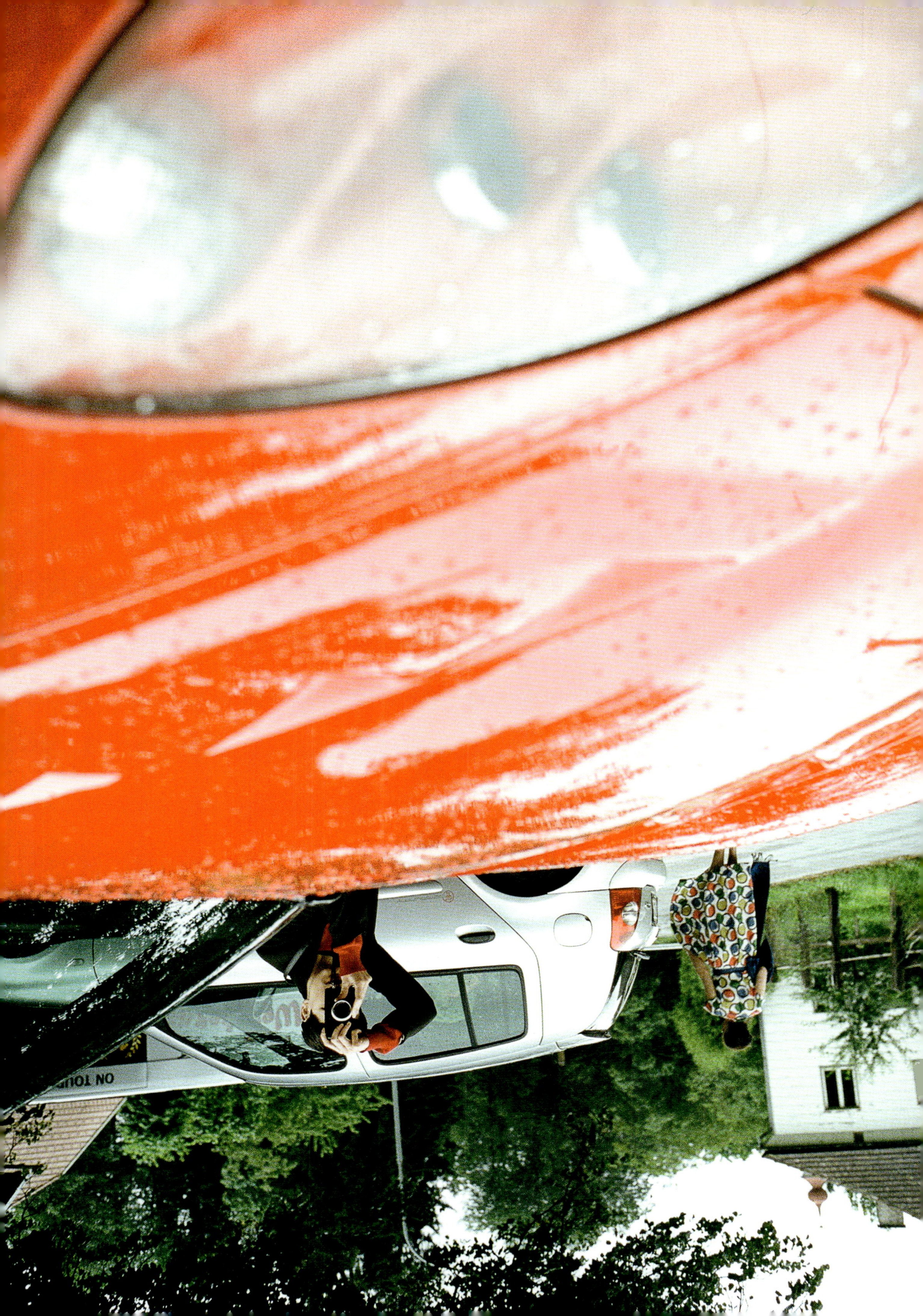

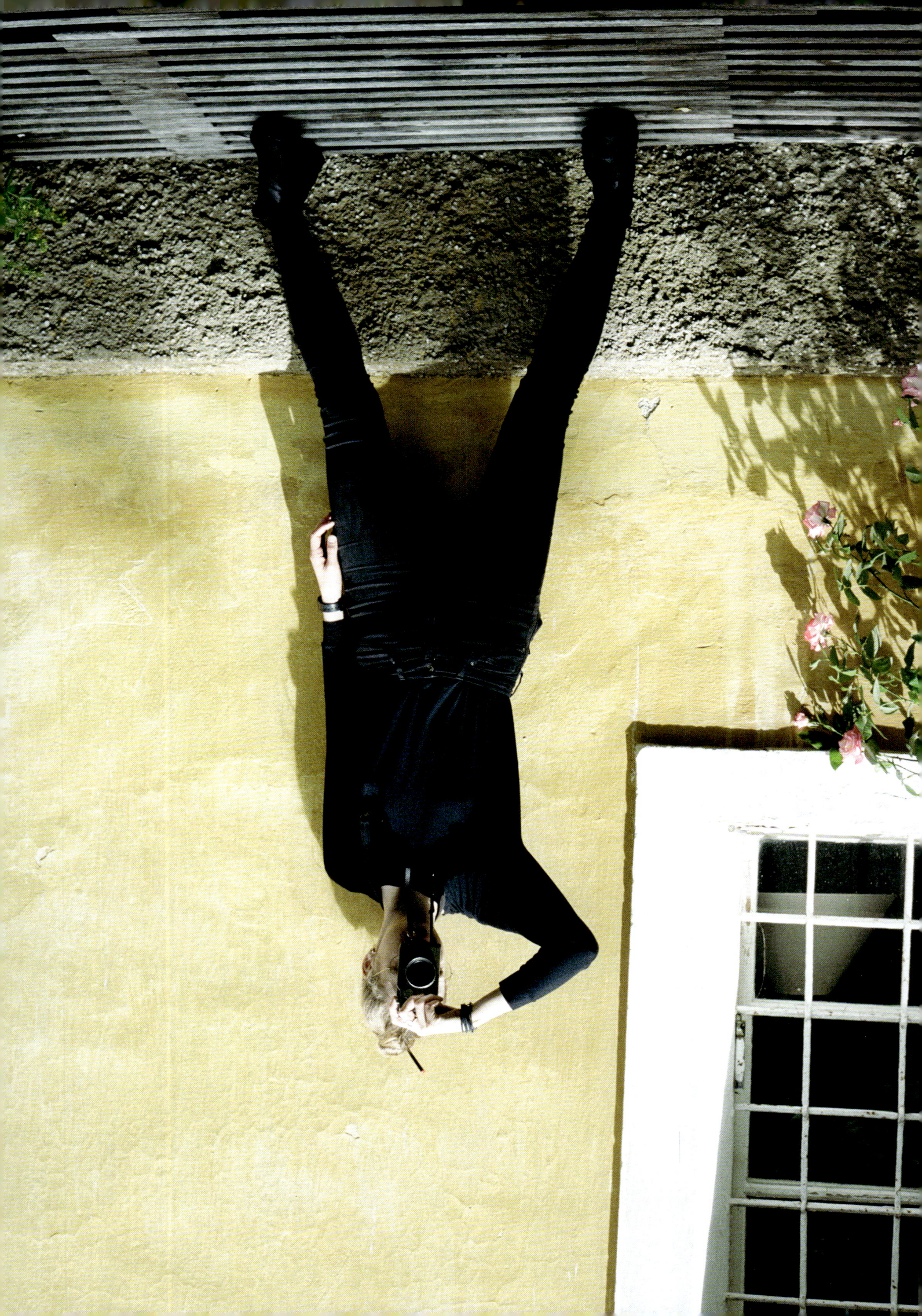

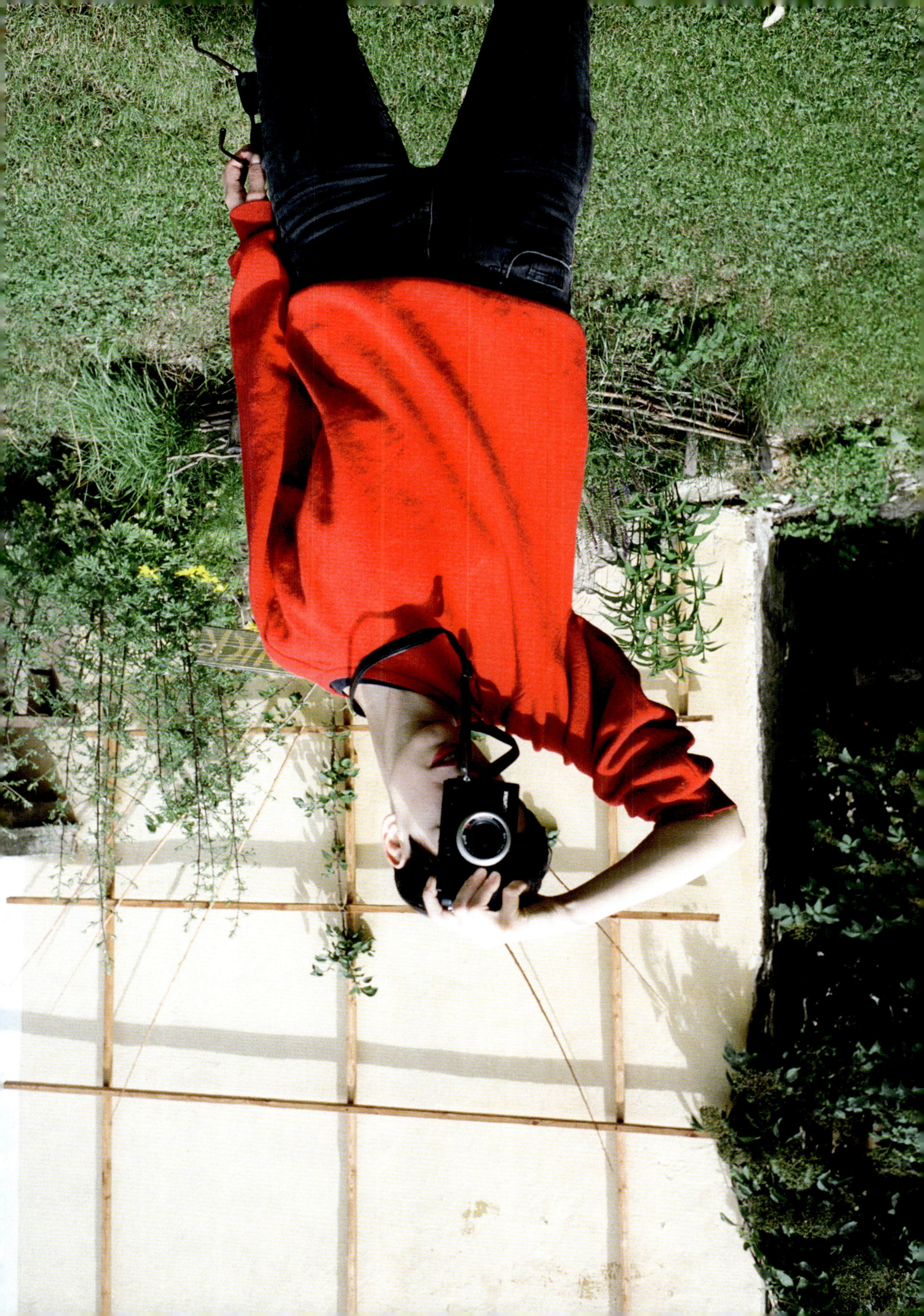

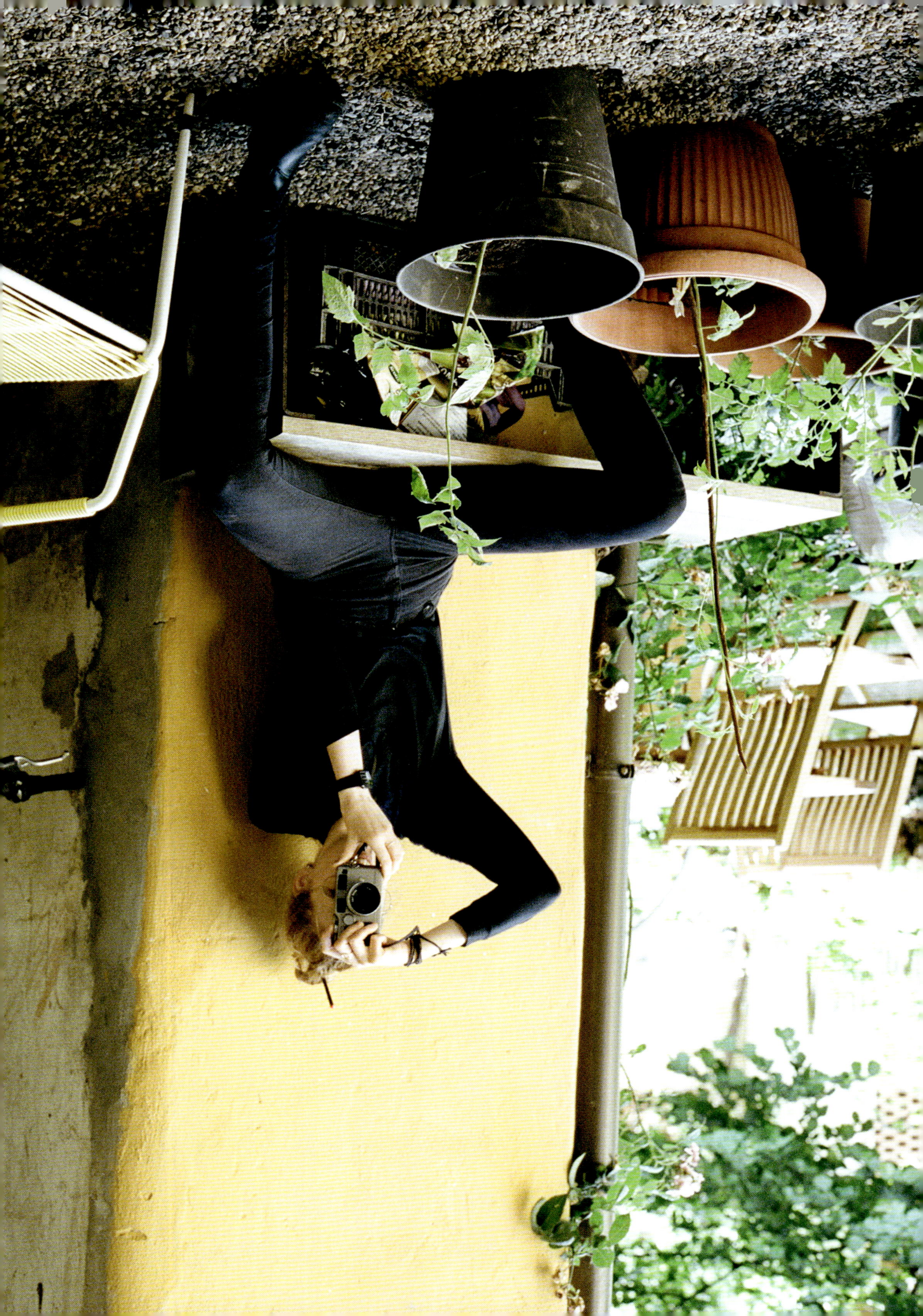

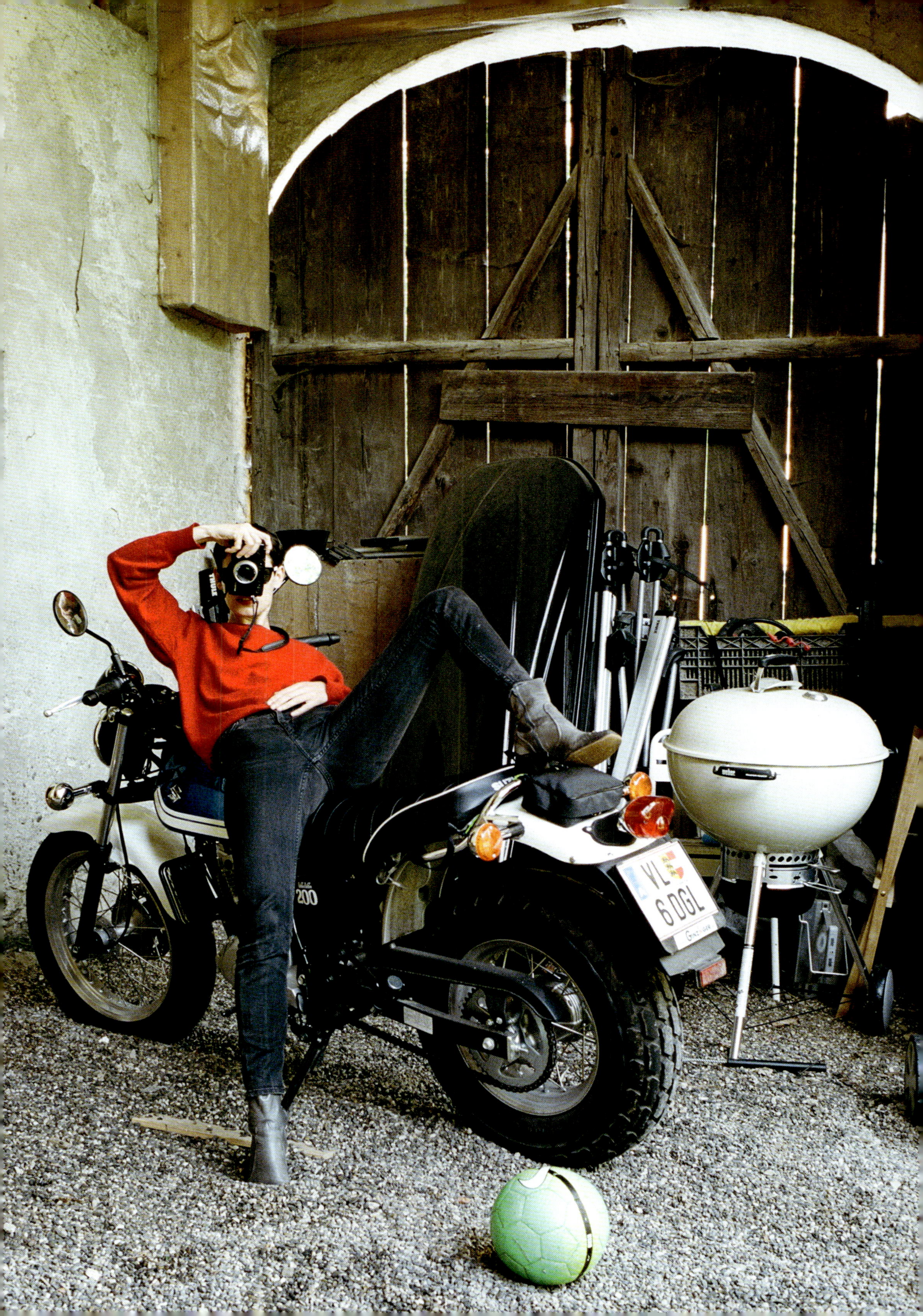
VL
6 DGL
200

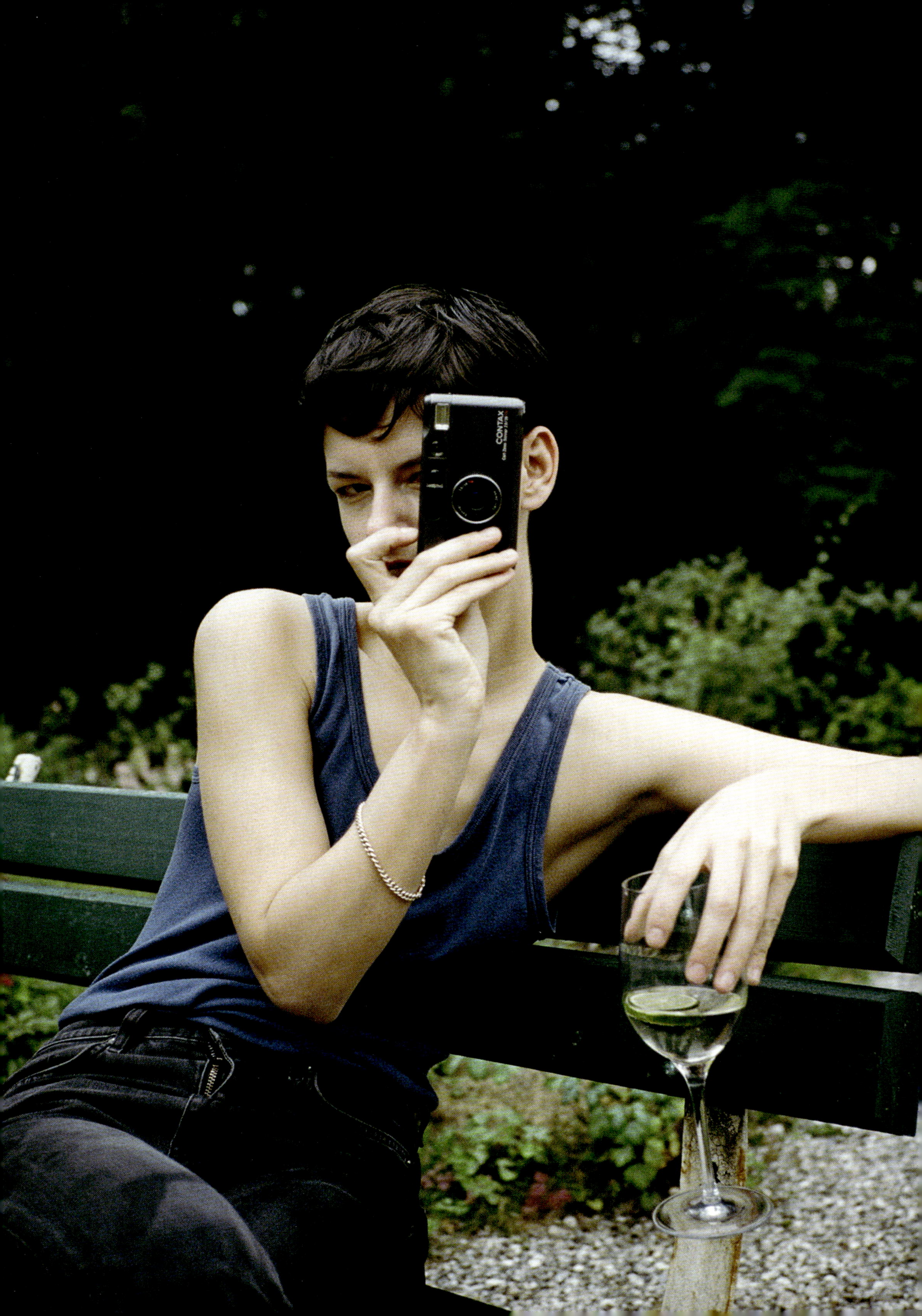
CONTAX

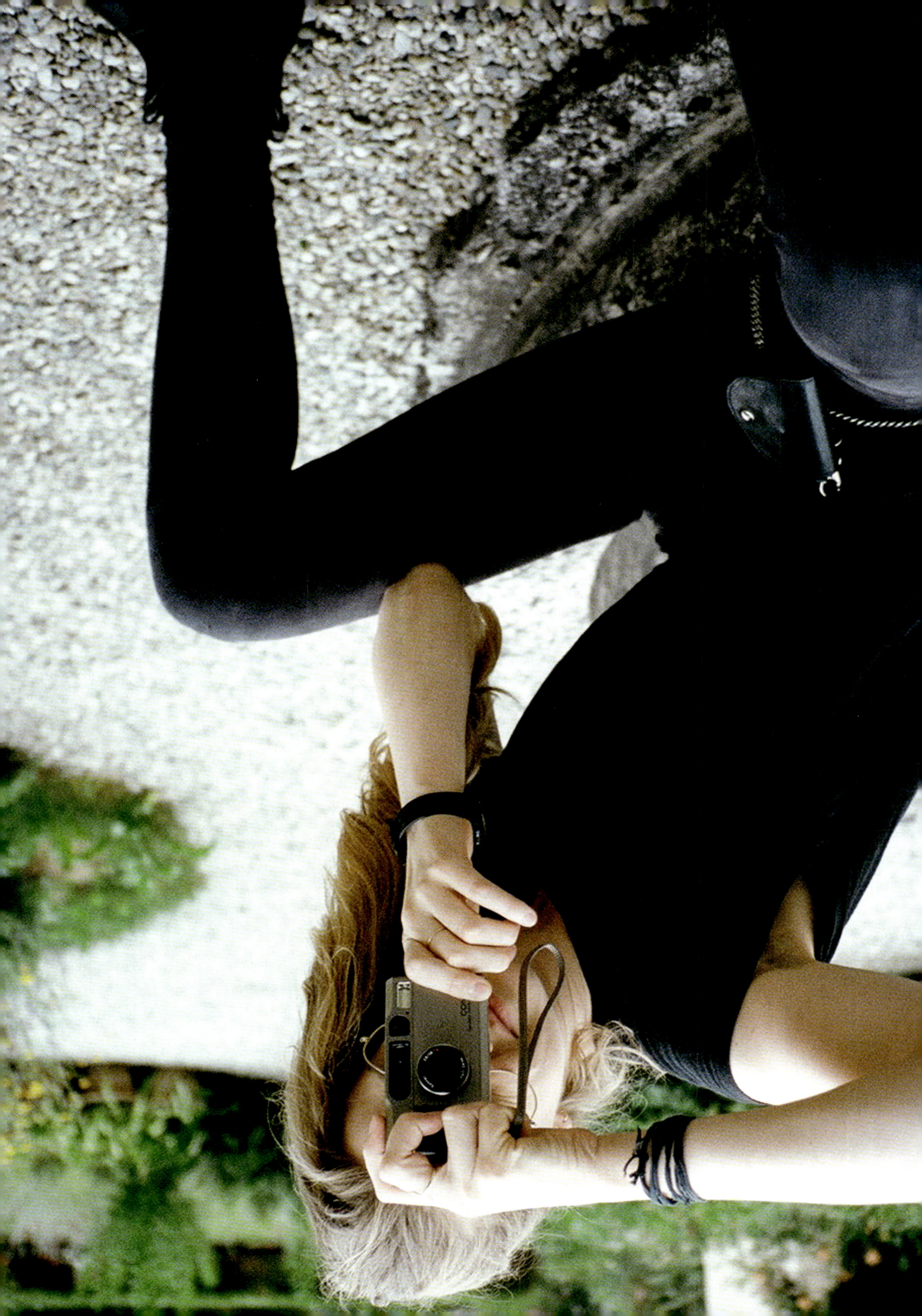

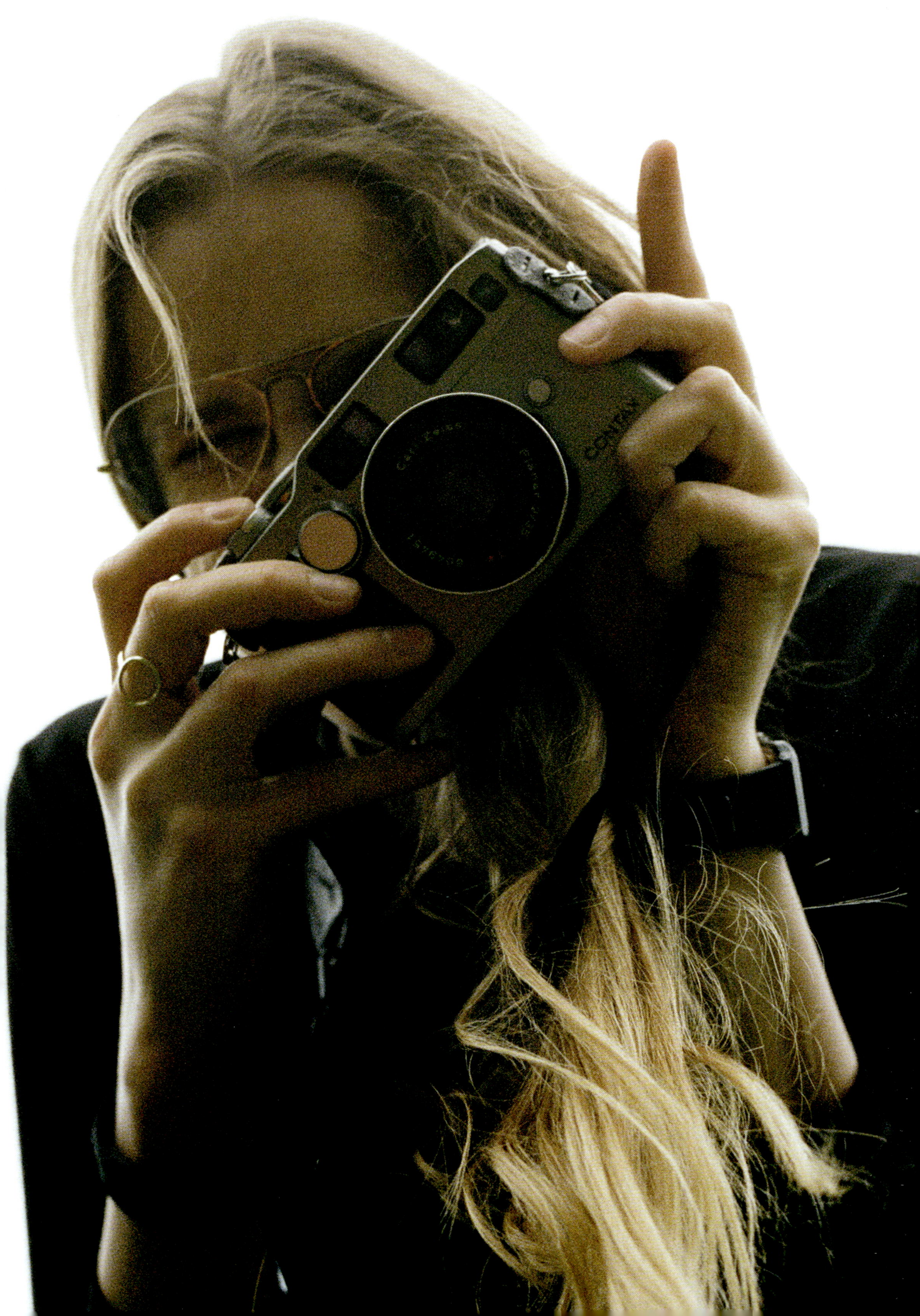
CONTAX

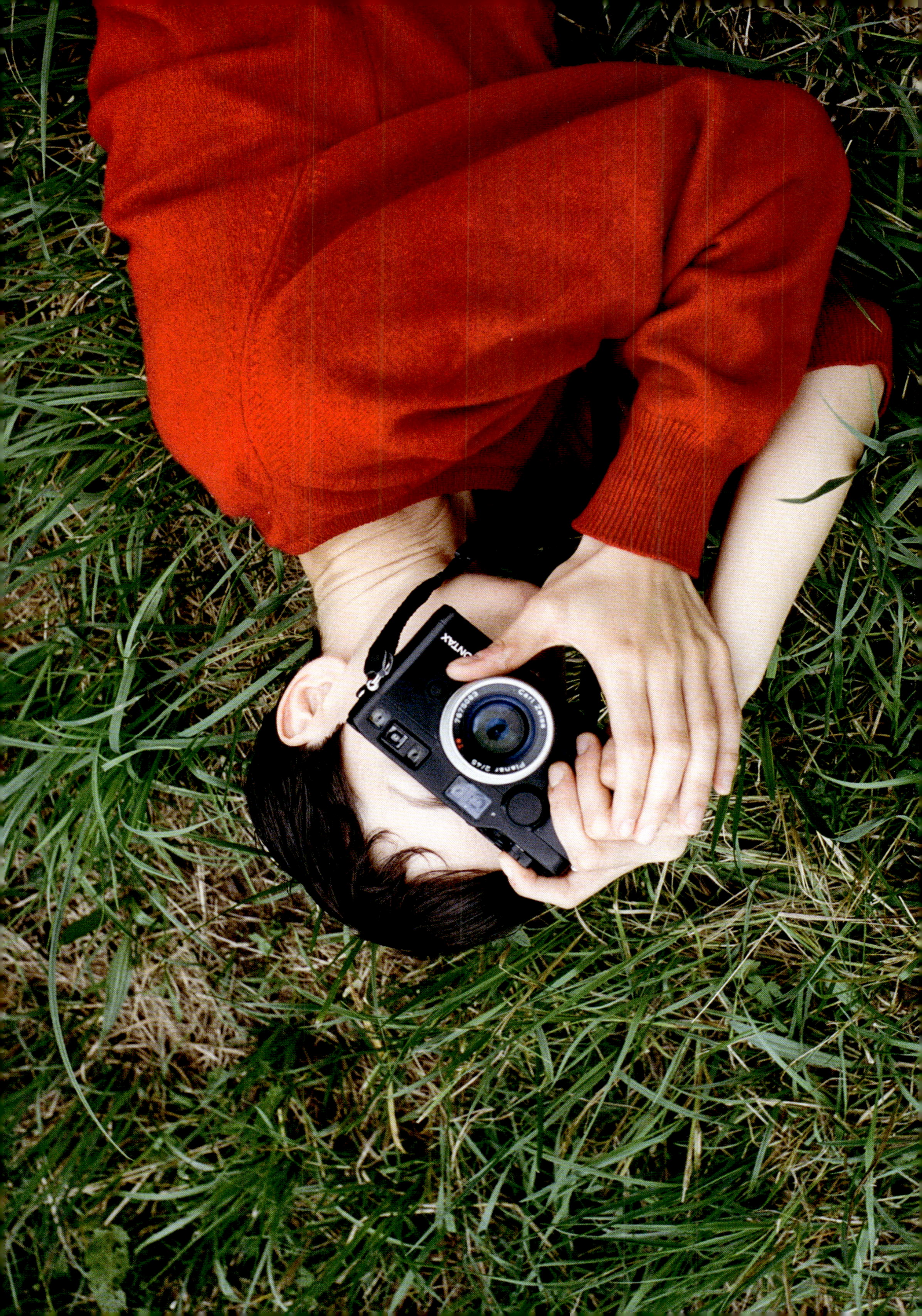
Carl Zeiss
Planar 2/45

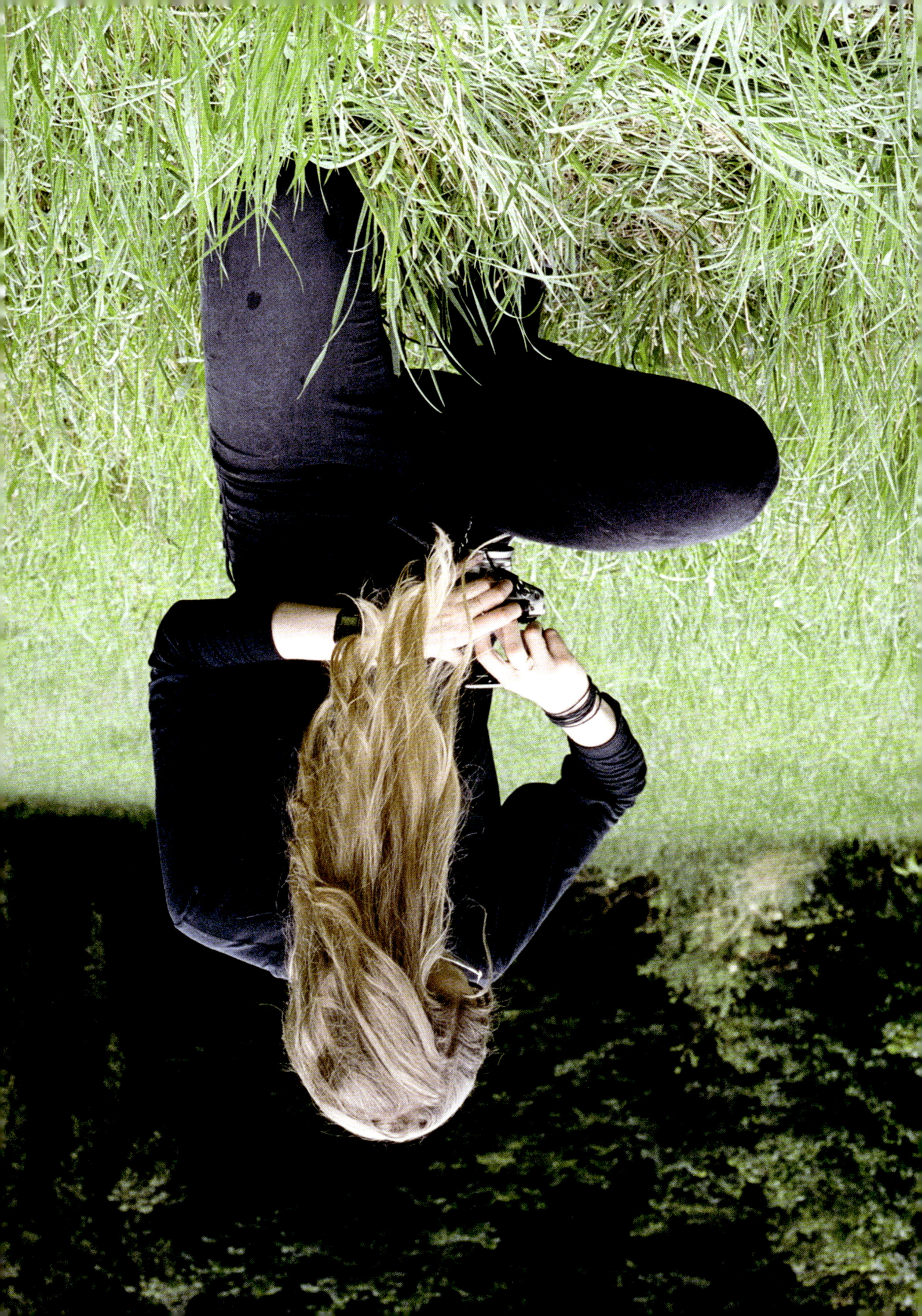

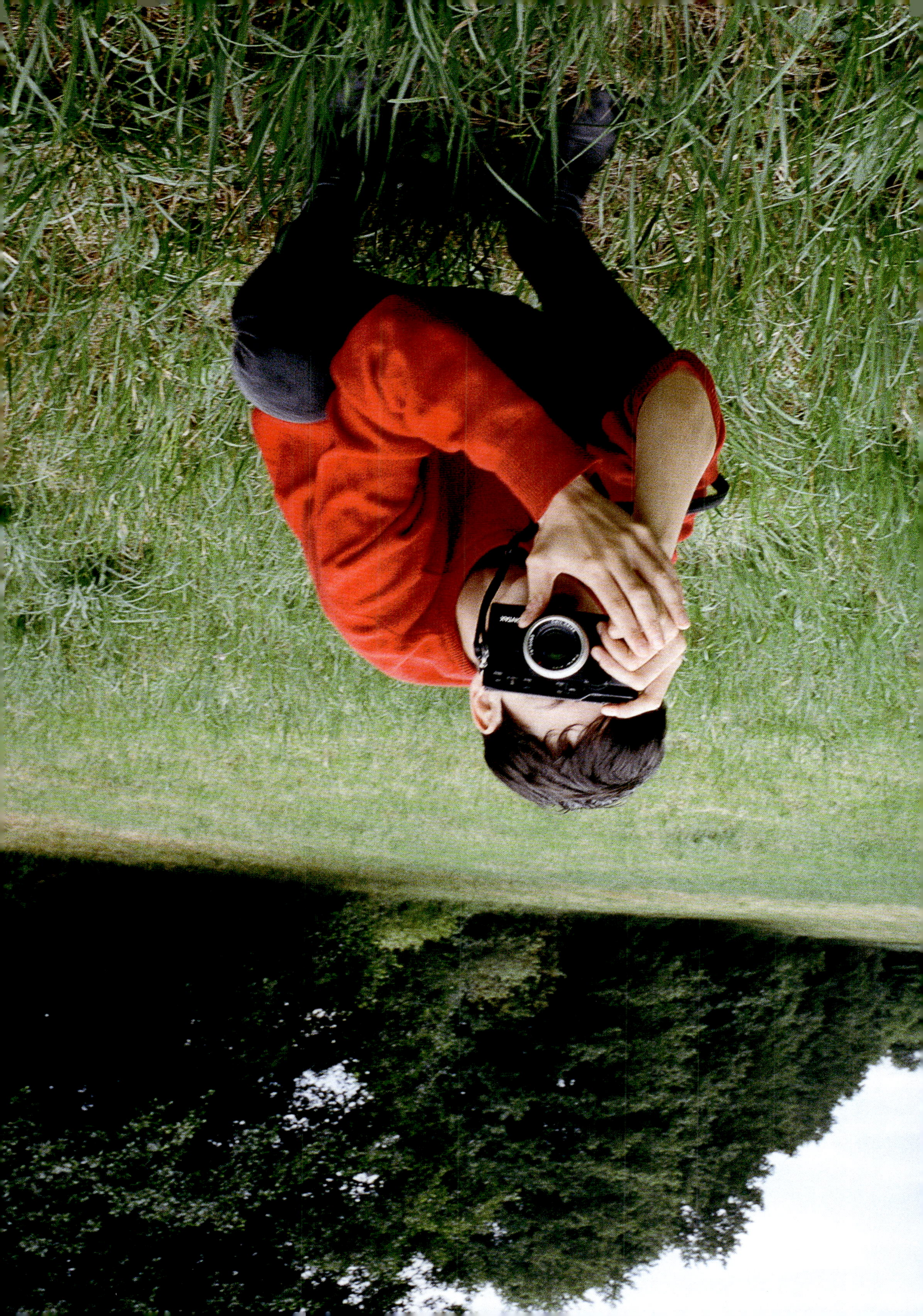

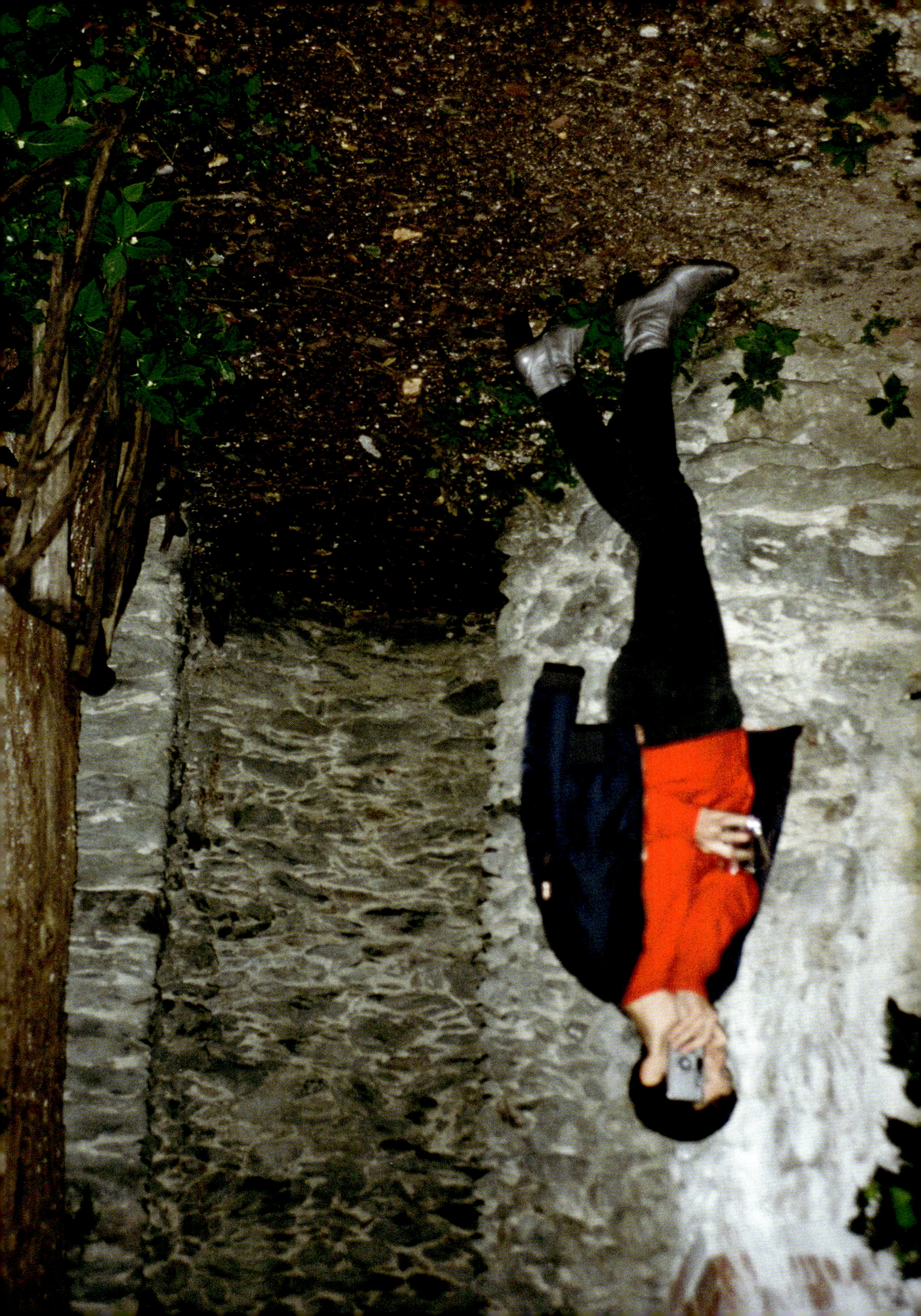

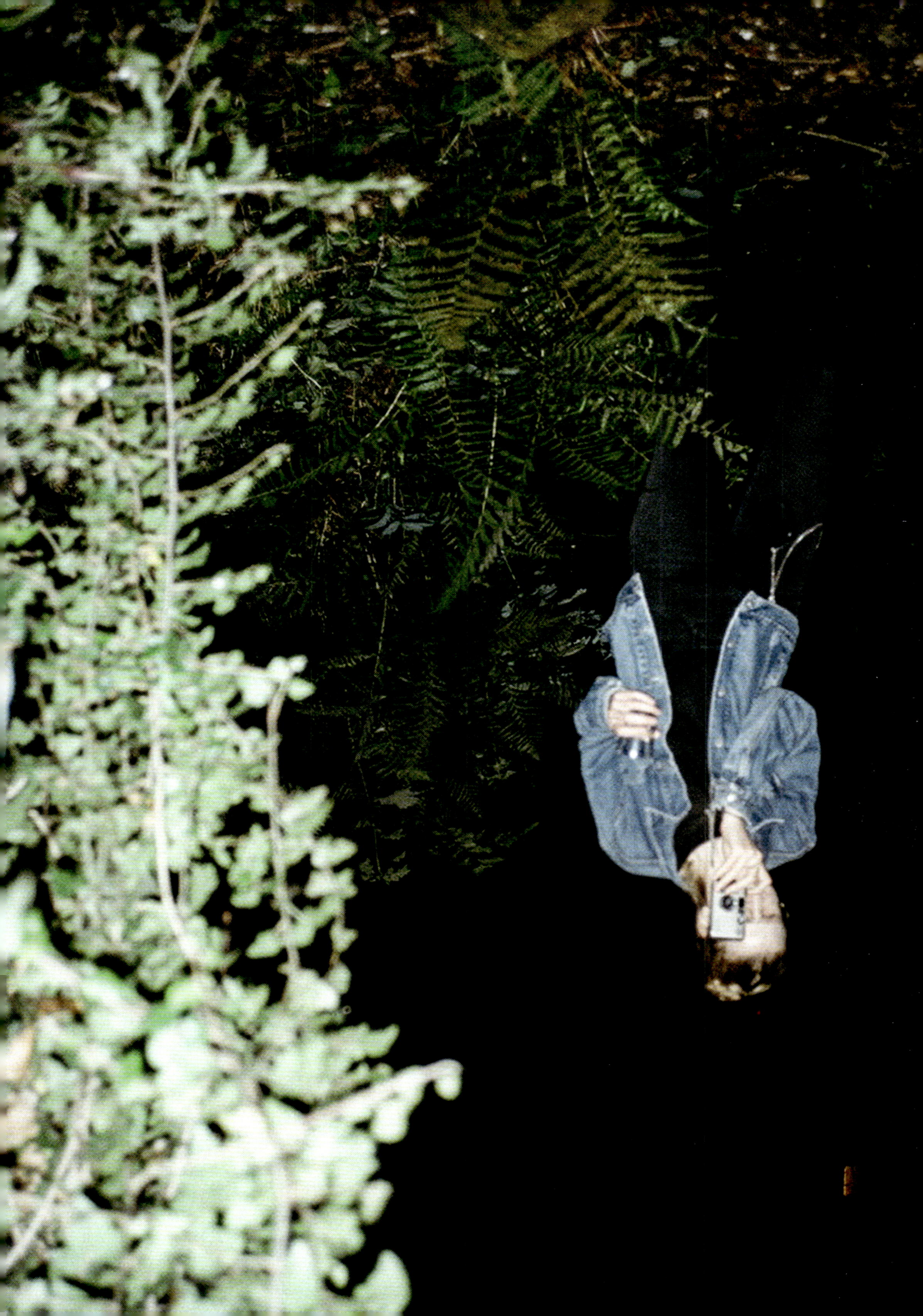

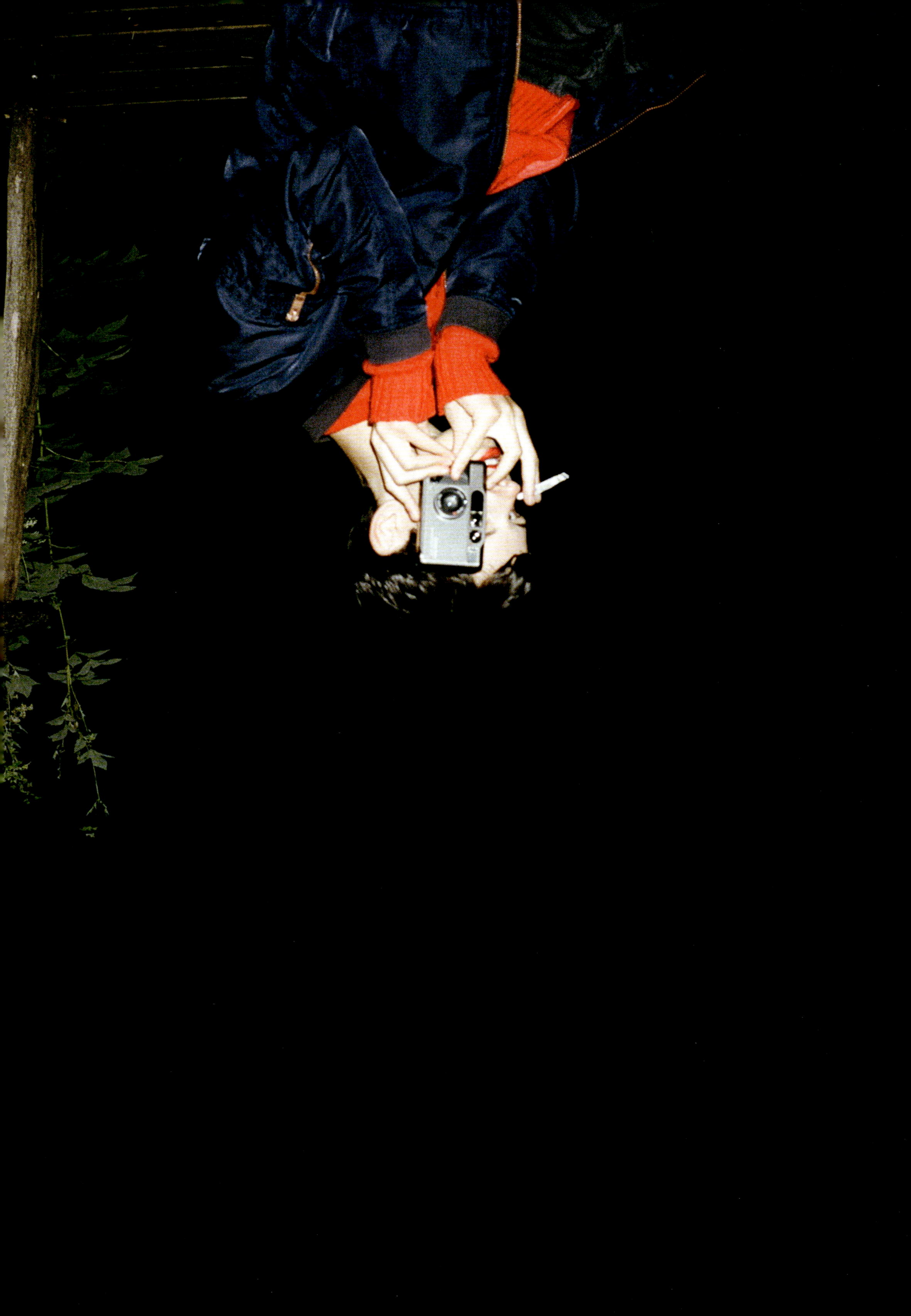

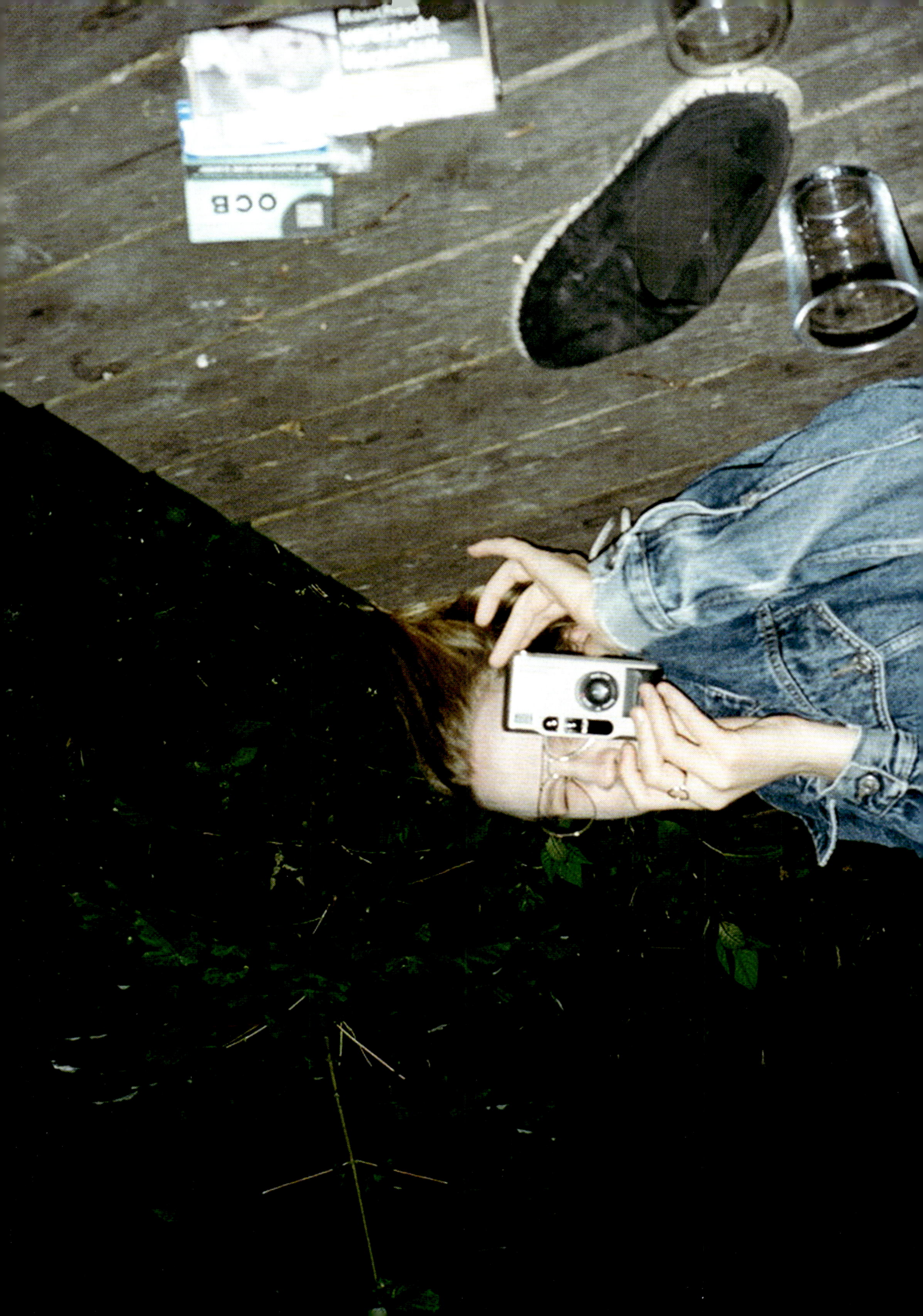
OCB

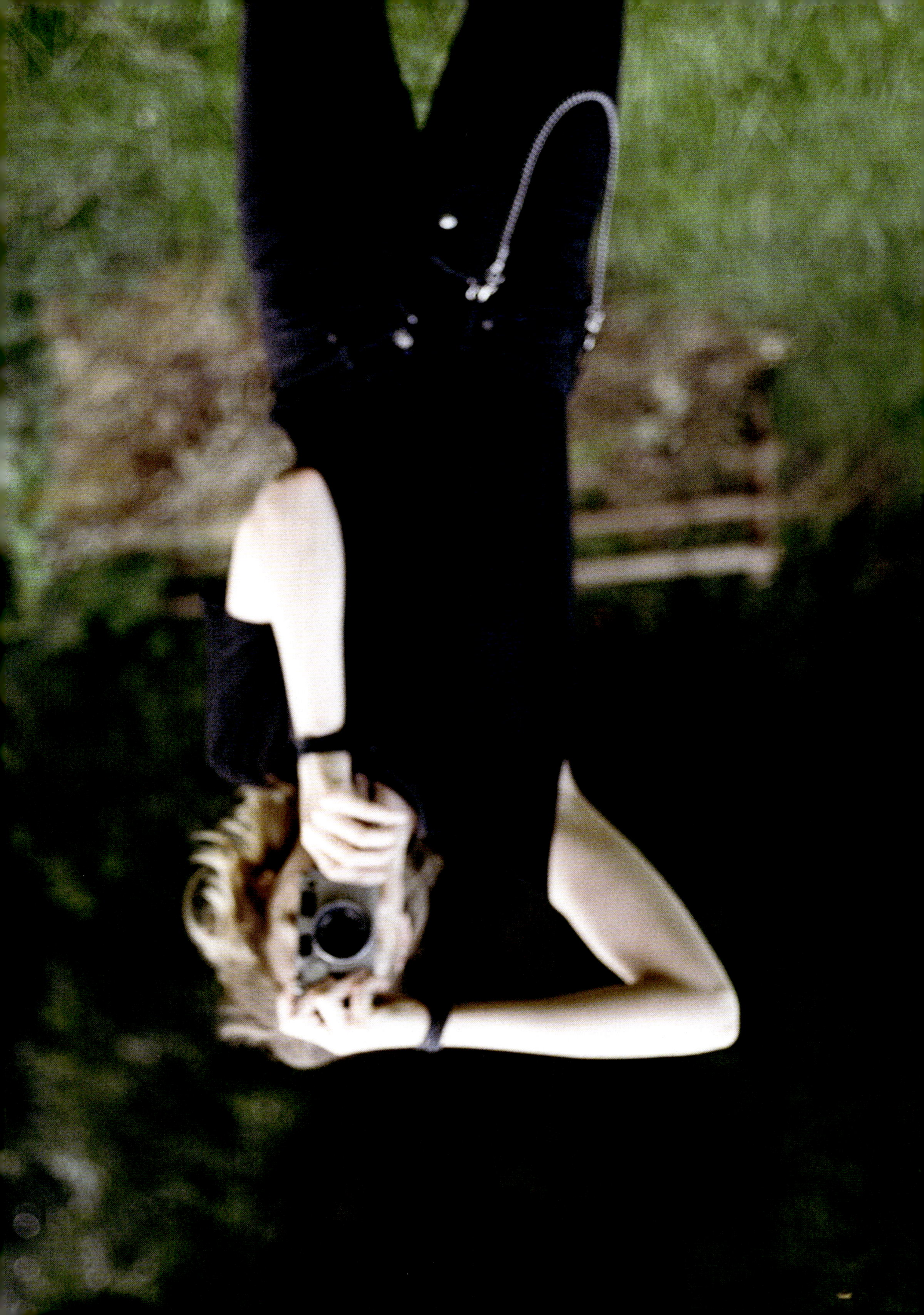

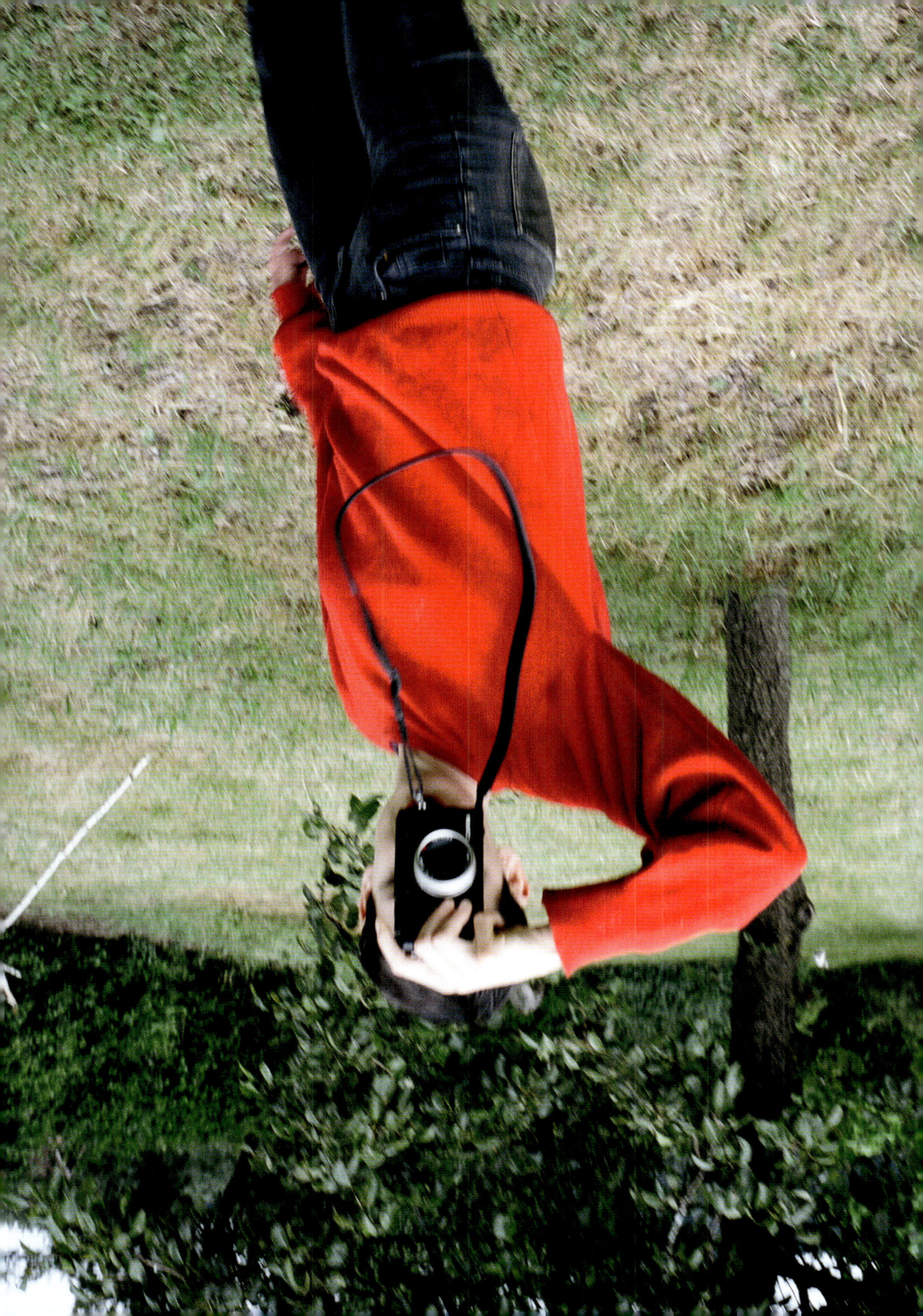

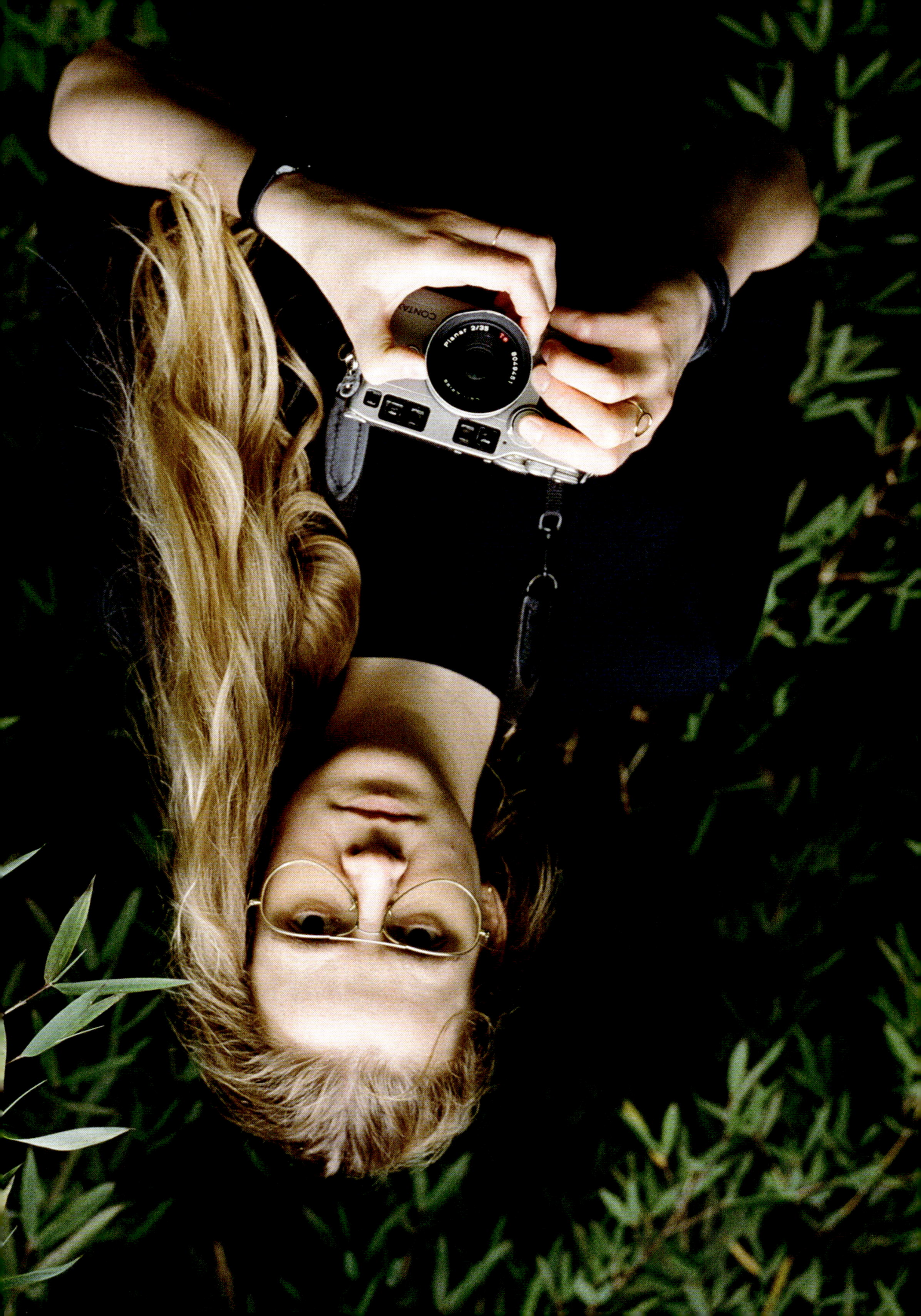

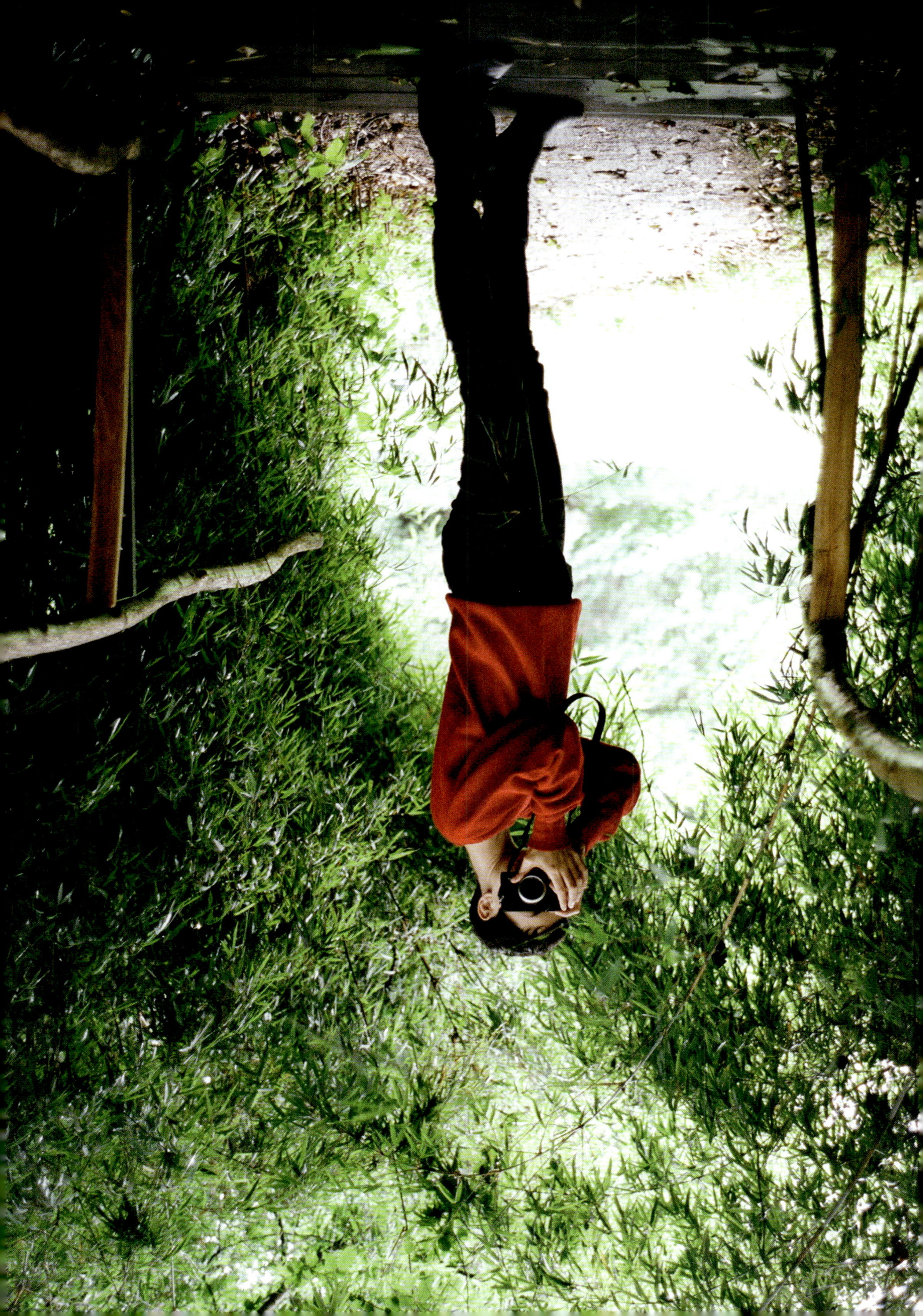

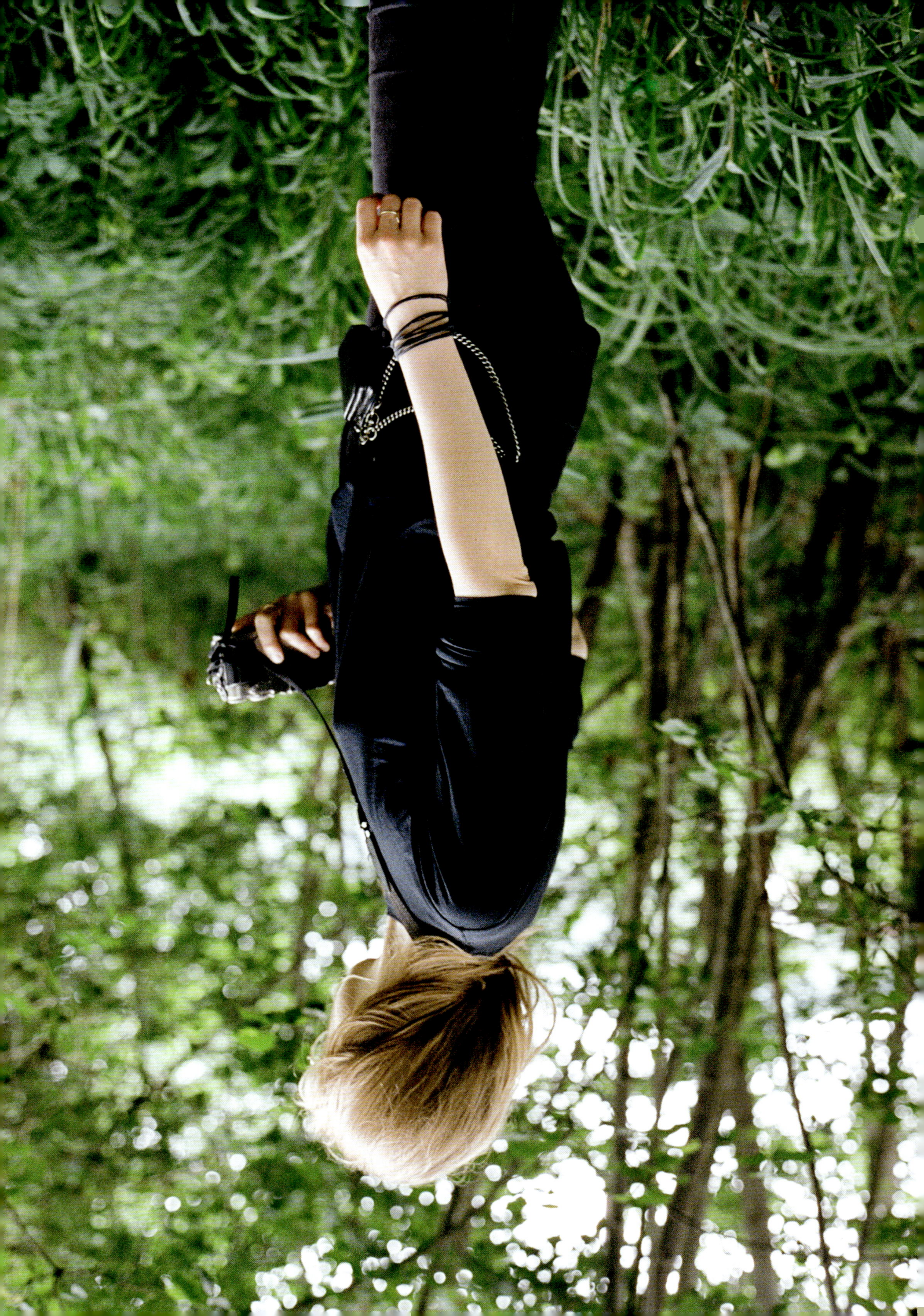

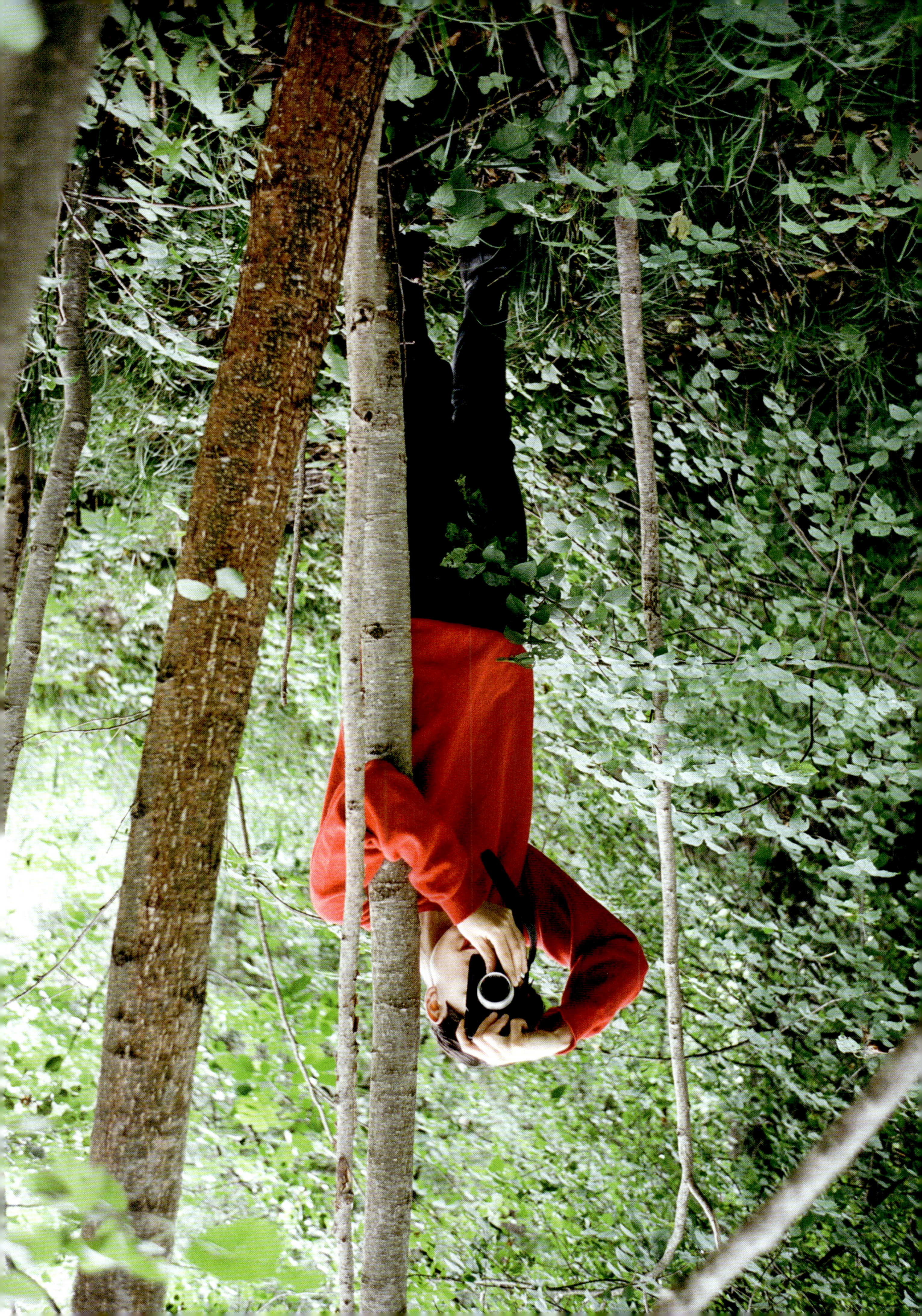

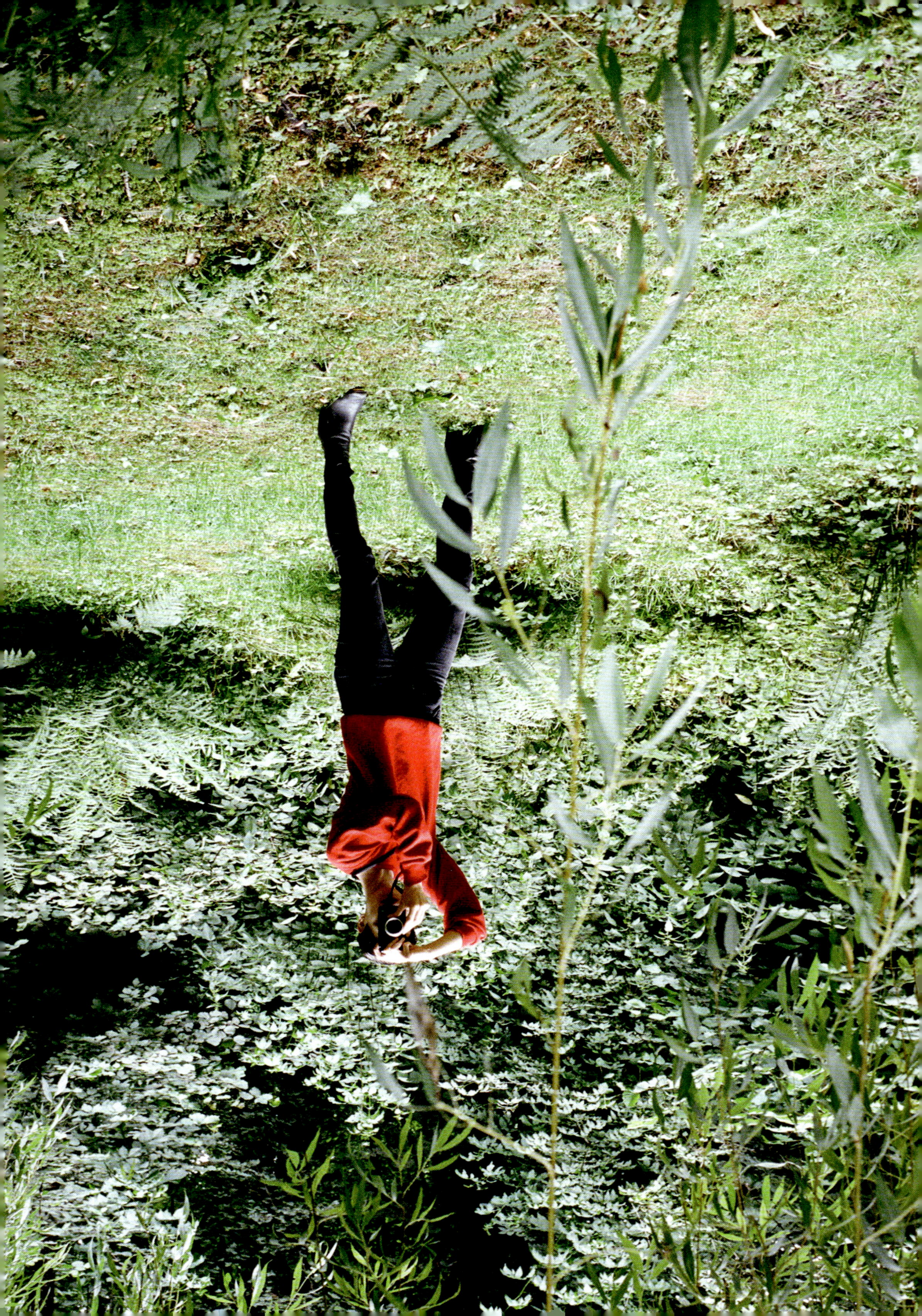

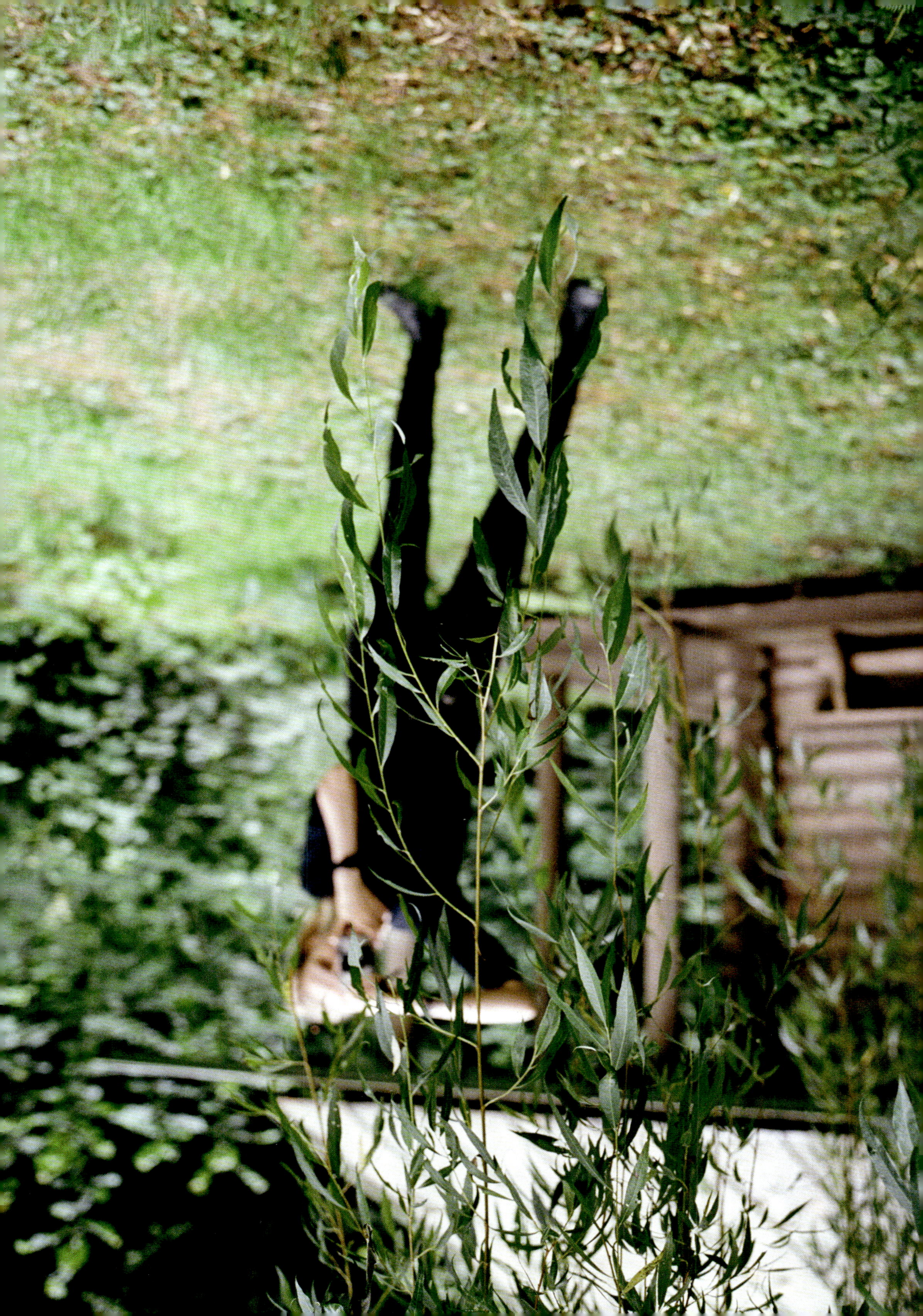

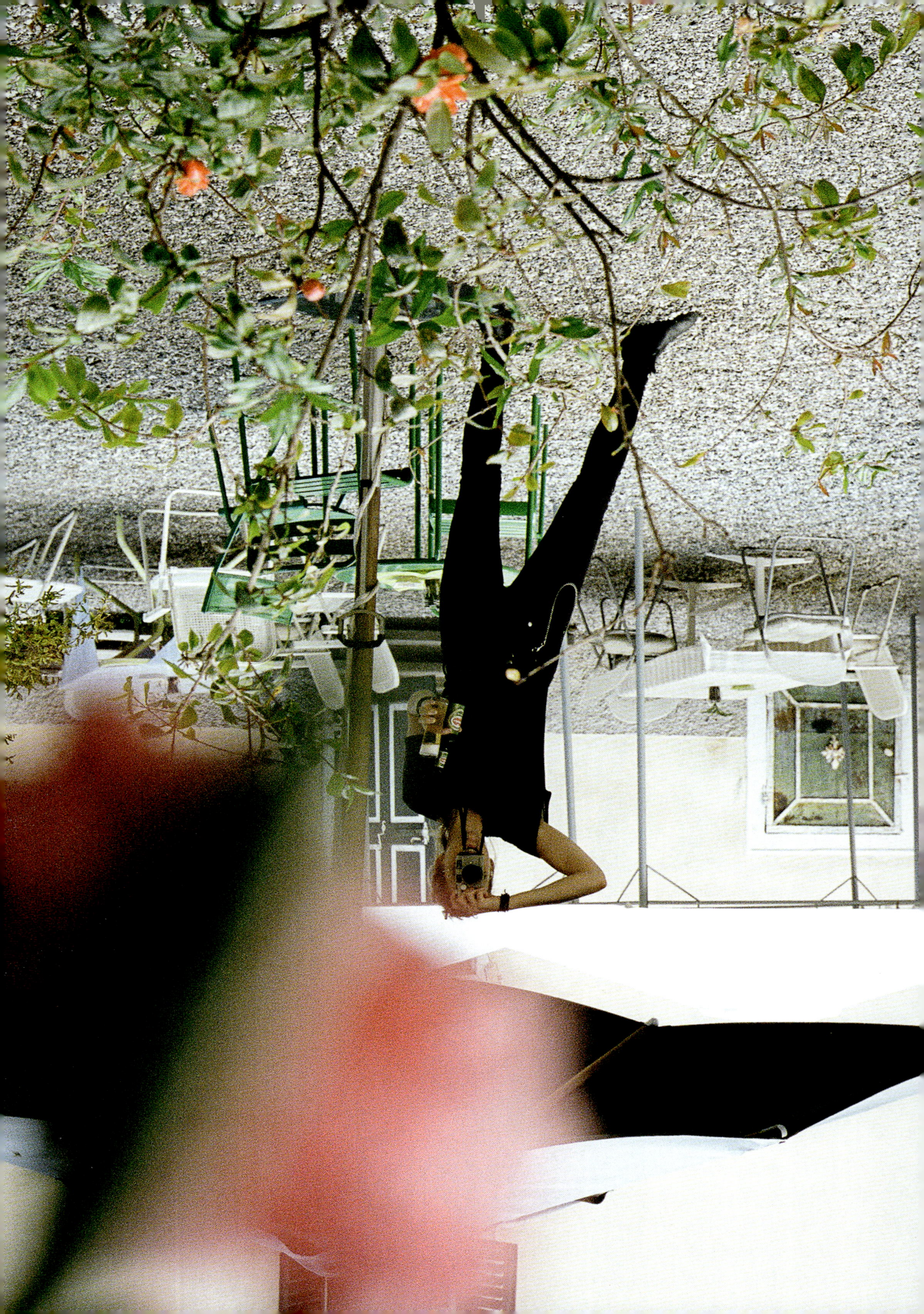

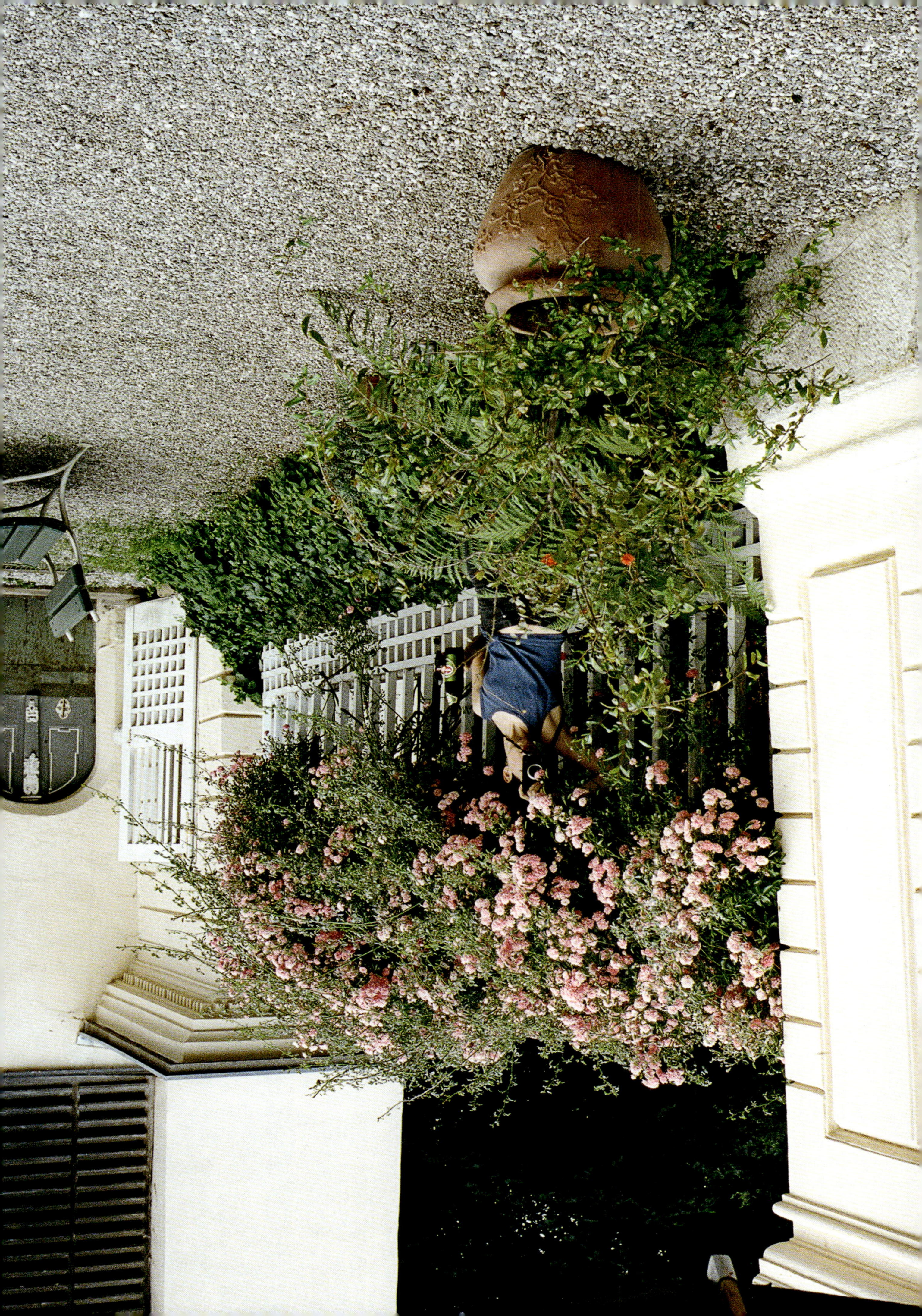

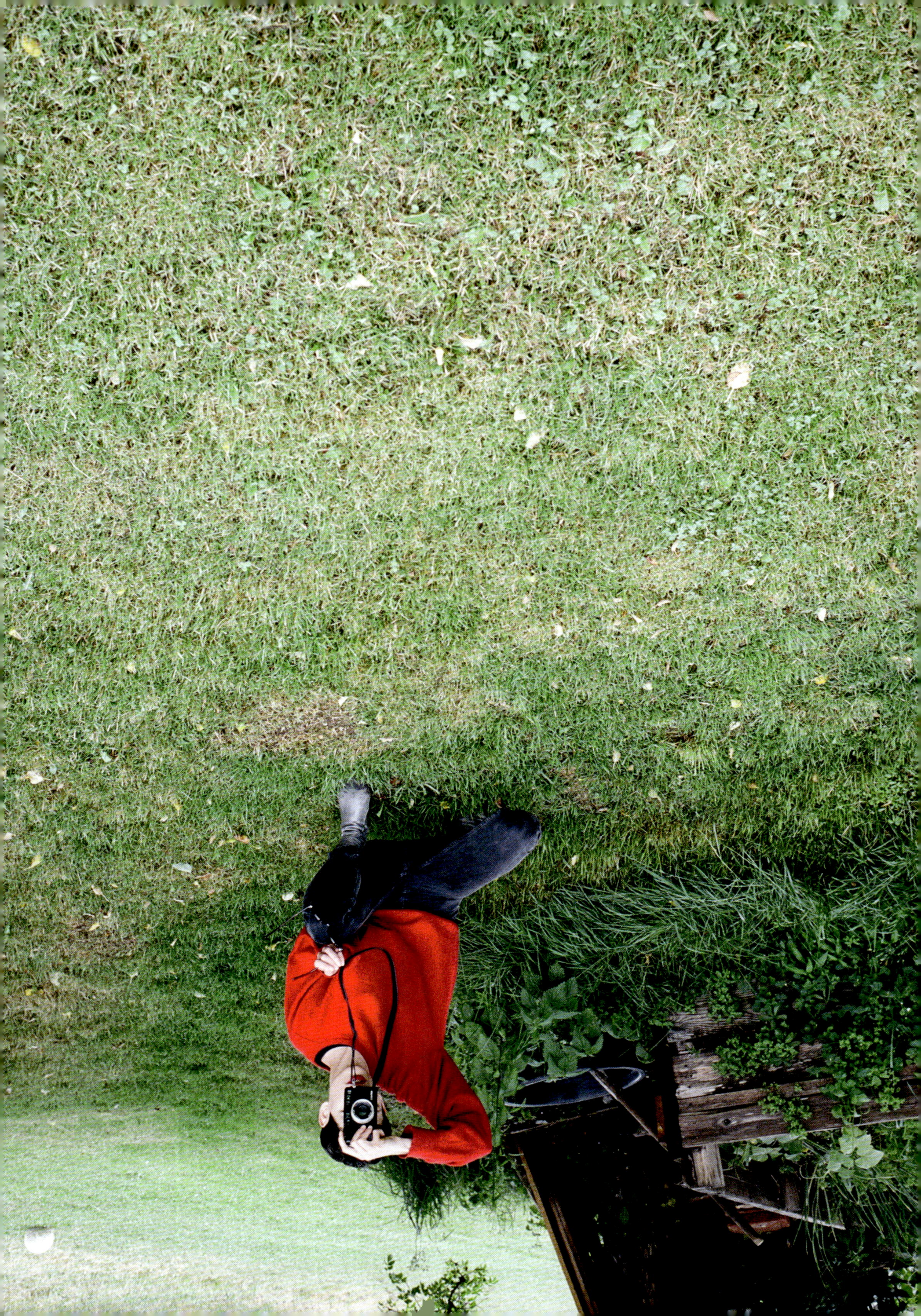

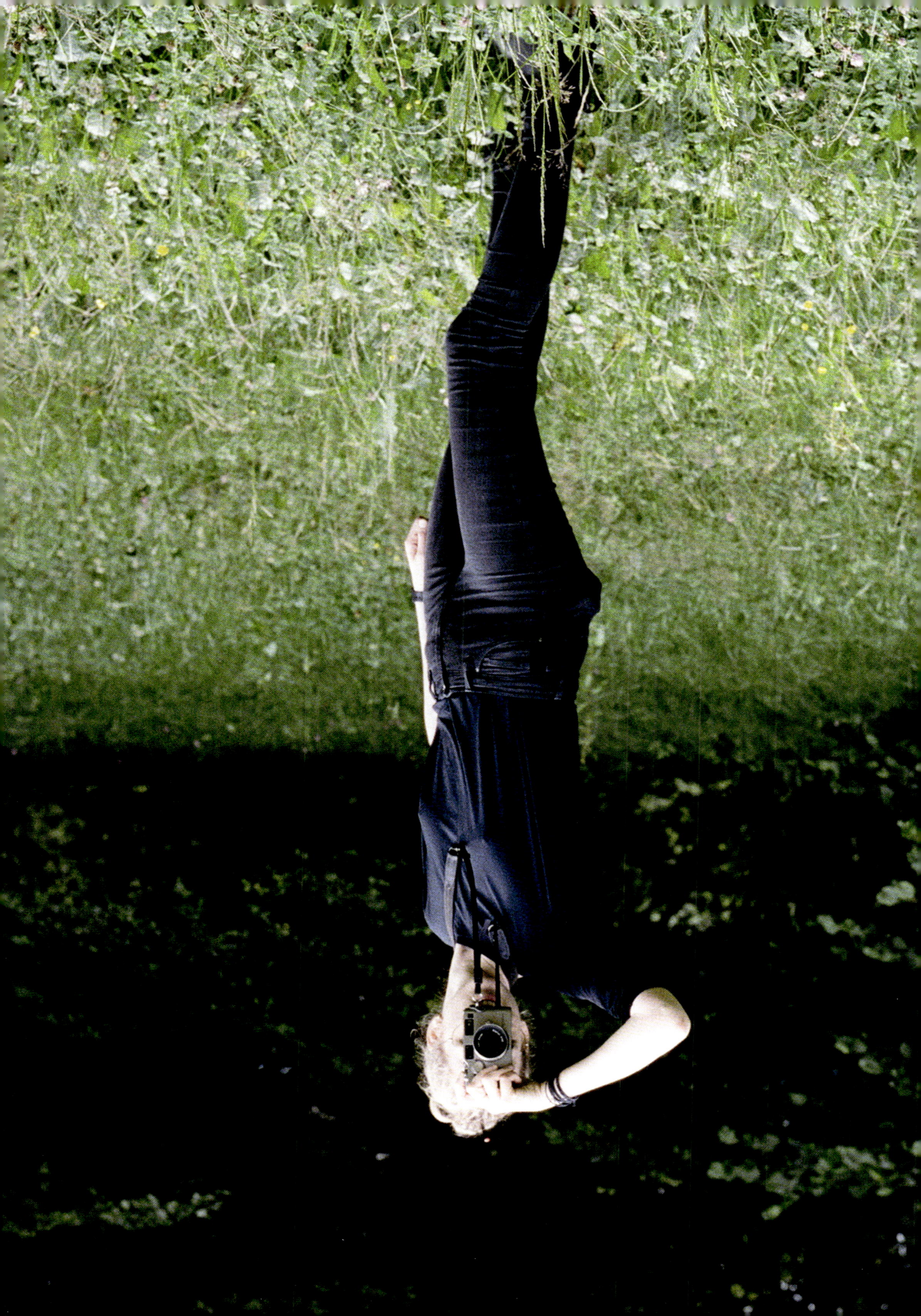

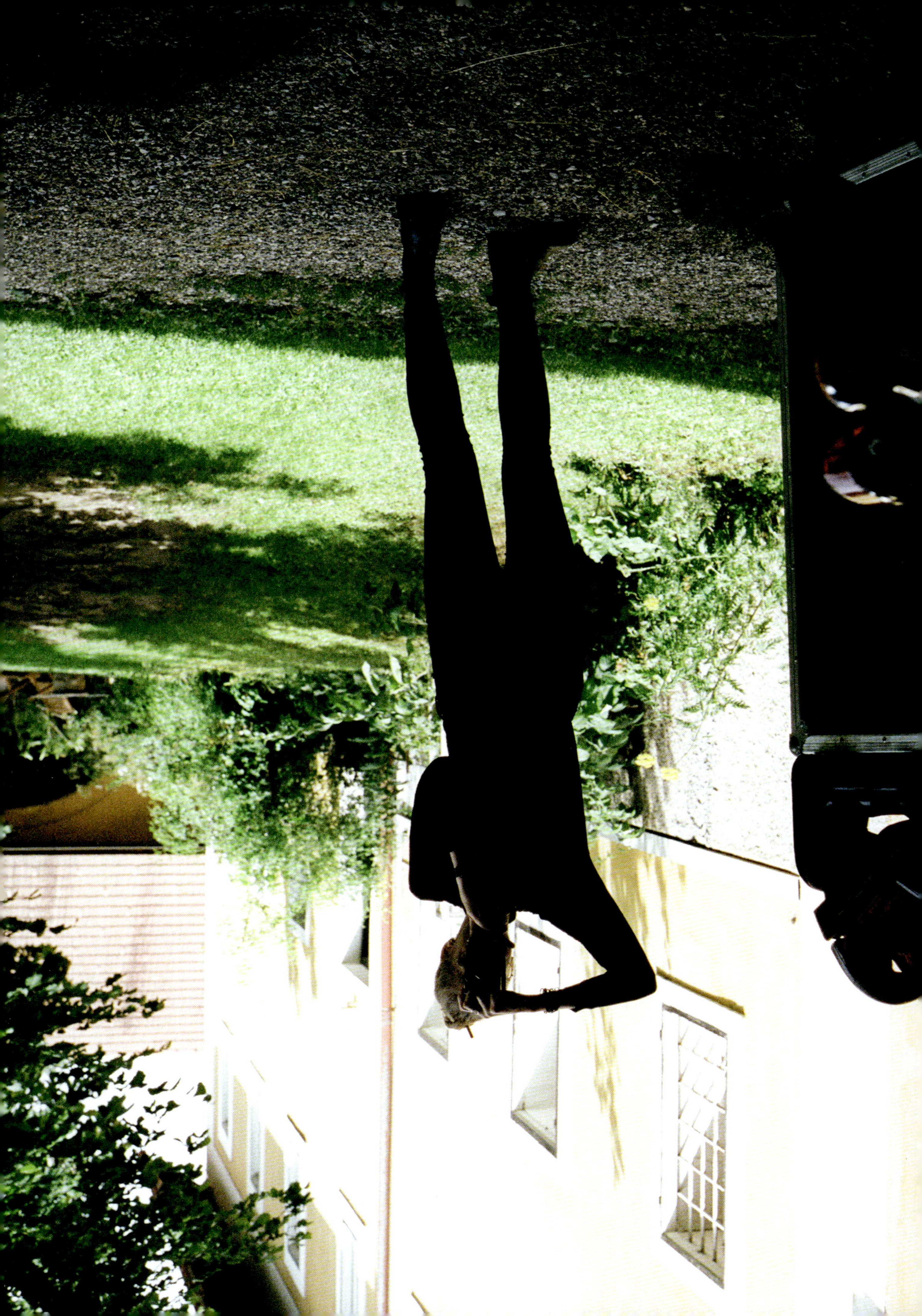

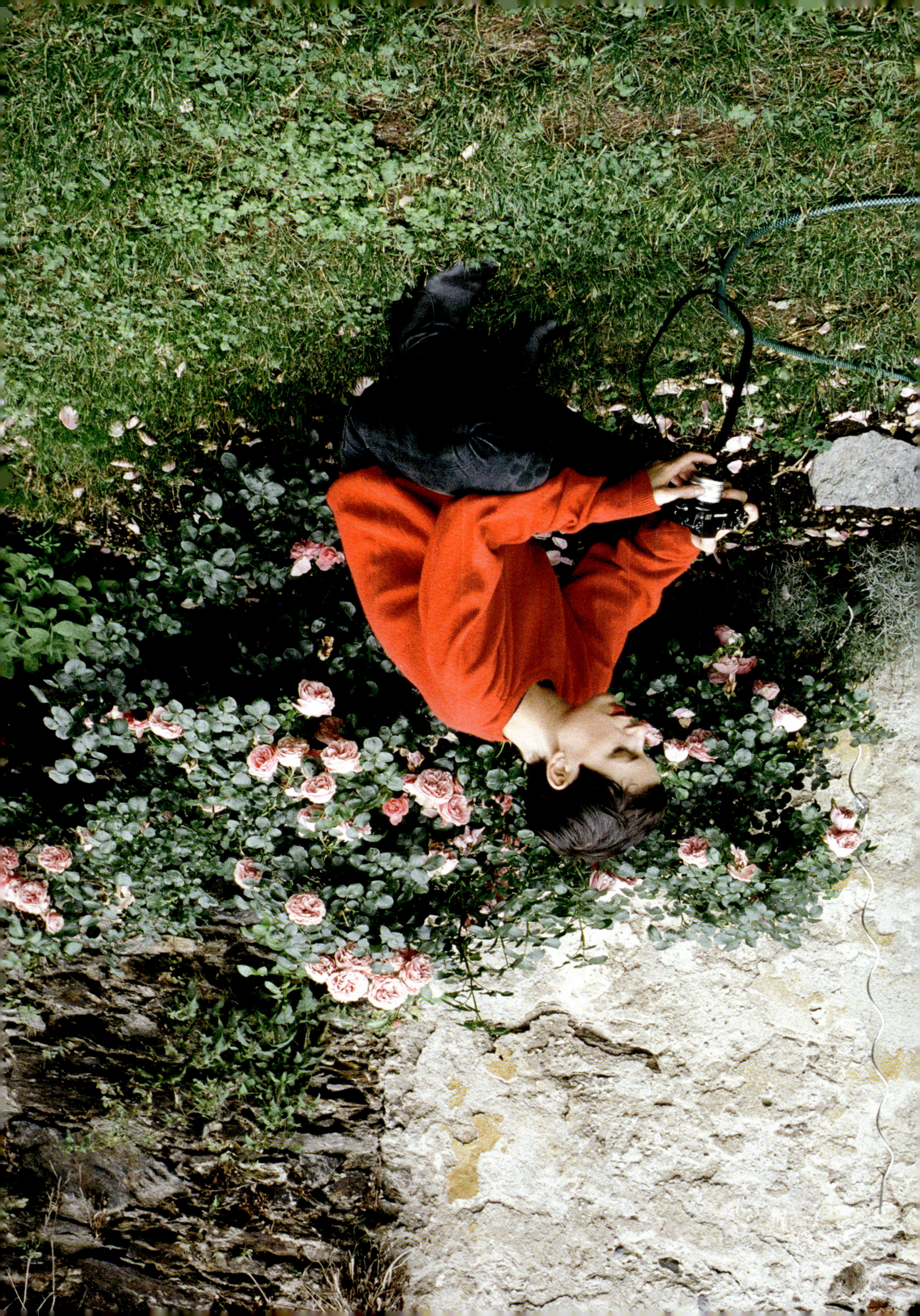

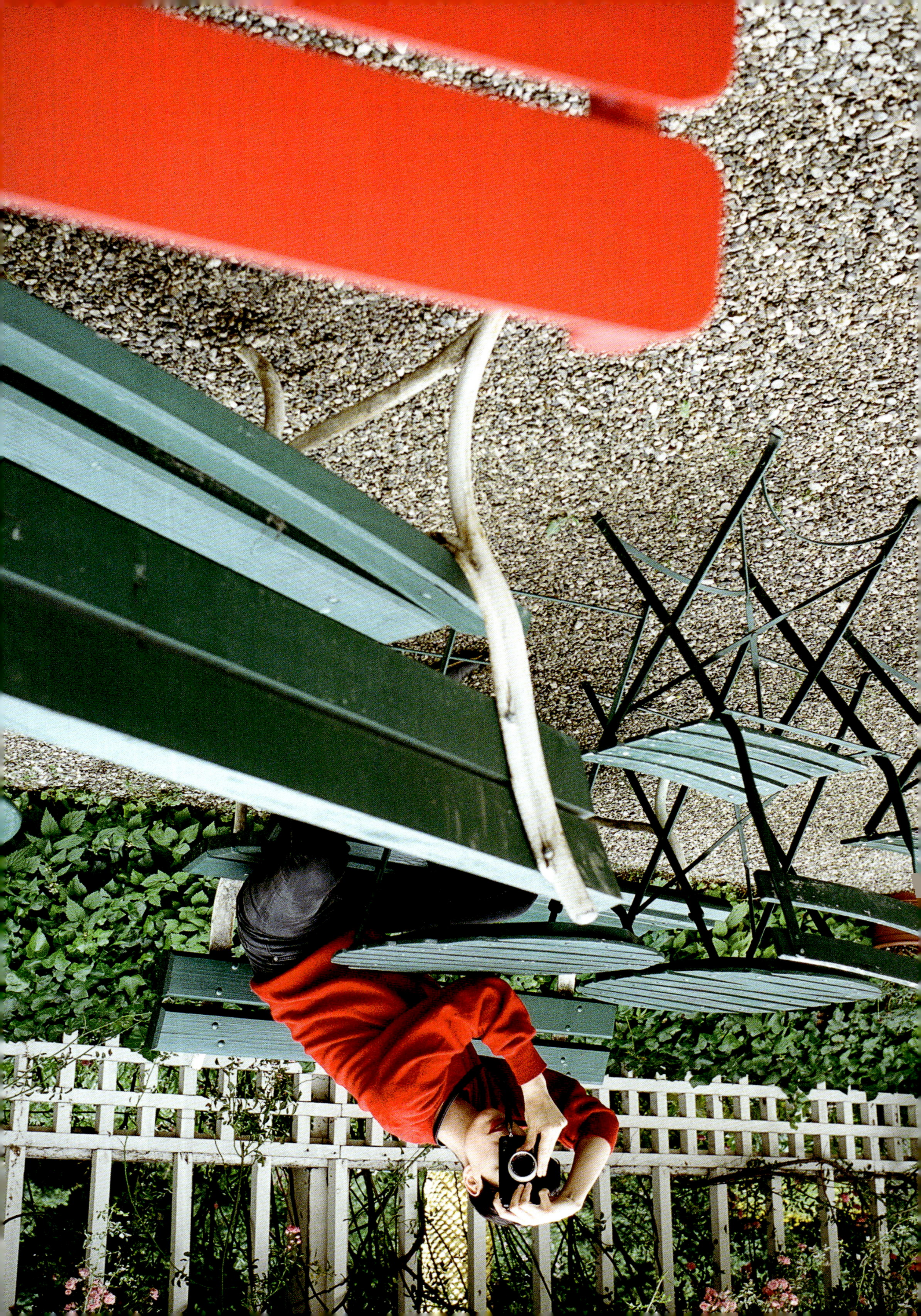

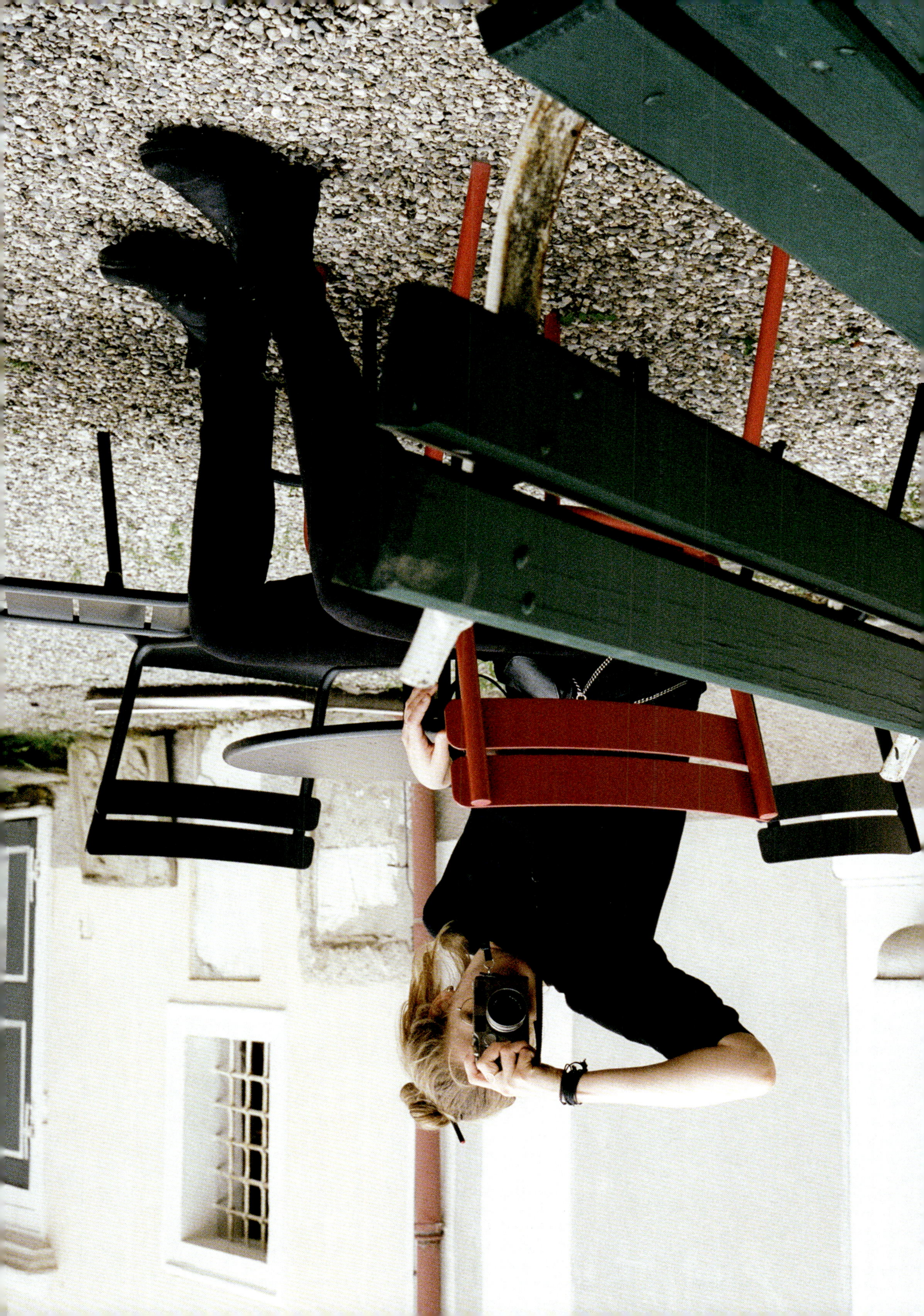

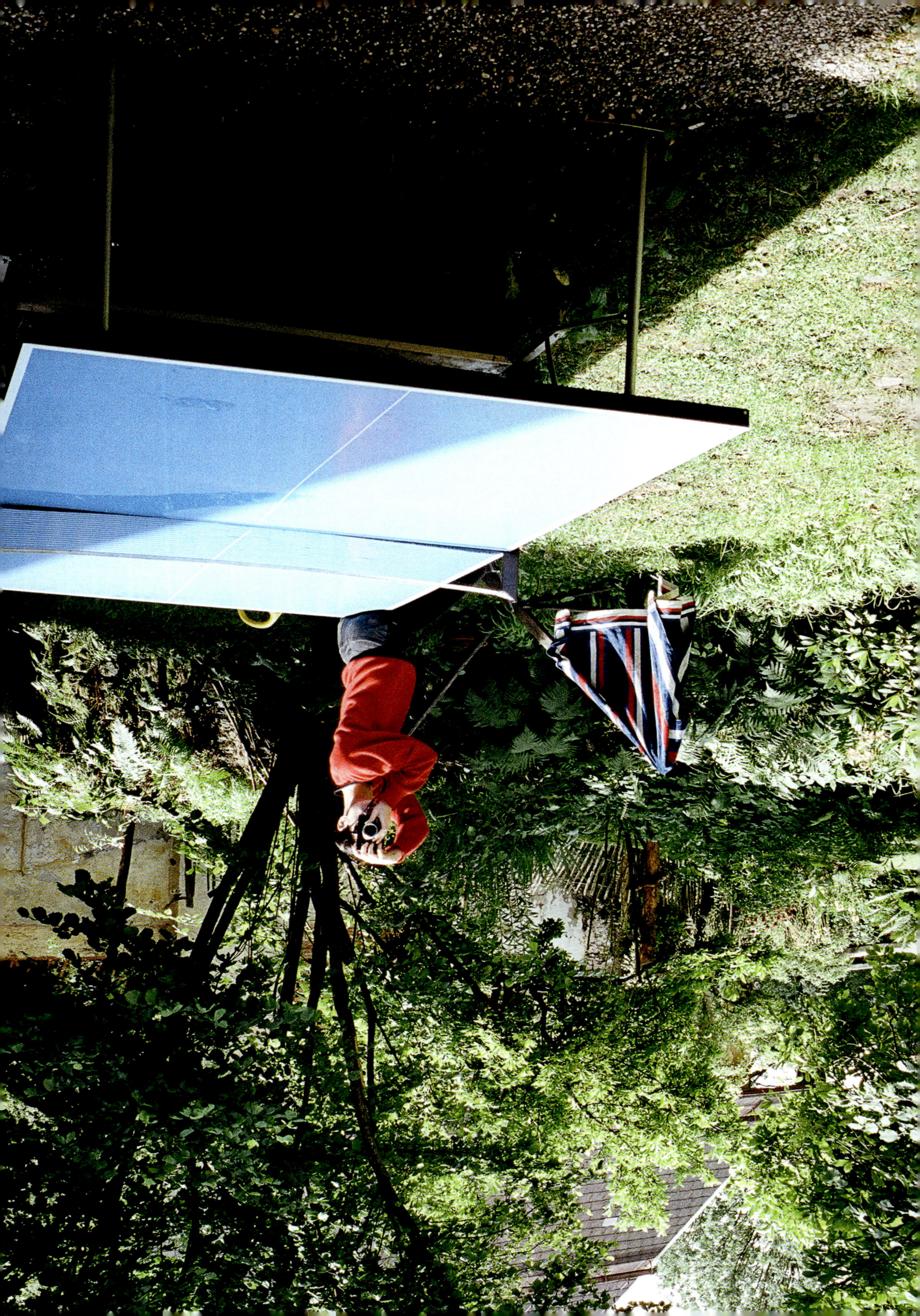

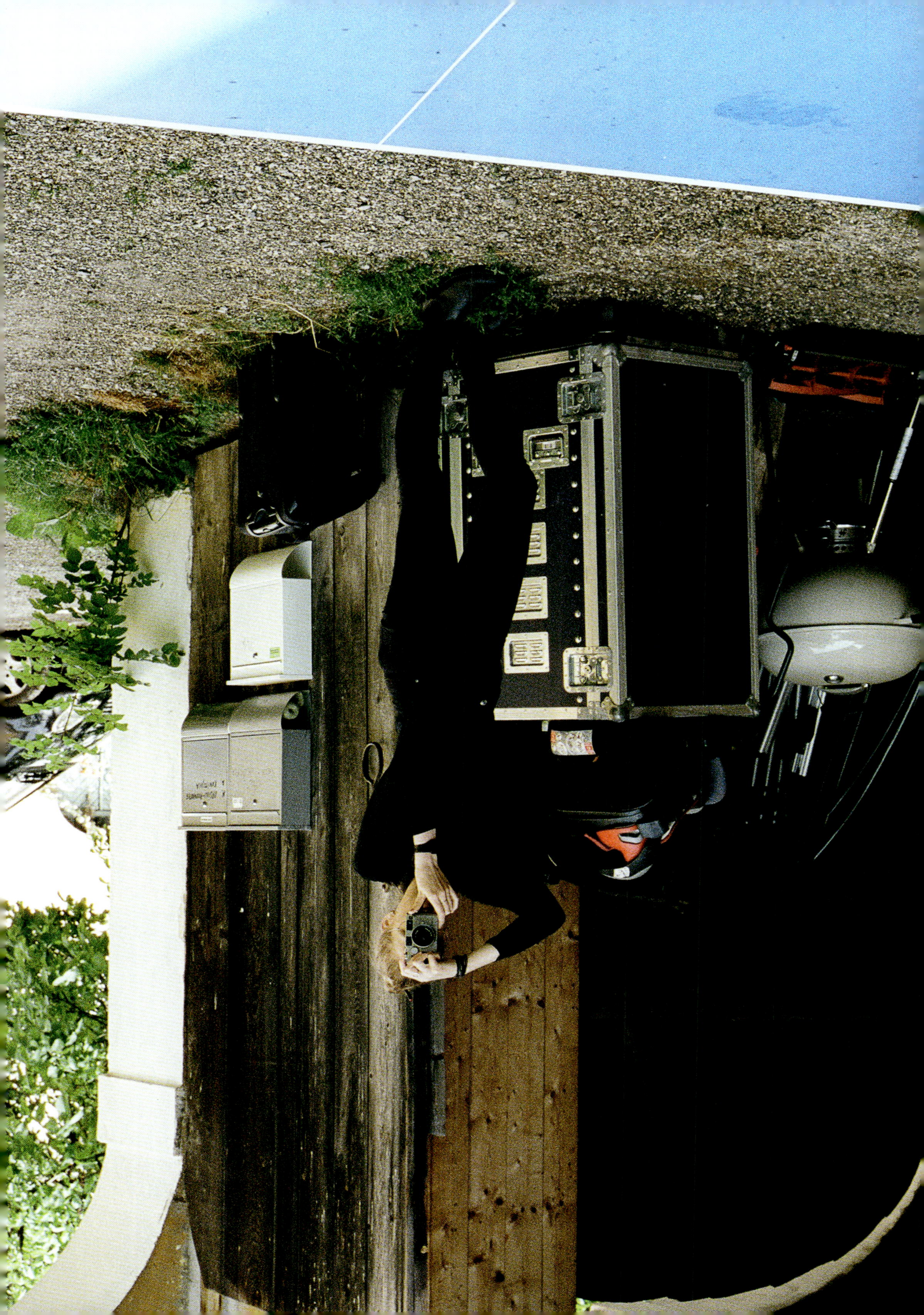

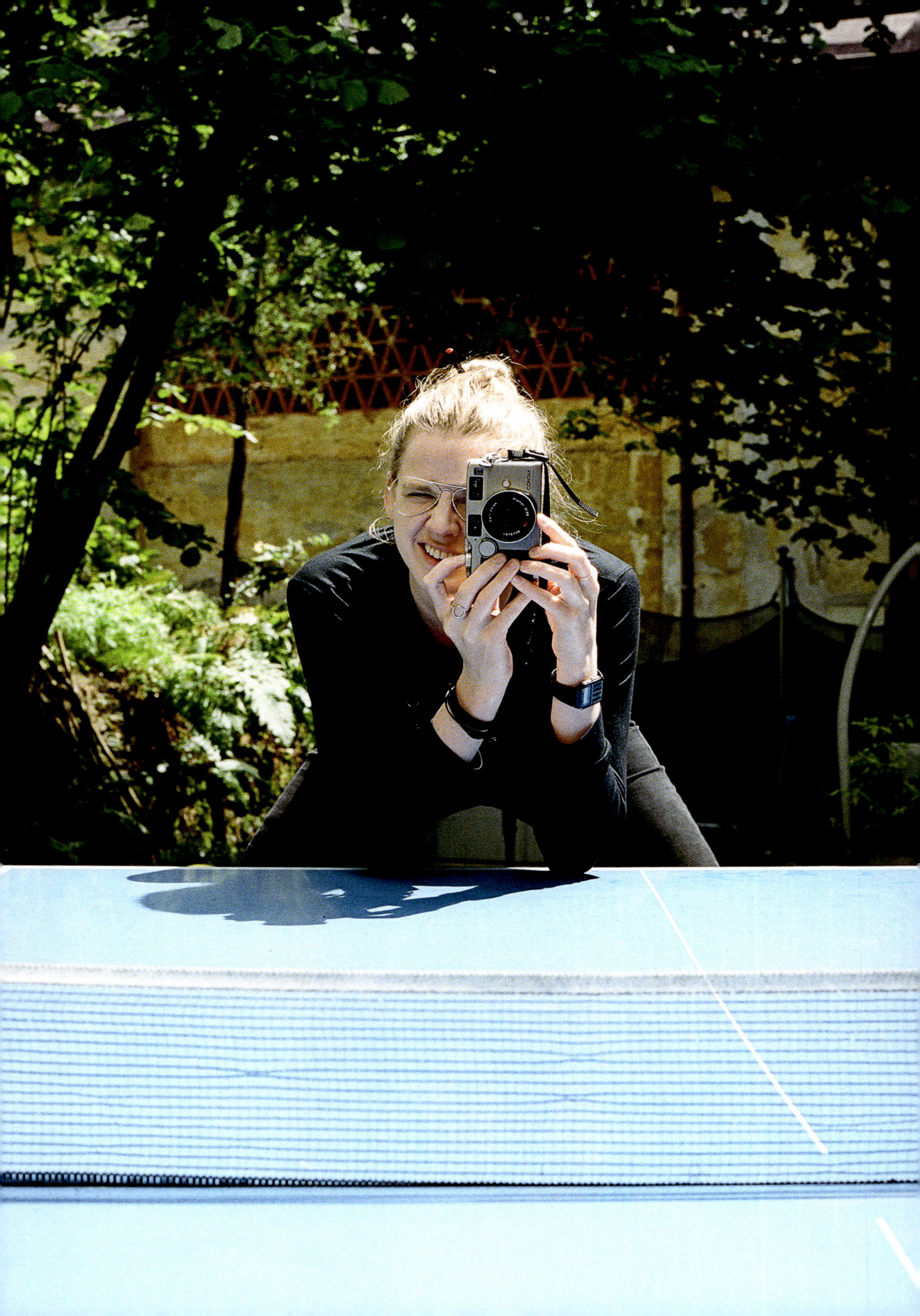

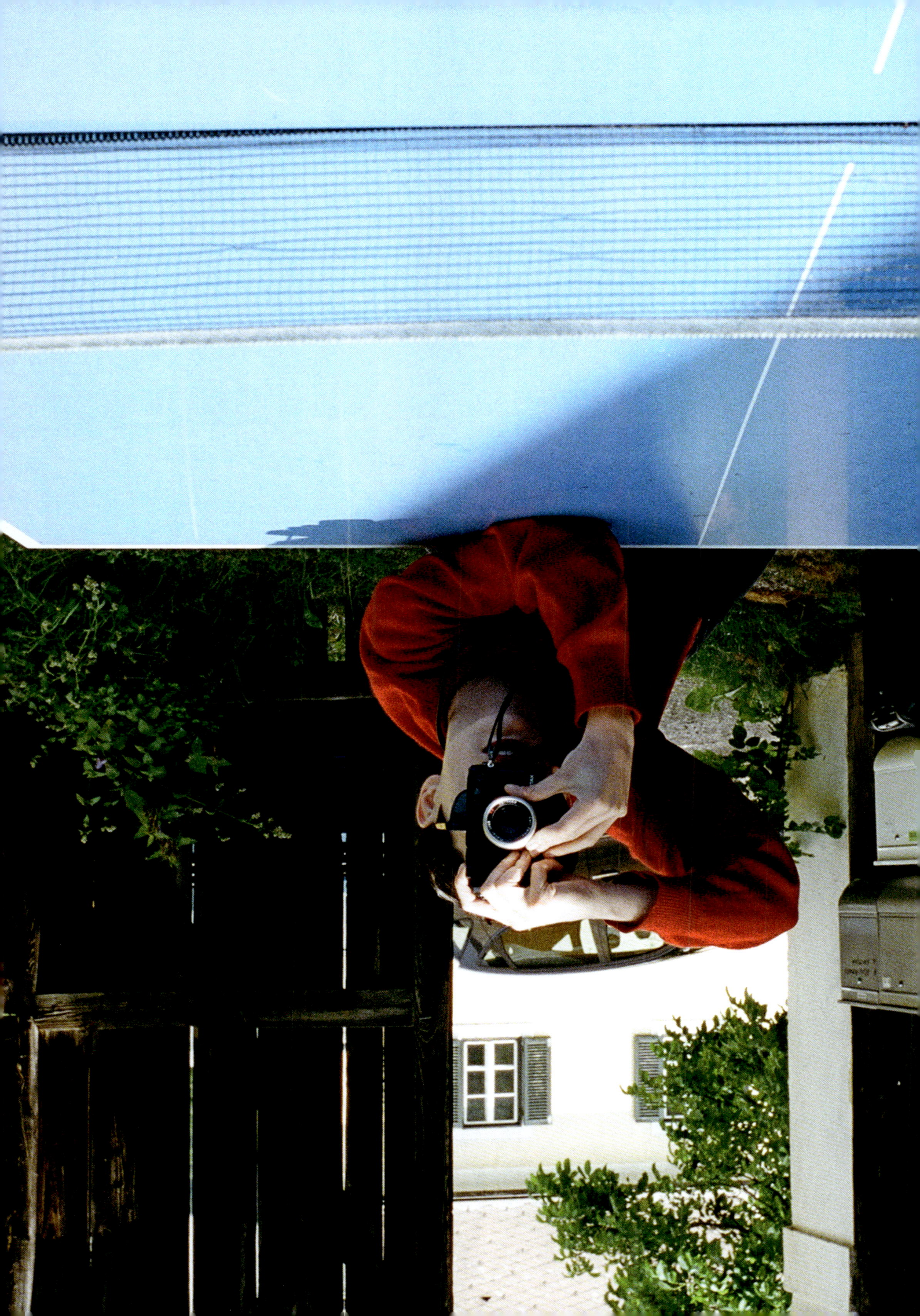

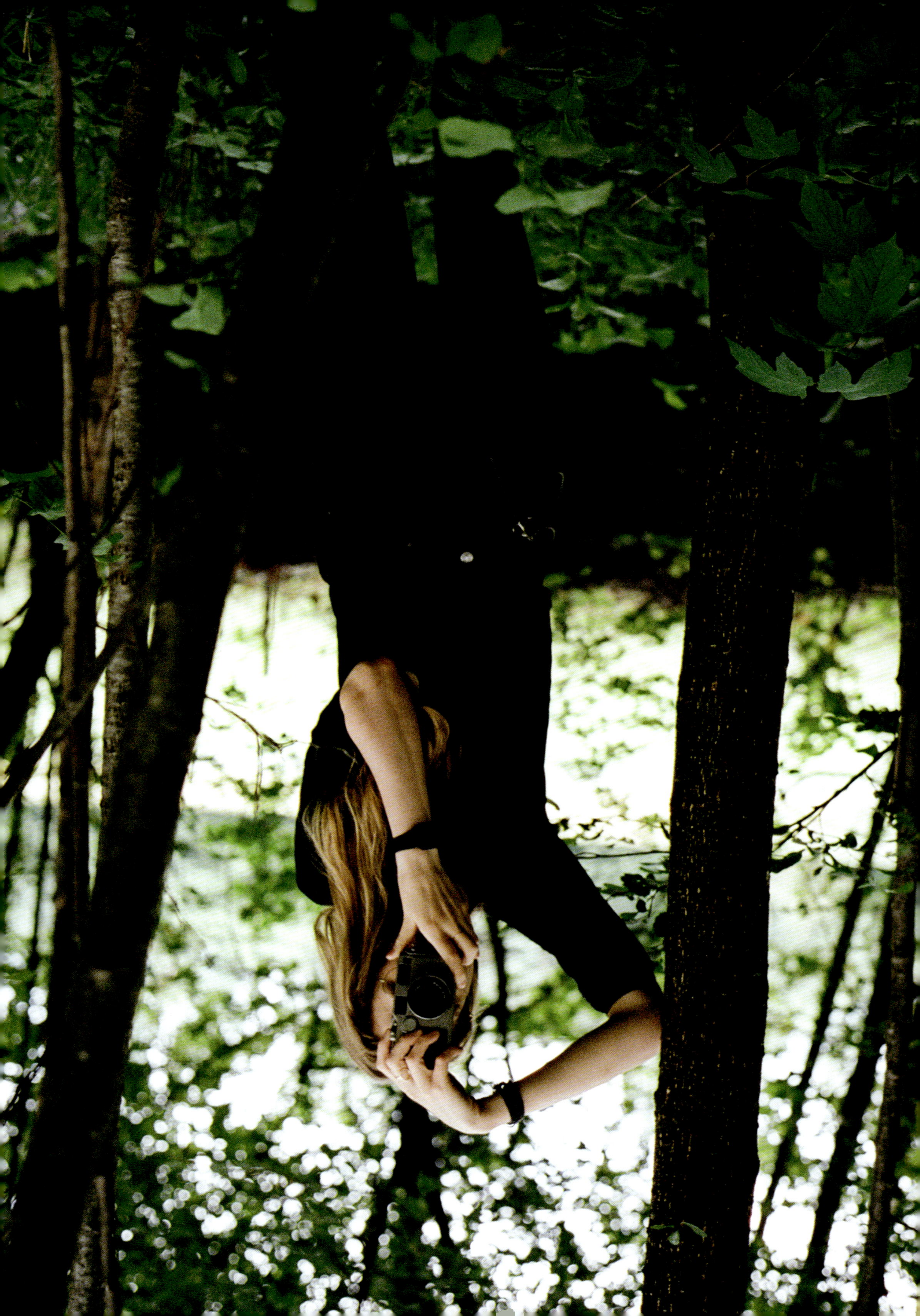

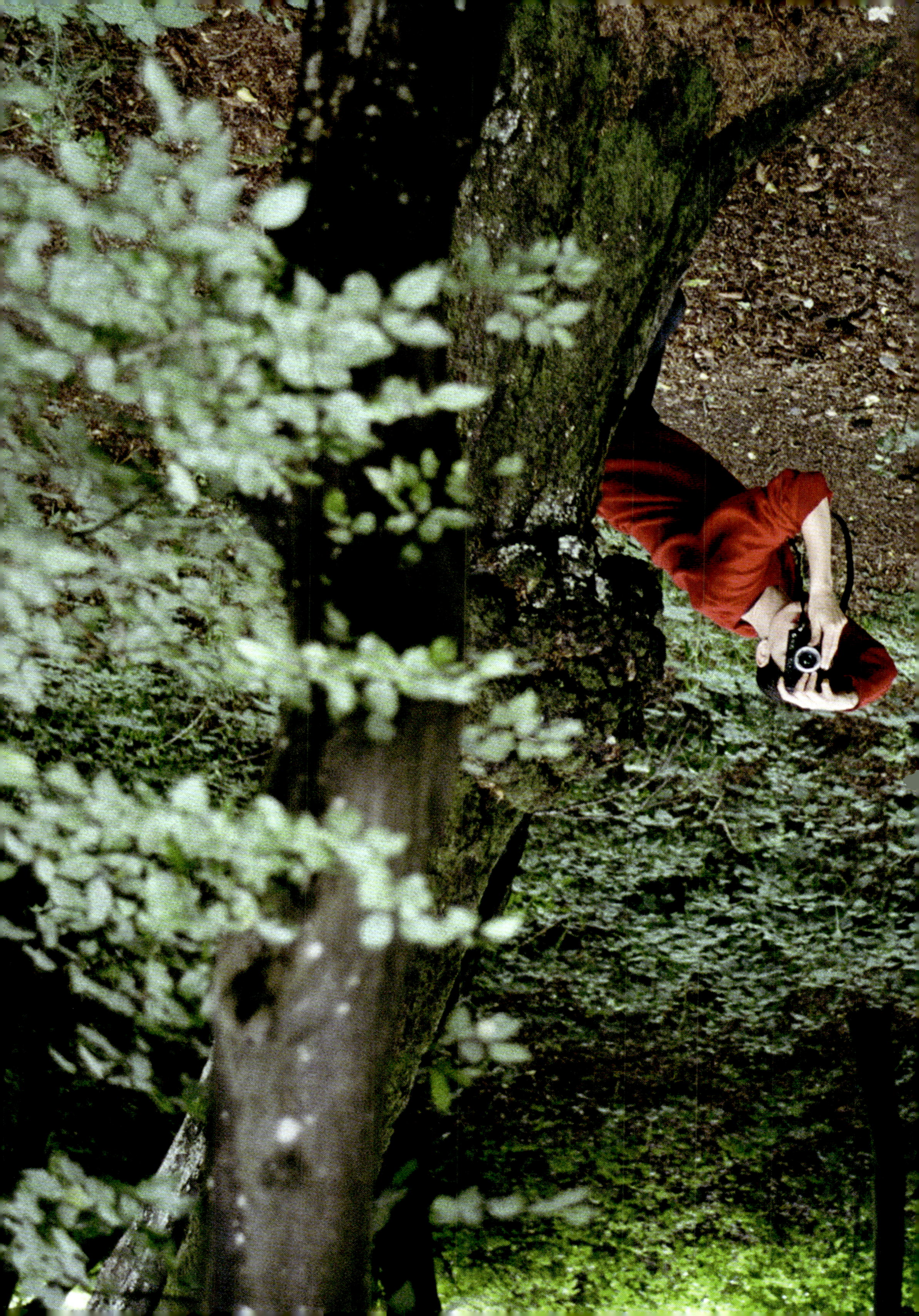

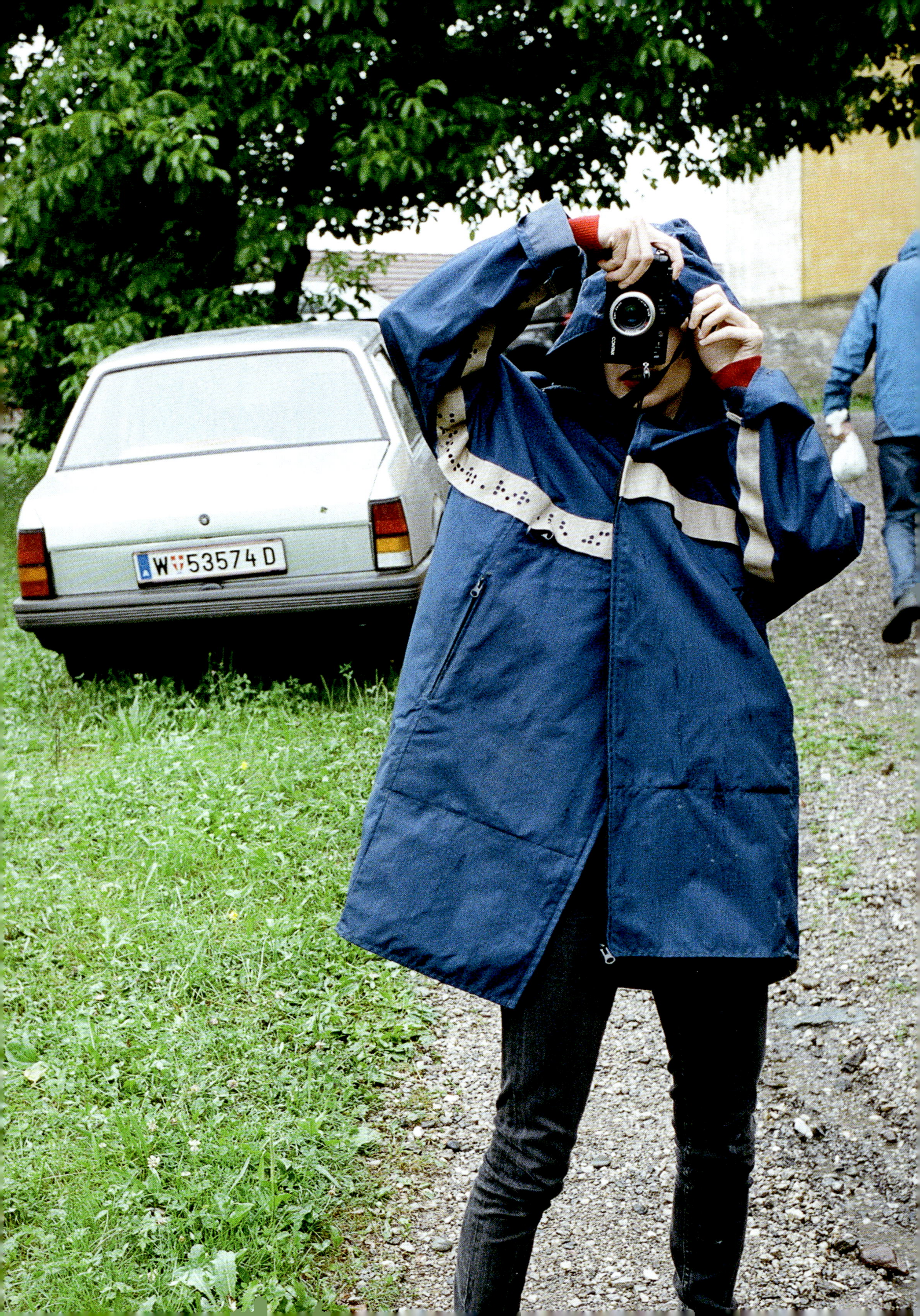
W 53574 D

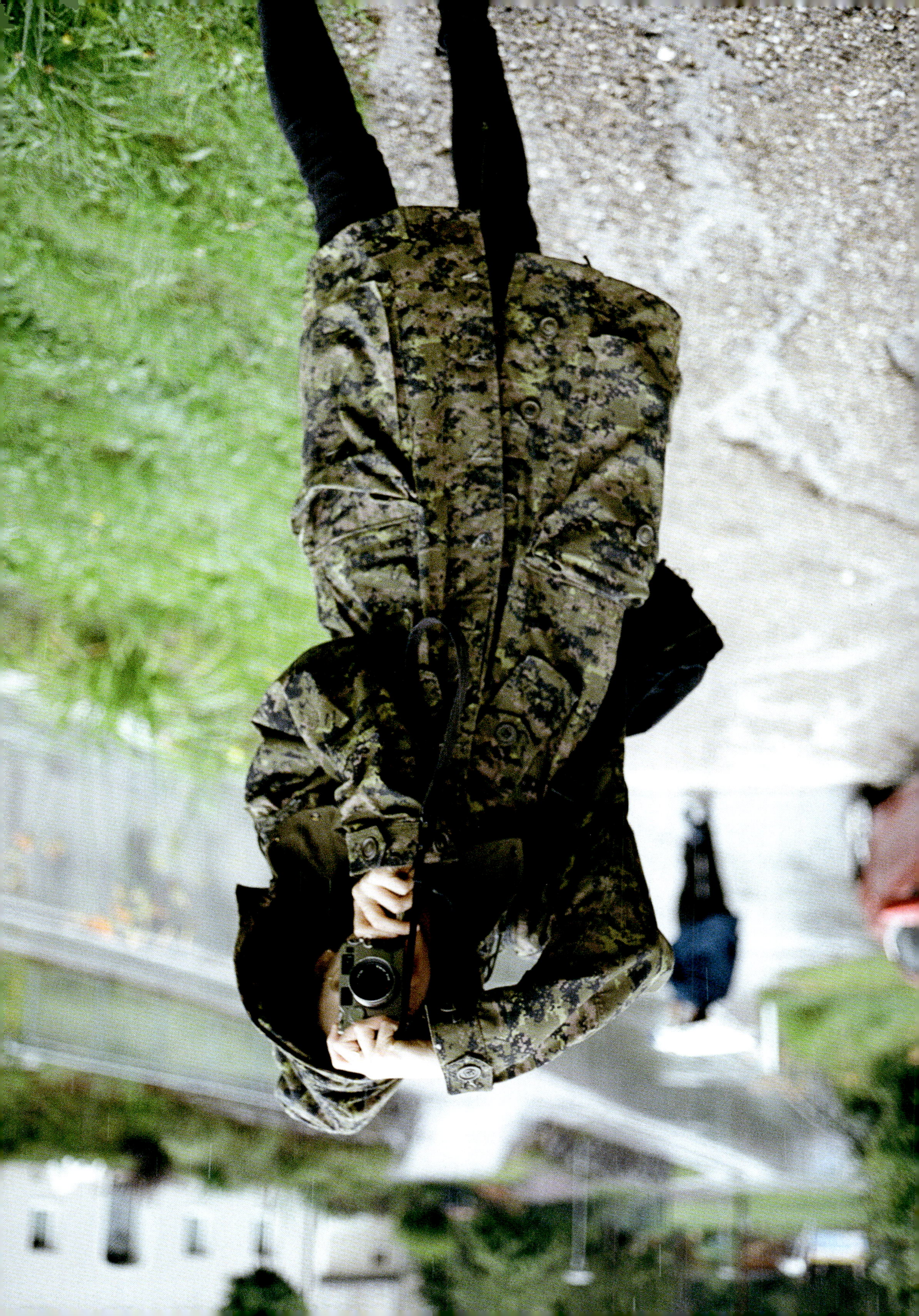

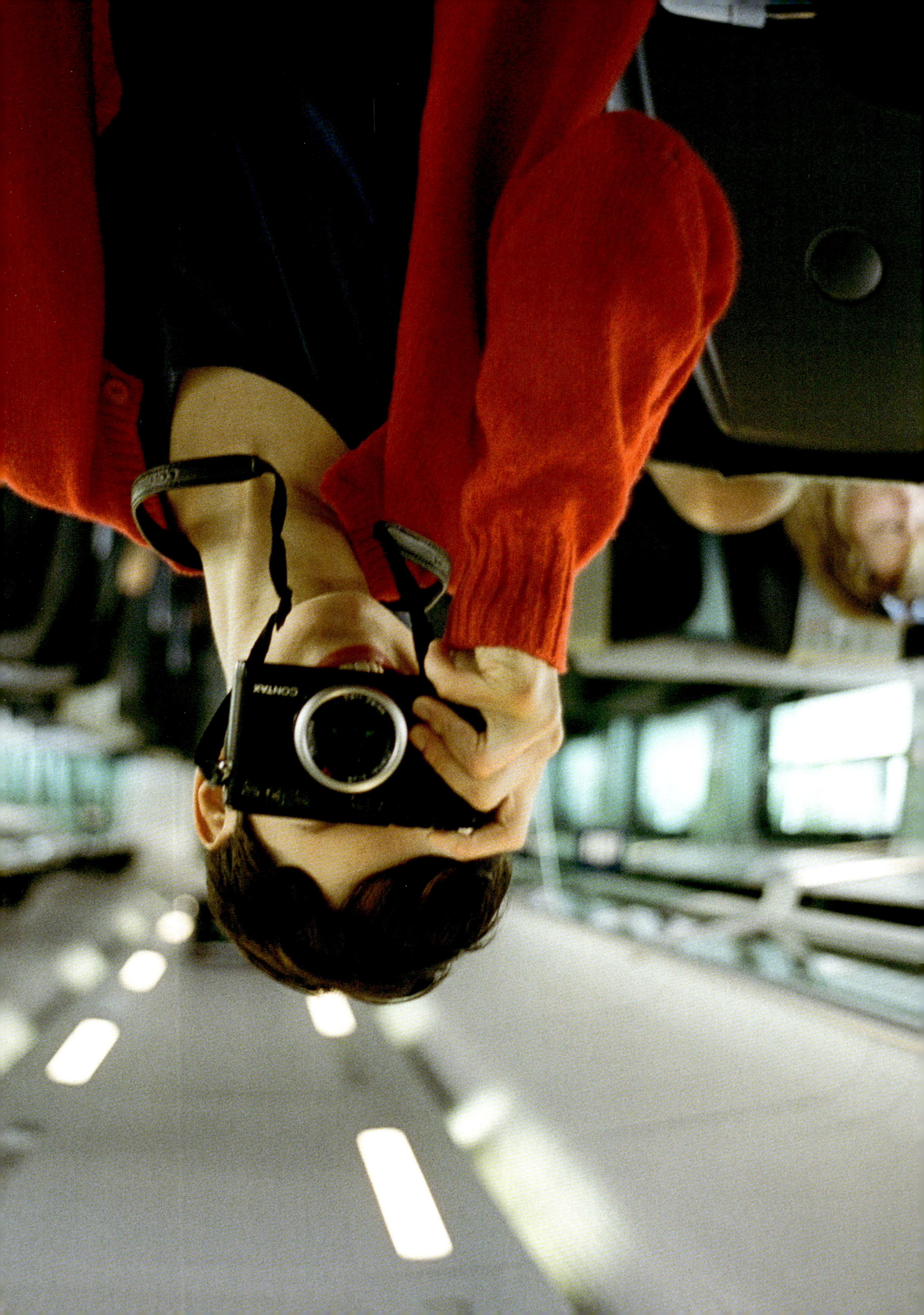

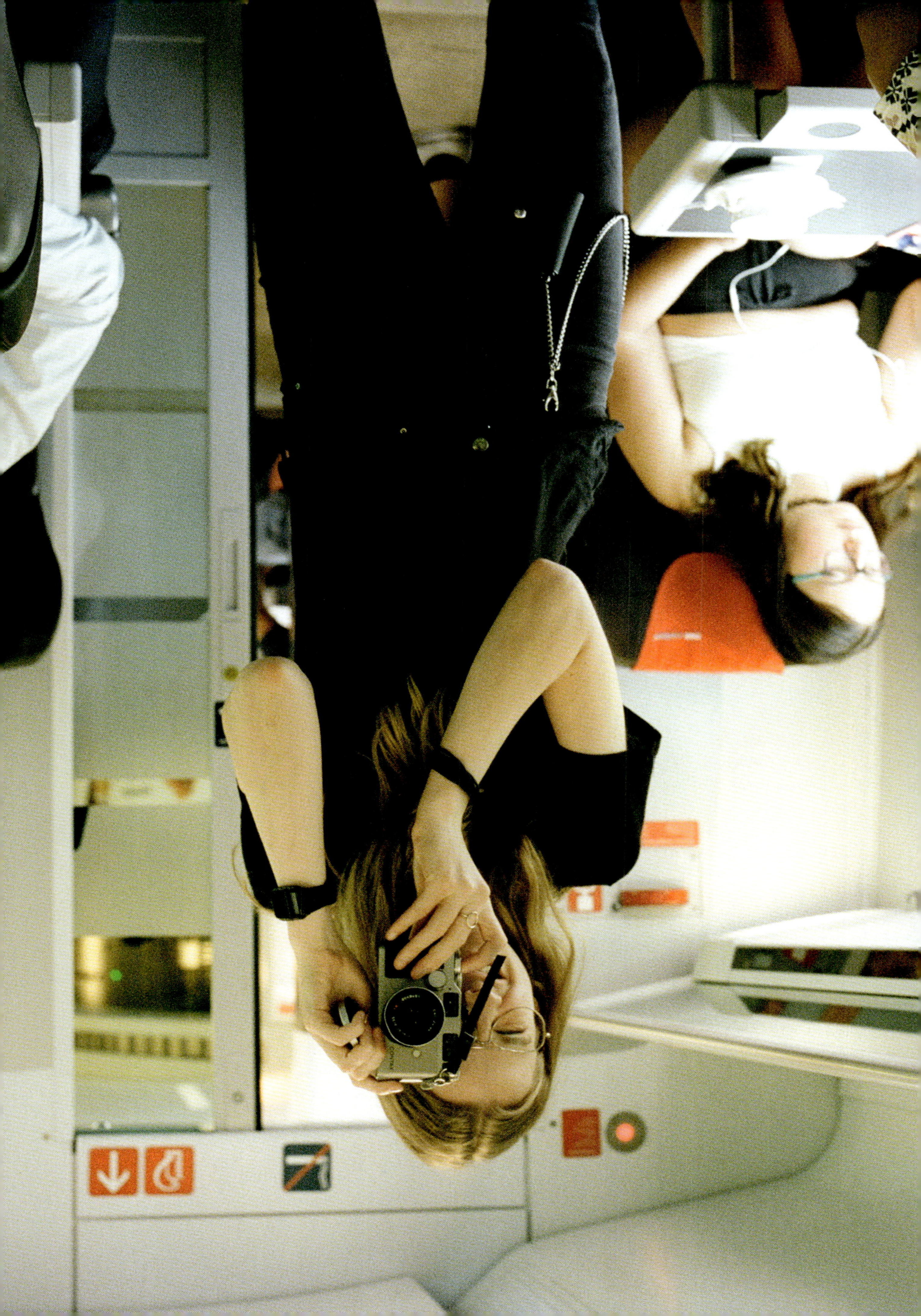

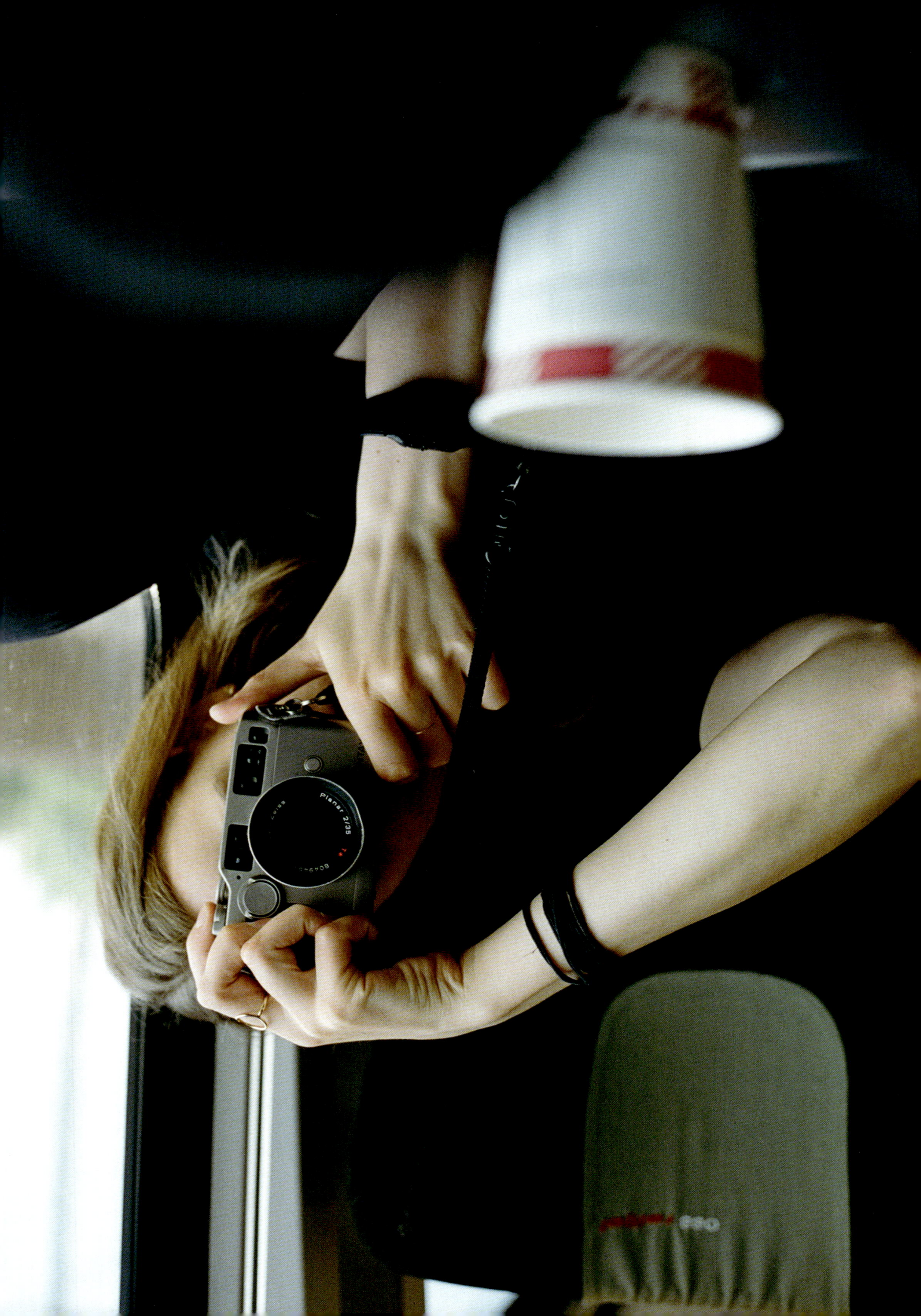
Planar 2/35

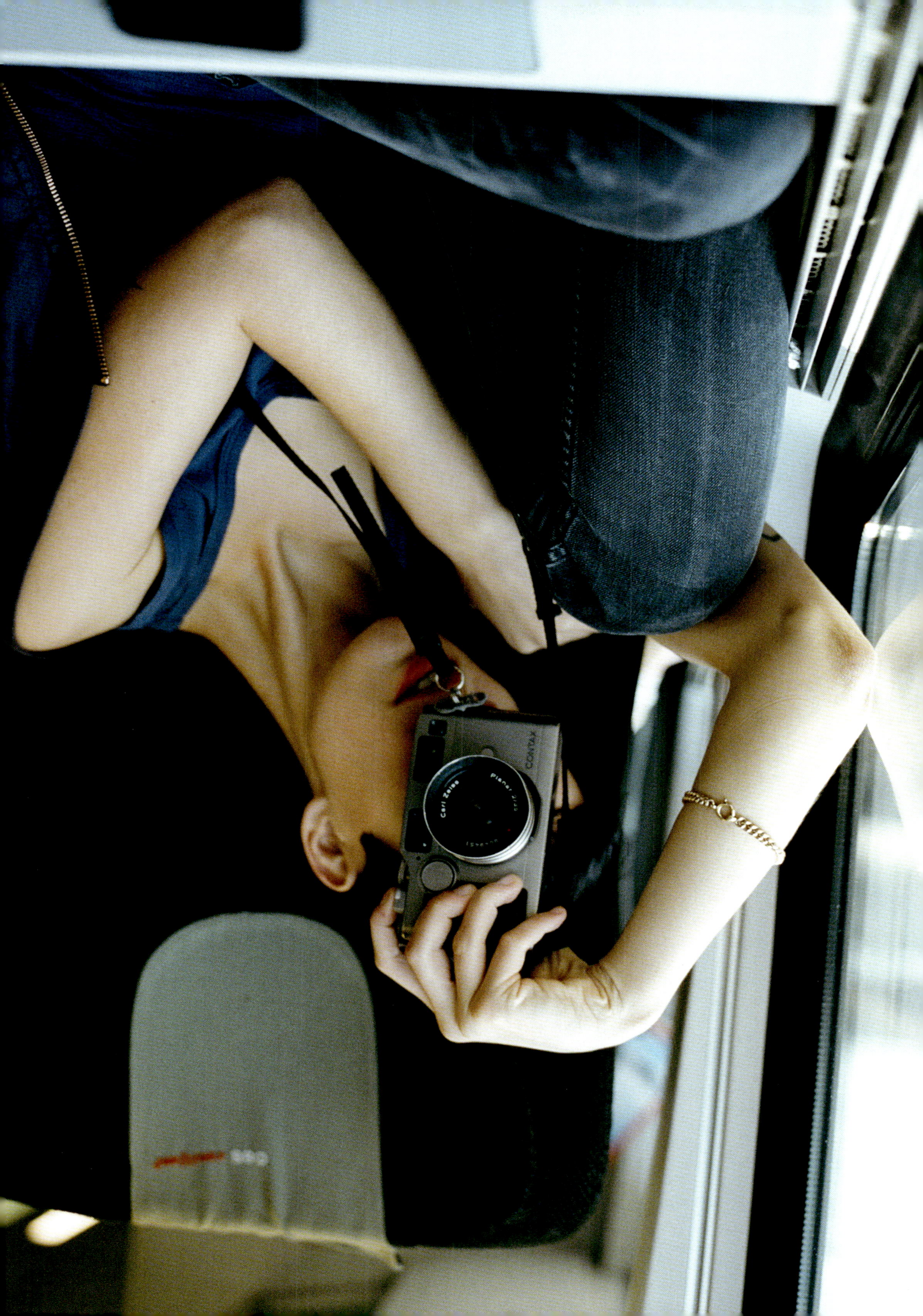
CONTAX
Carl Zeiss

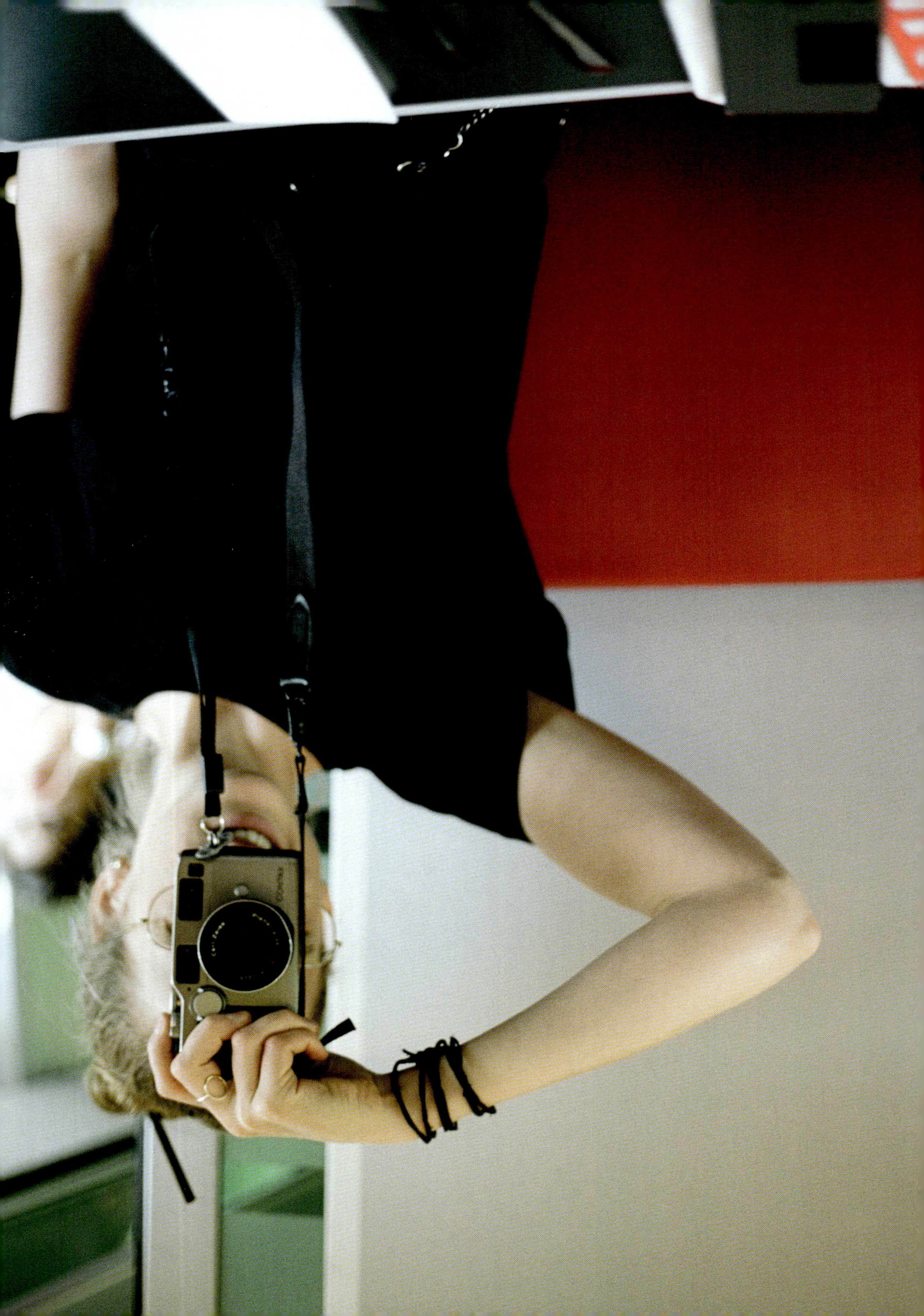

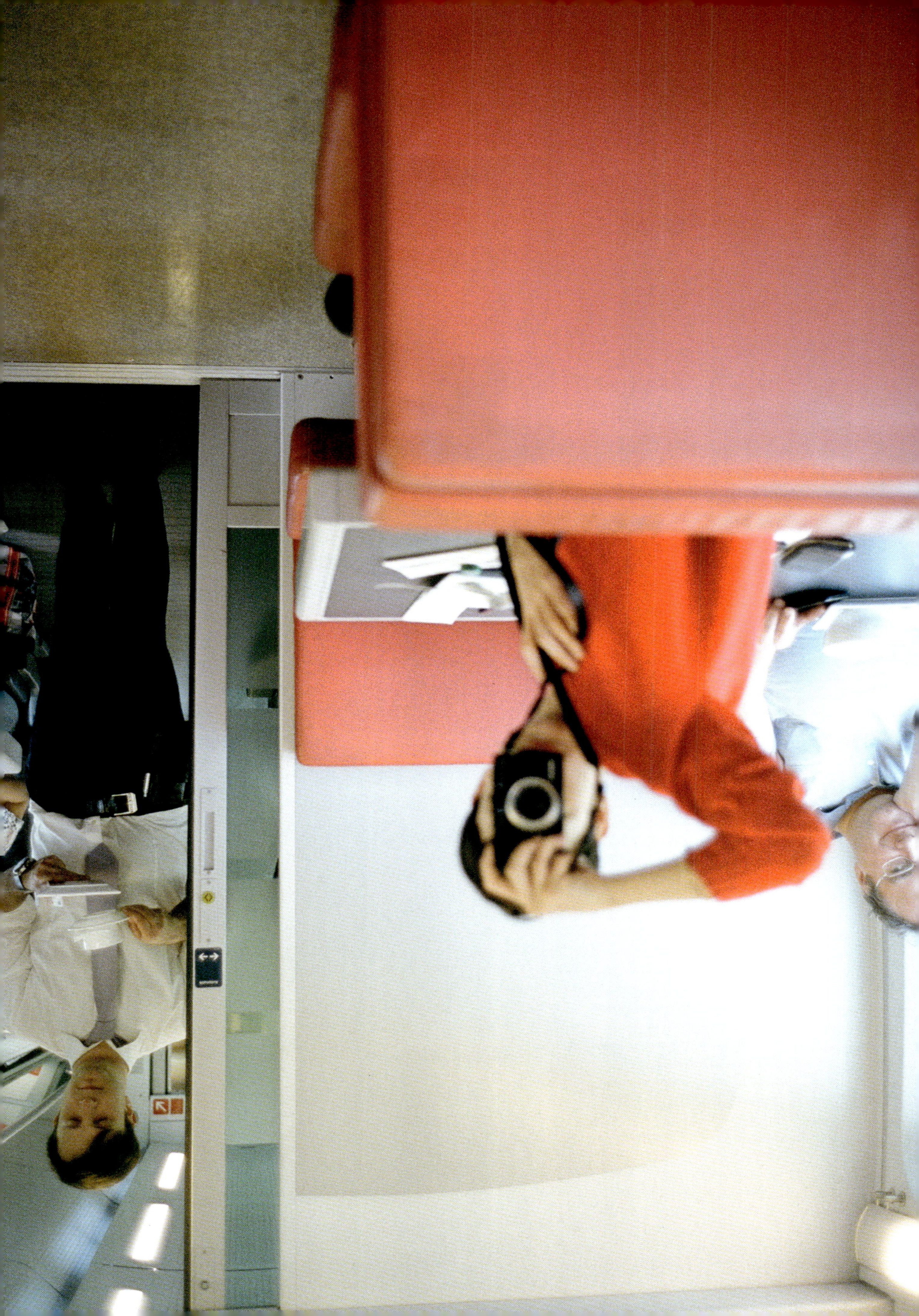

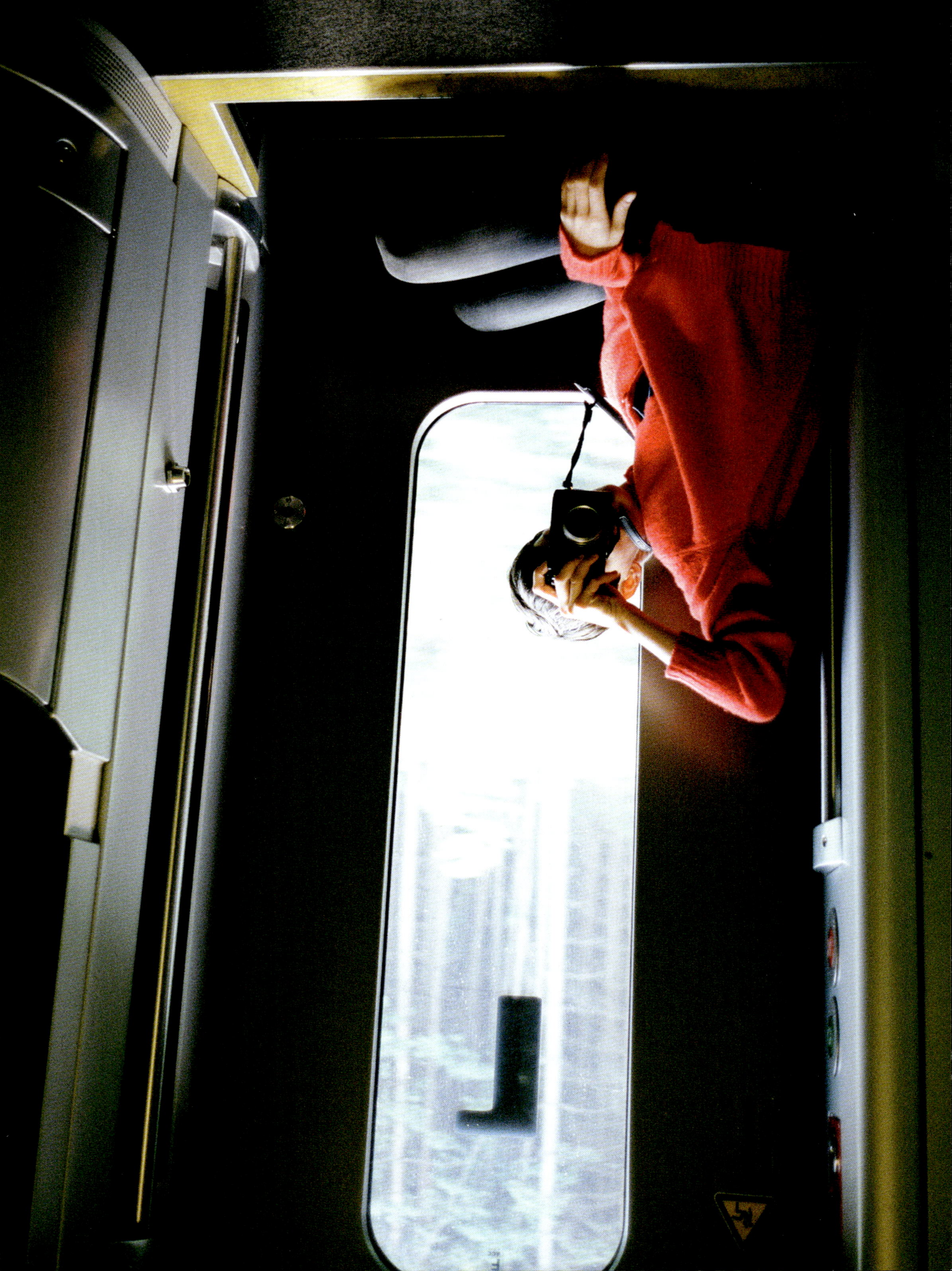

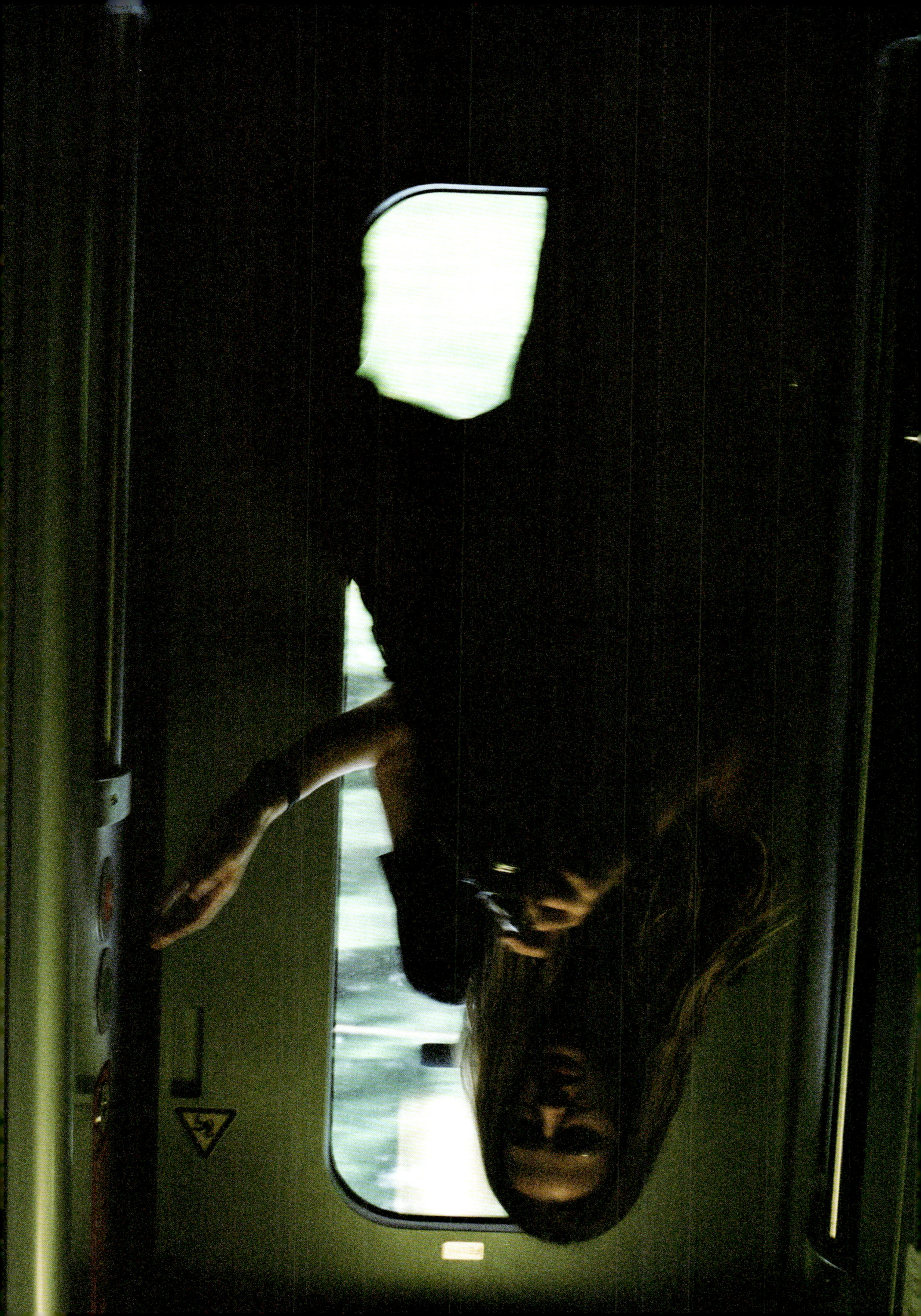

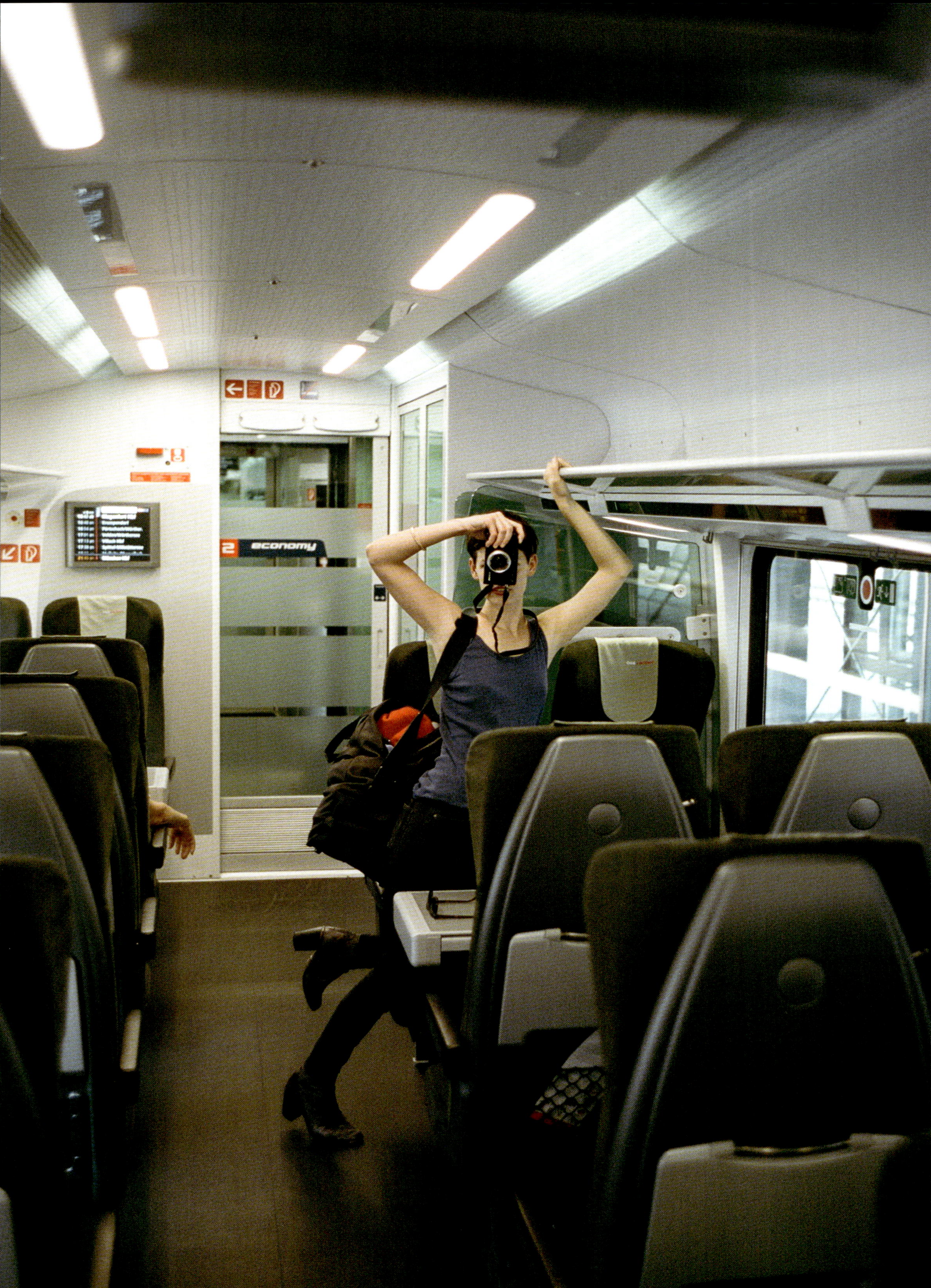
2 economy

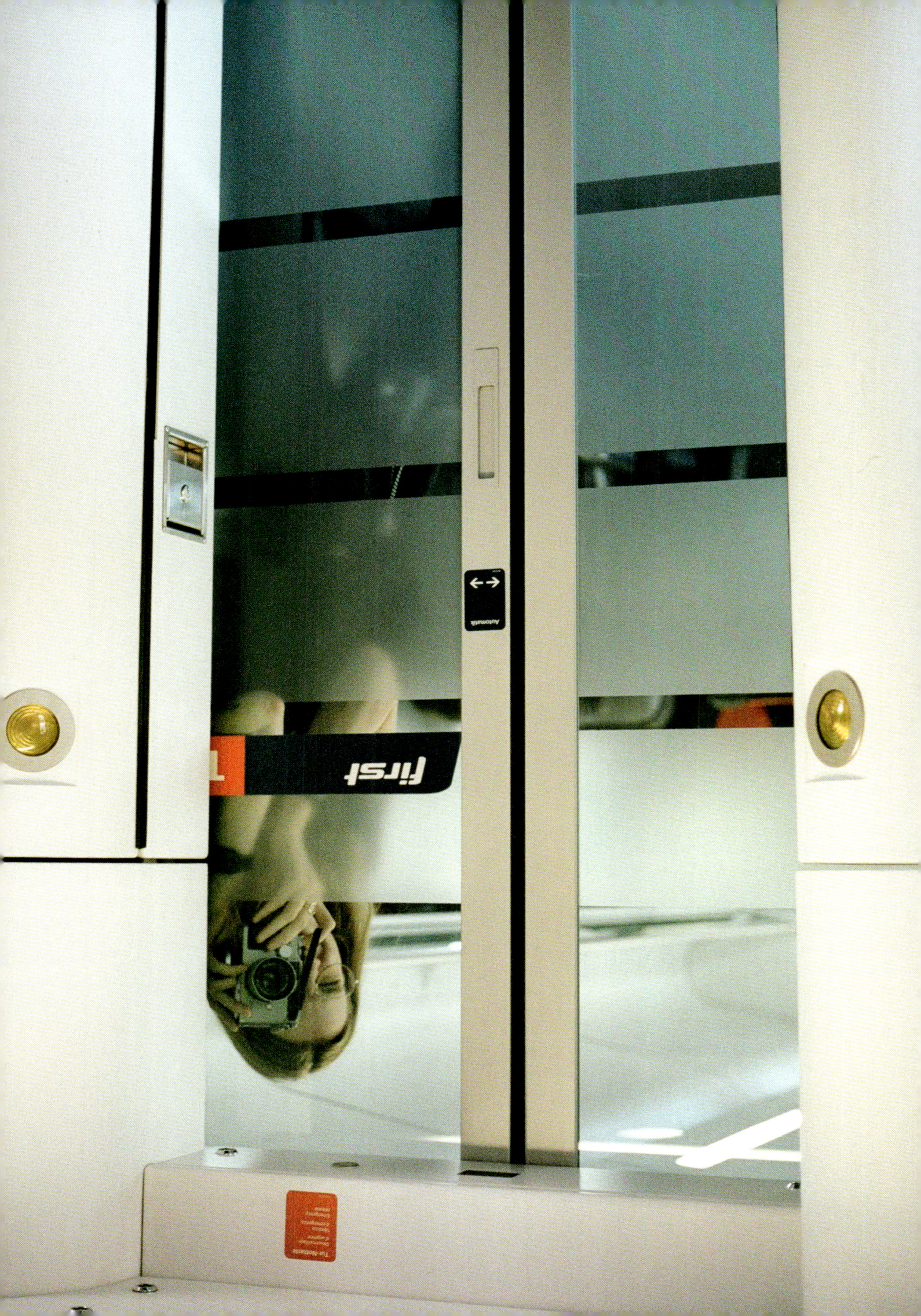
first

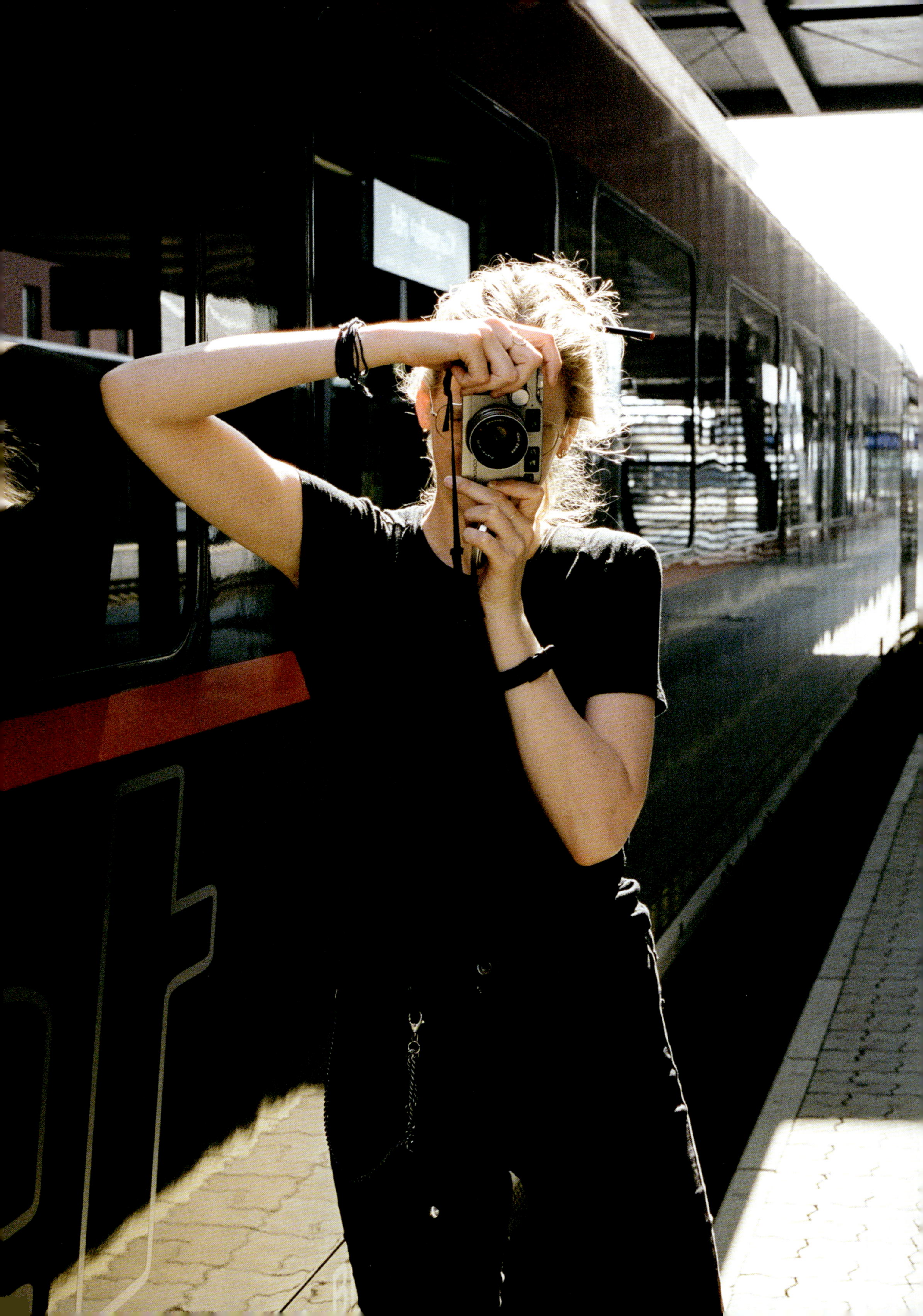

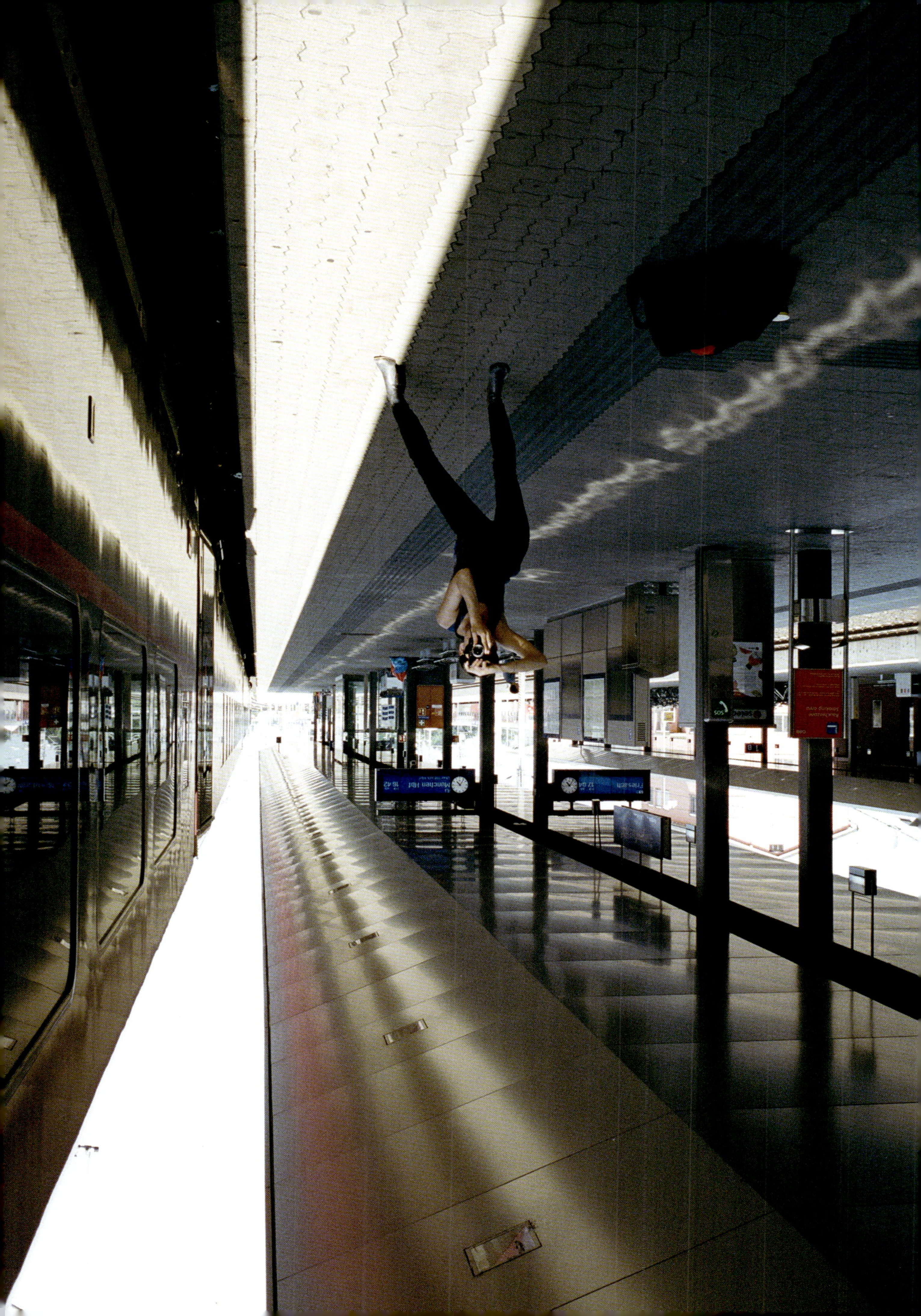
München Hbf
Friesach

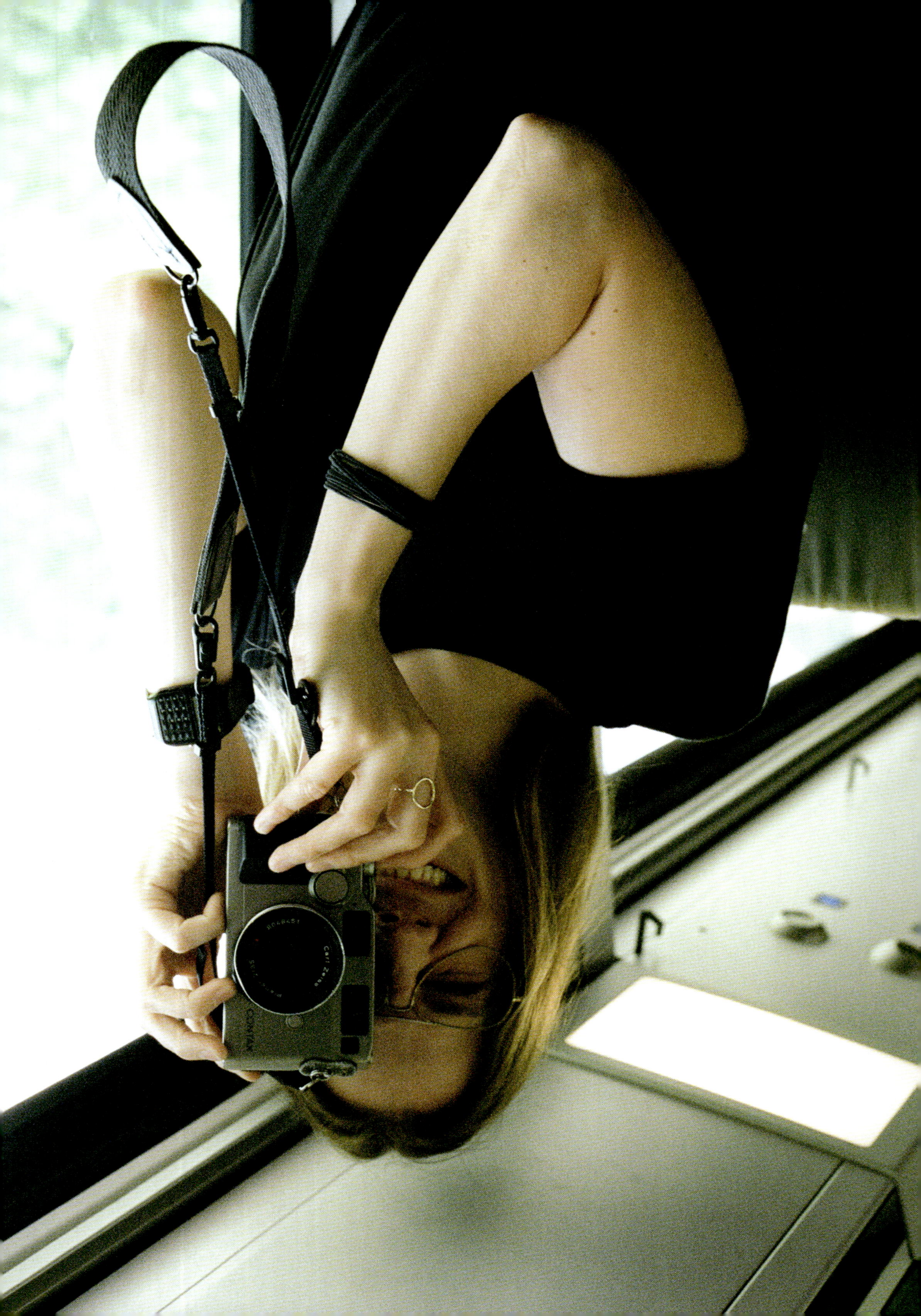
CONTAX
Carl Zeiss

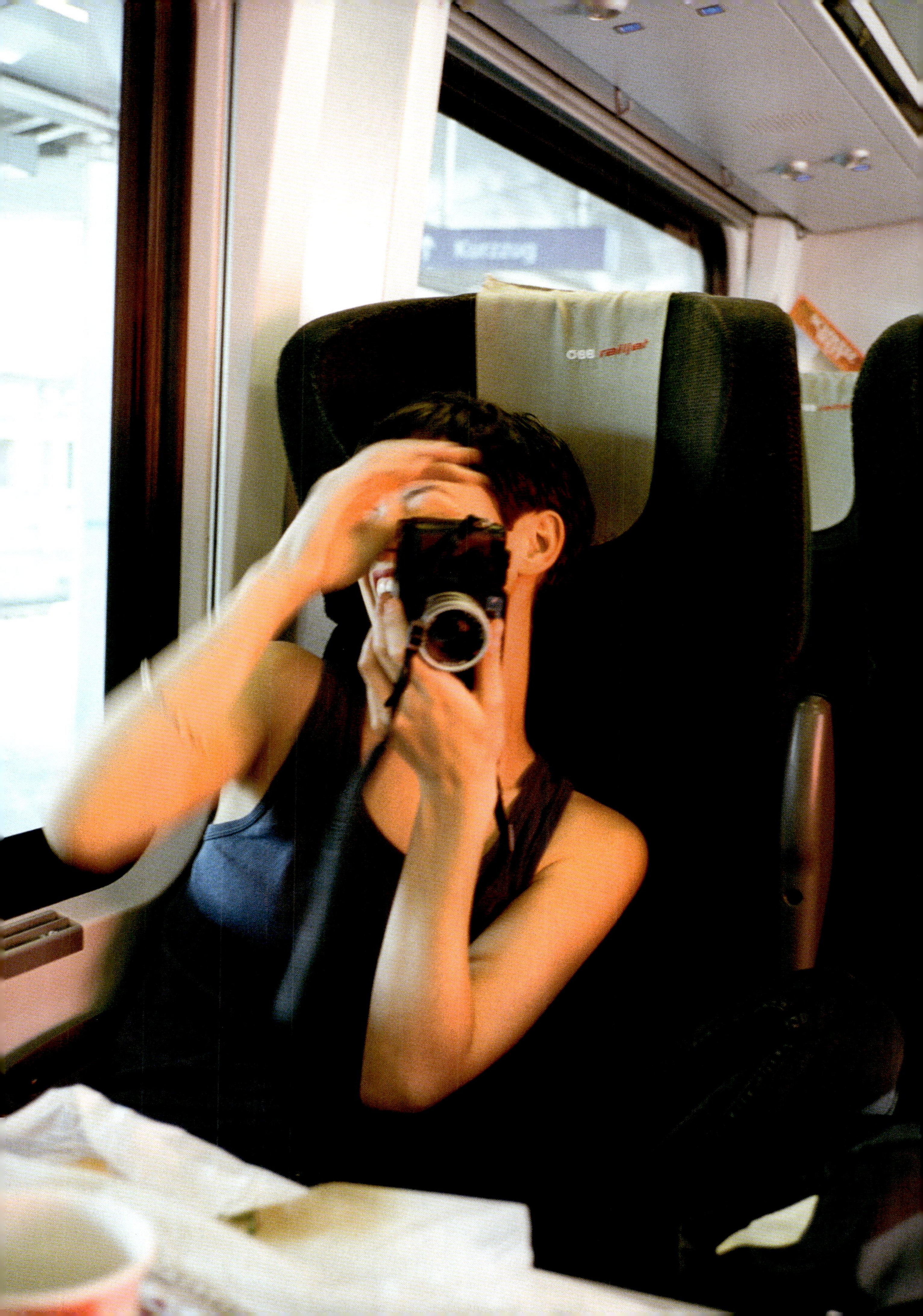
ÖBB railjet

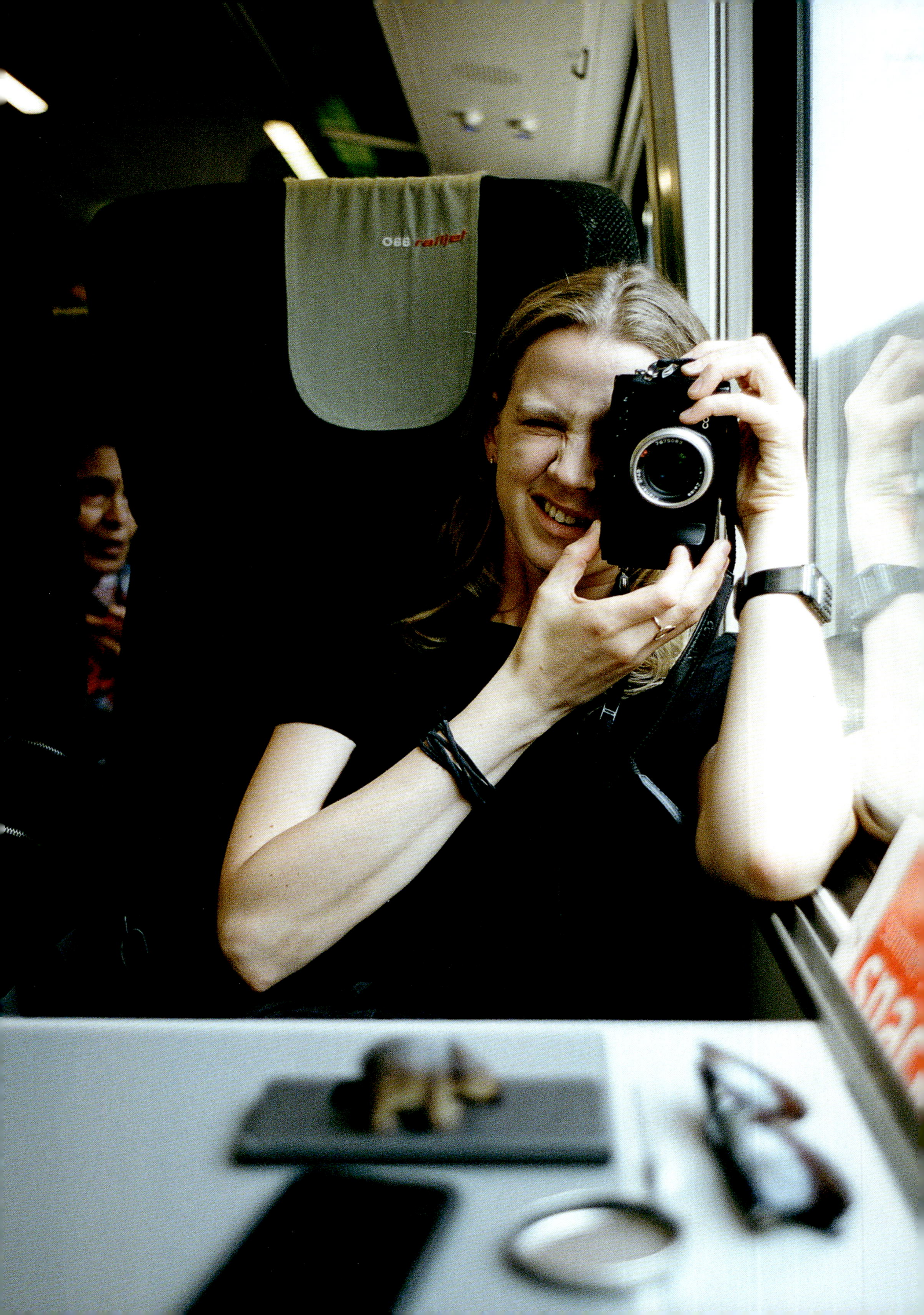

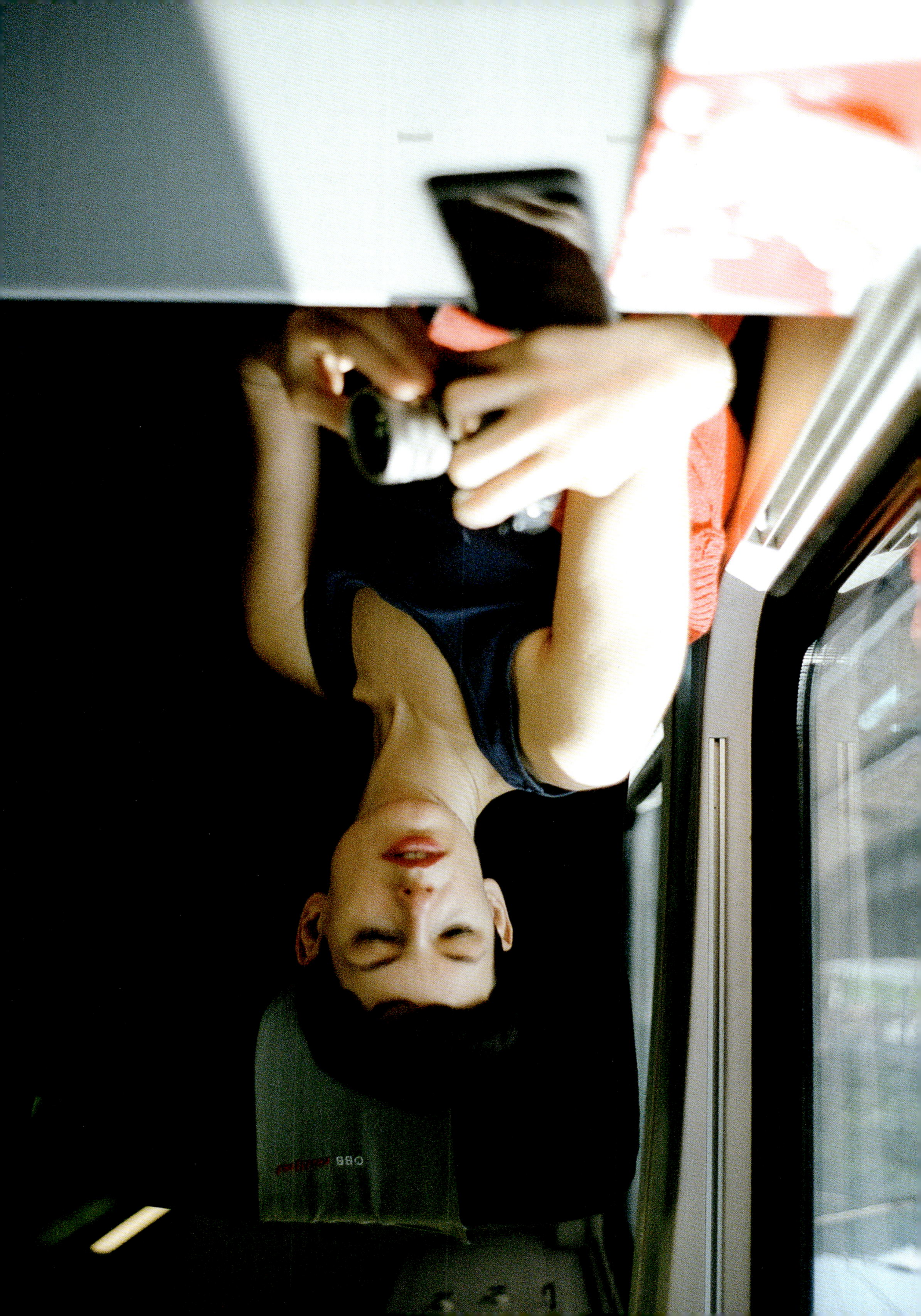

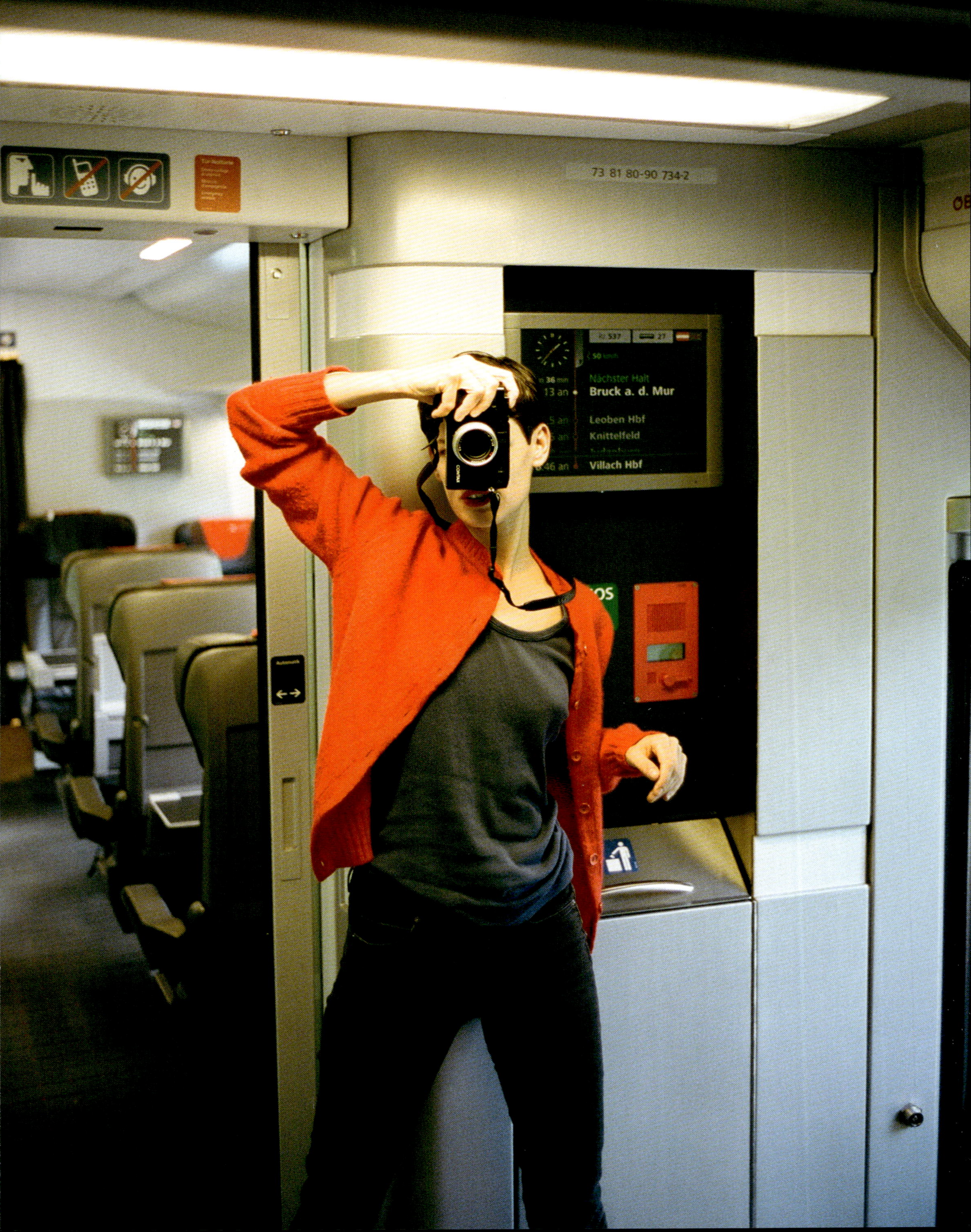
73 81 80-90 734-2
Nächster Halt
Bruck a. d. Mur
Leoben Hbf
Knittelfeld
Villach Hbf

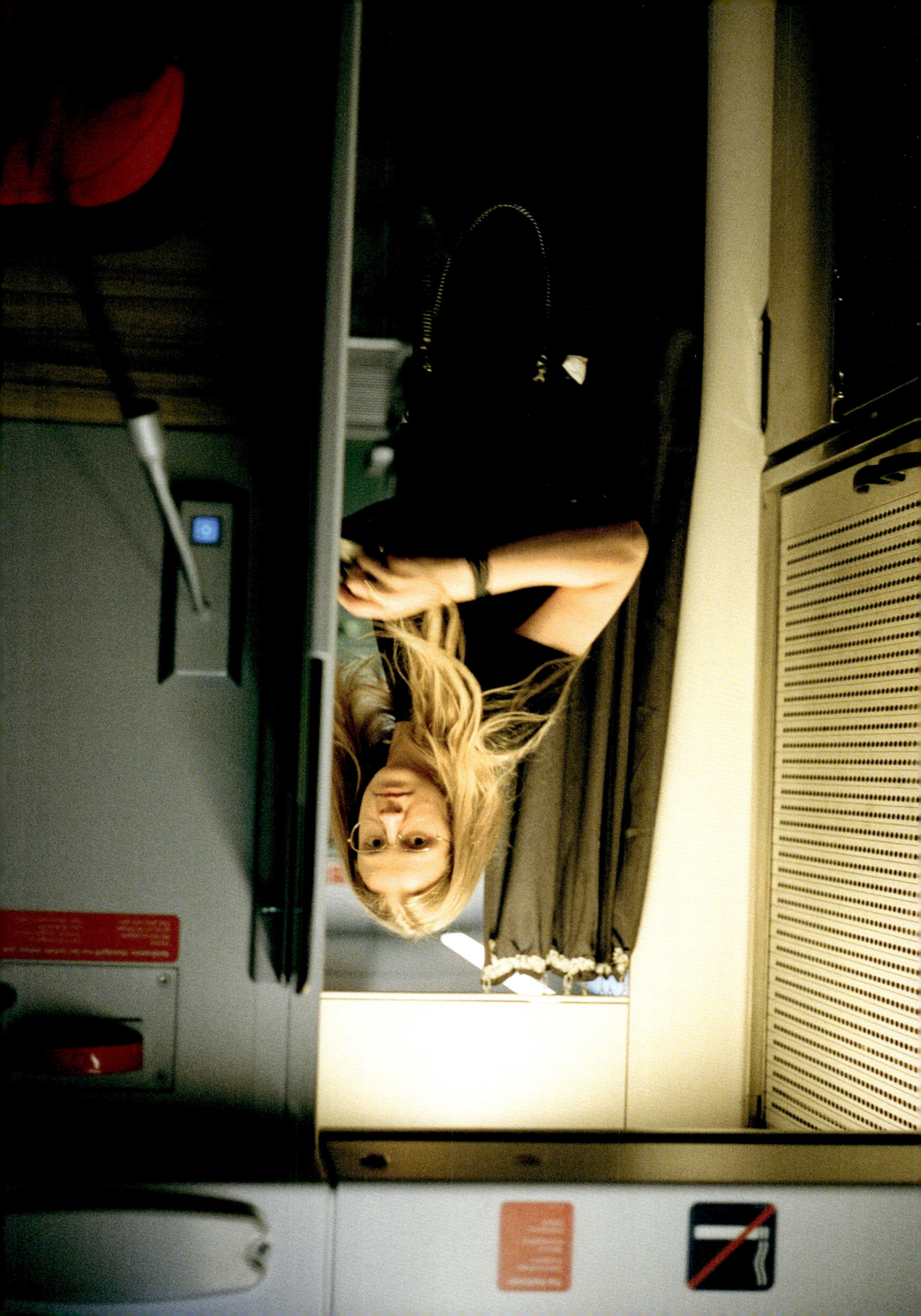

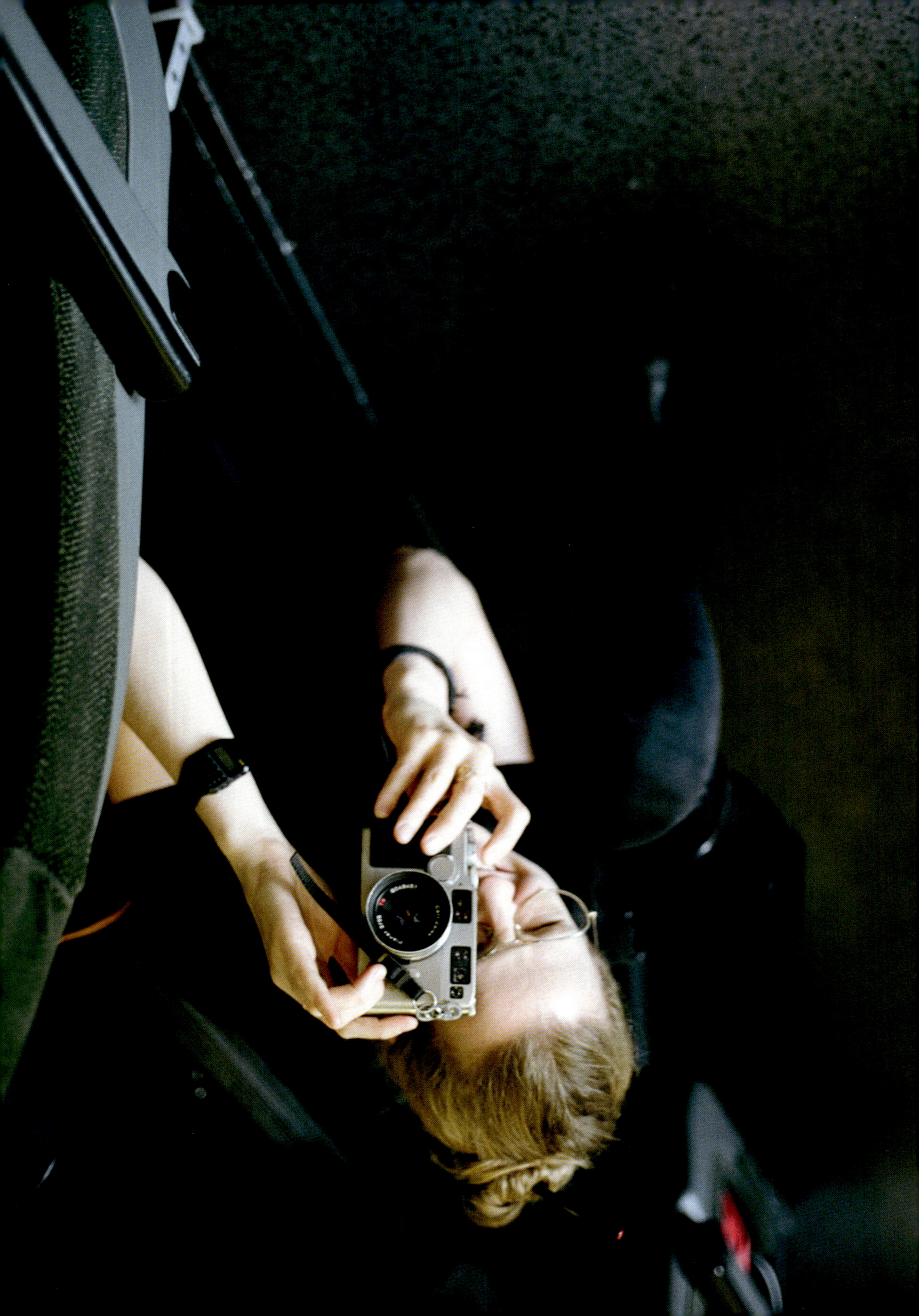

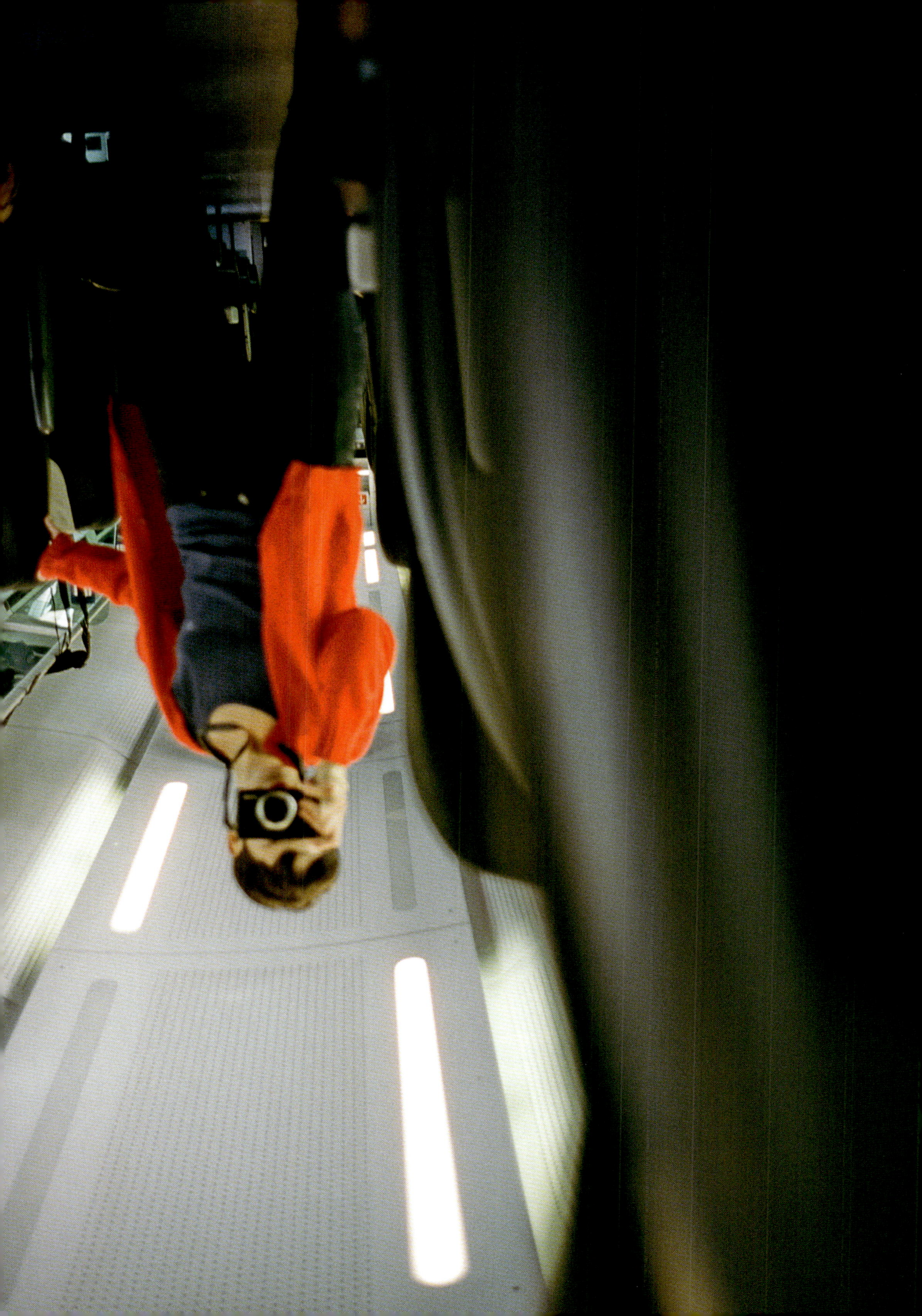

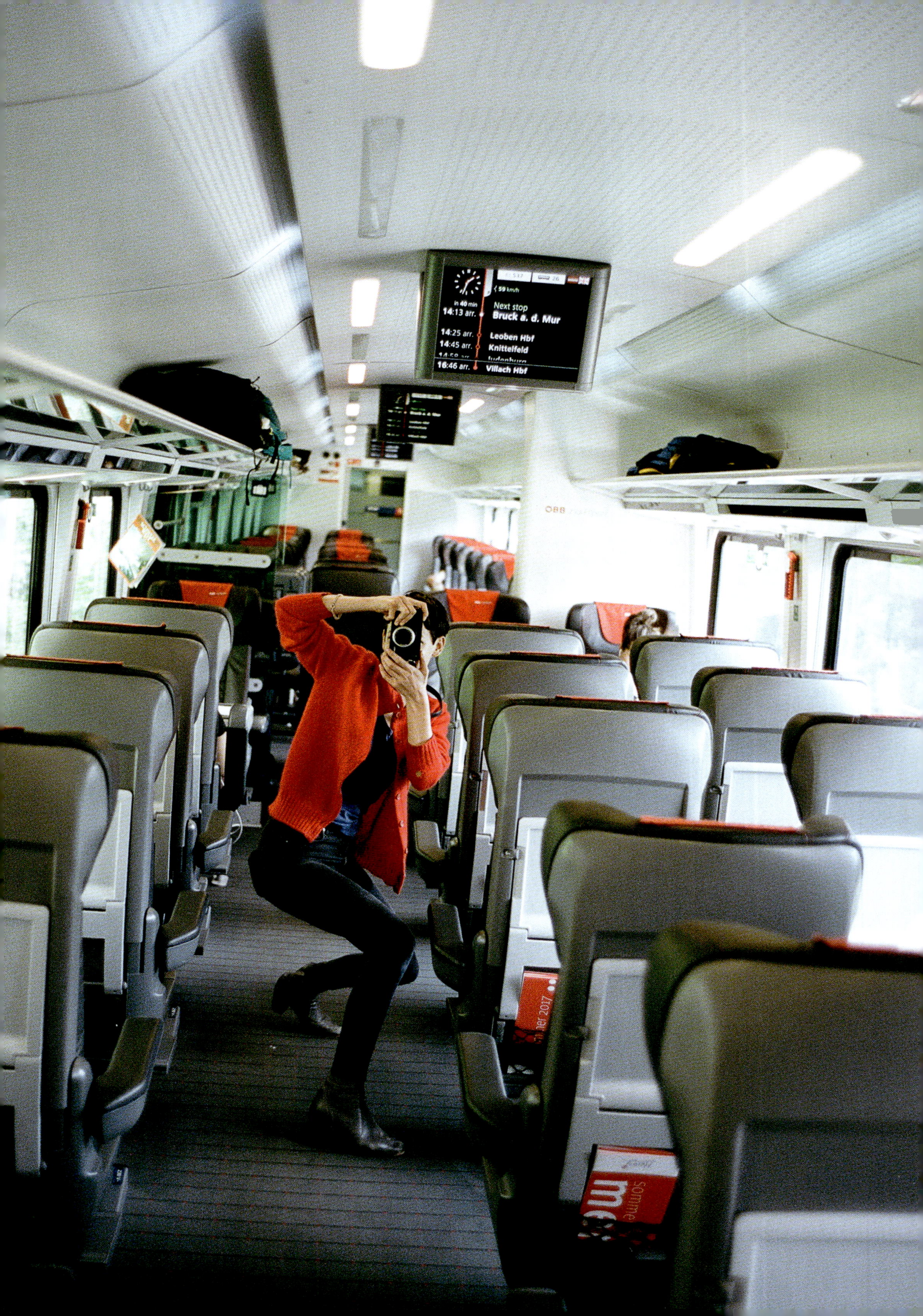
Next stop
Bruck a. d. Mur
14:13 arr.
14:25 arr.
Leoben Hbf
14:45 arr.
Knittelfeld
16:46 arr.
Villach Hbf

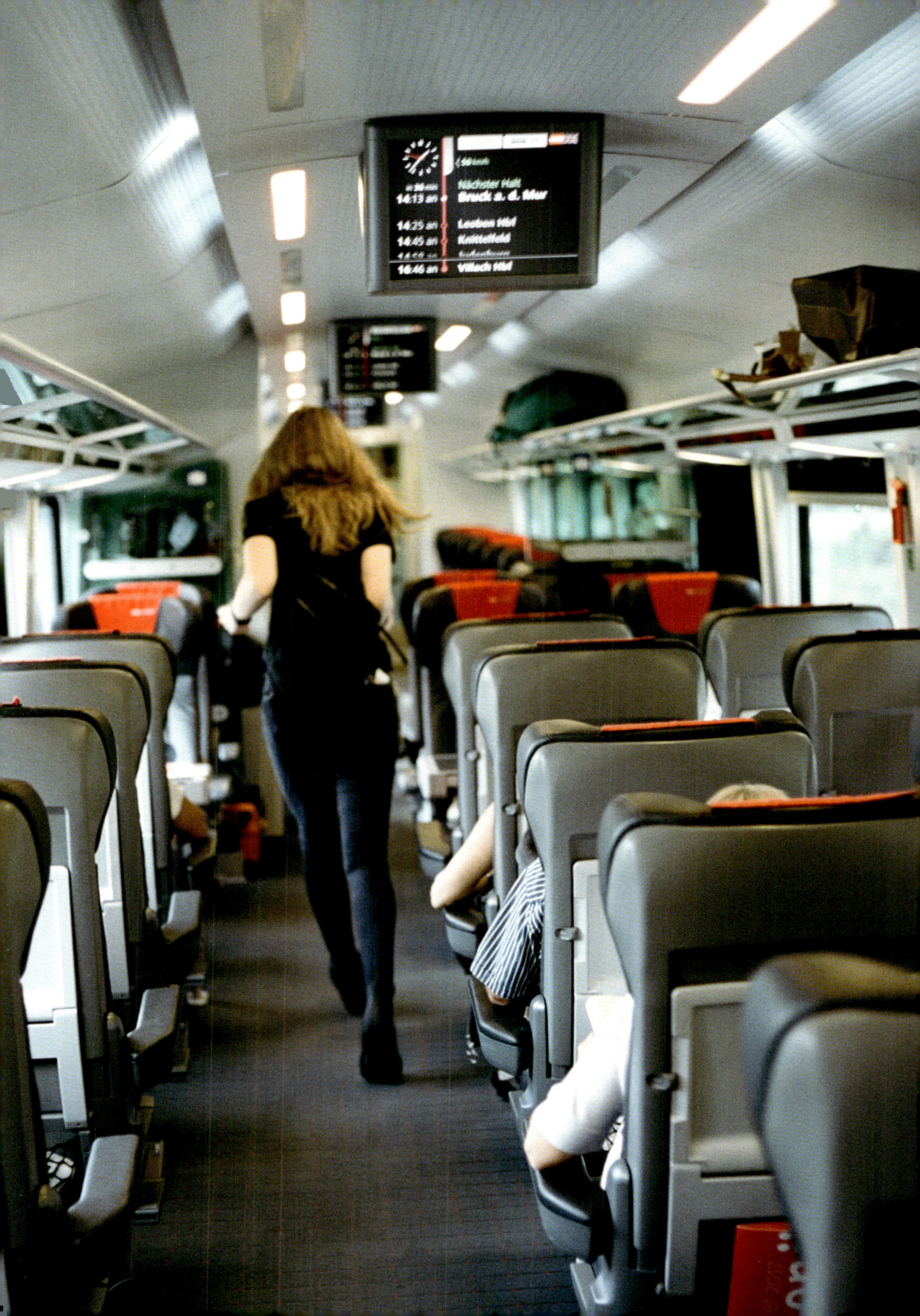
Nächster Halt
14:13 an Bruck a. d. Mur
14:25 an Leoben Hbf
14:45 an Knittelfeld
16:46 an Villach Hbf

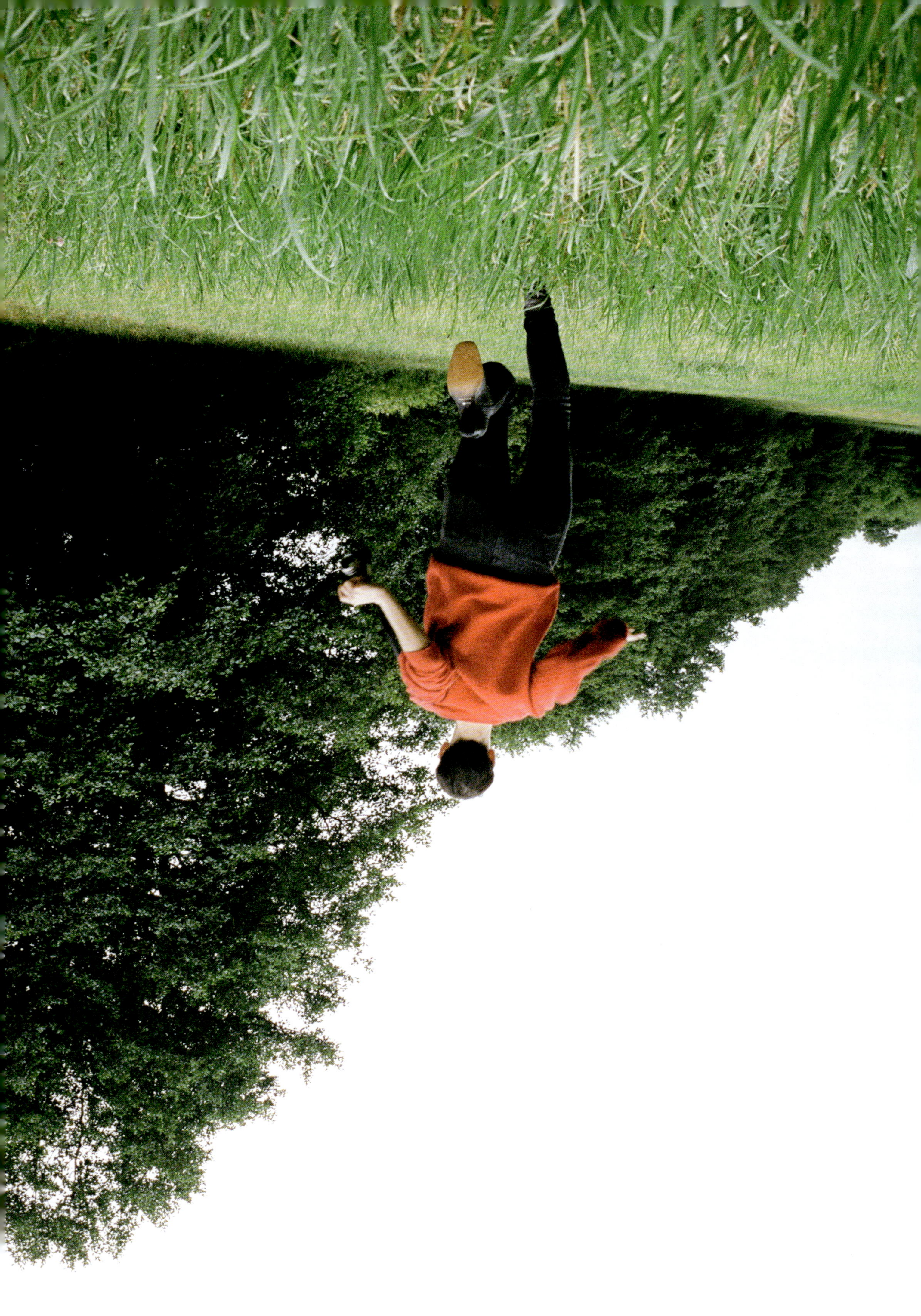

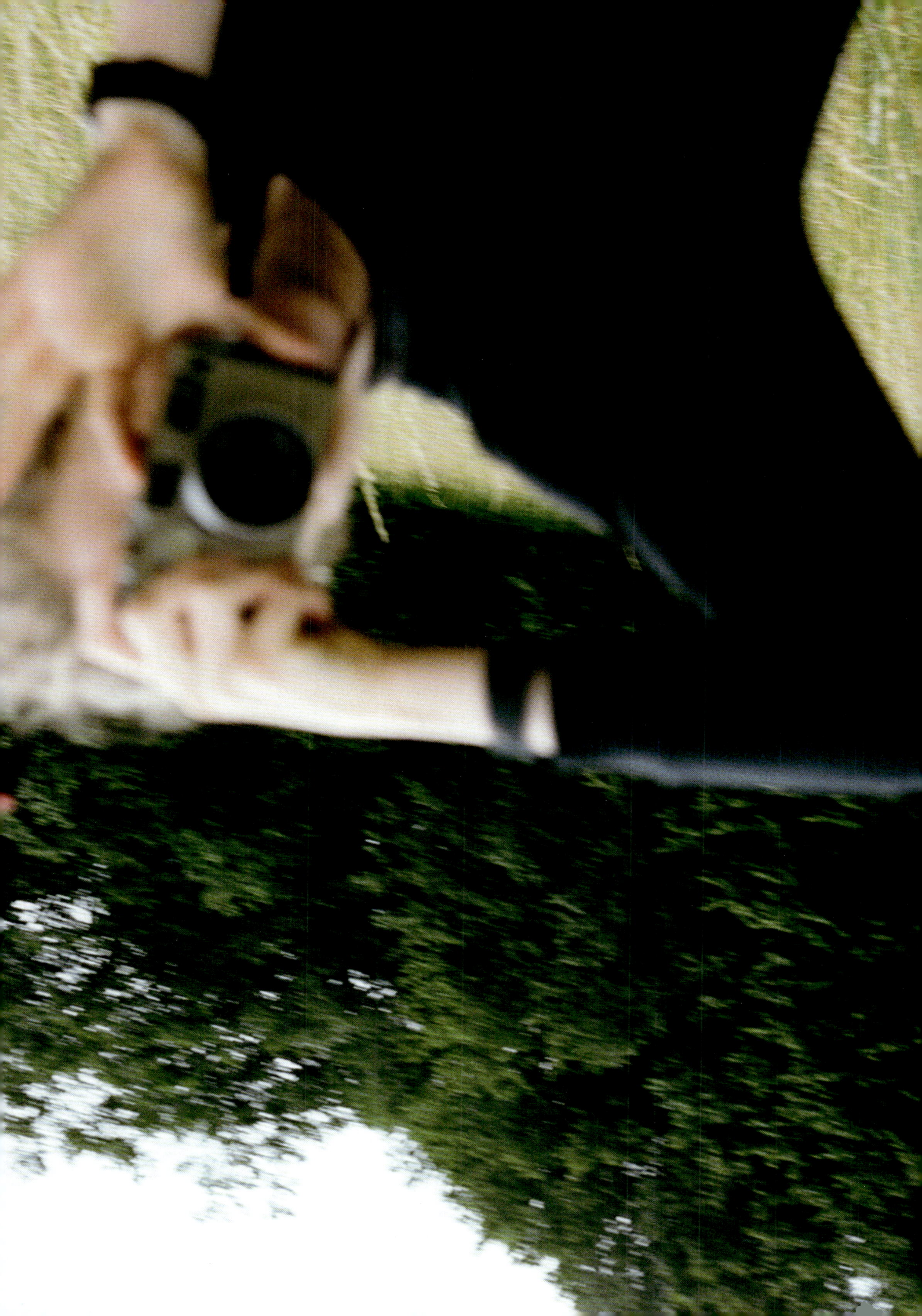

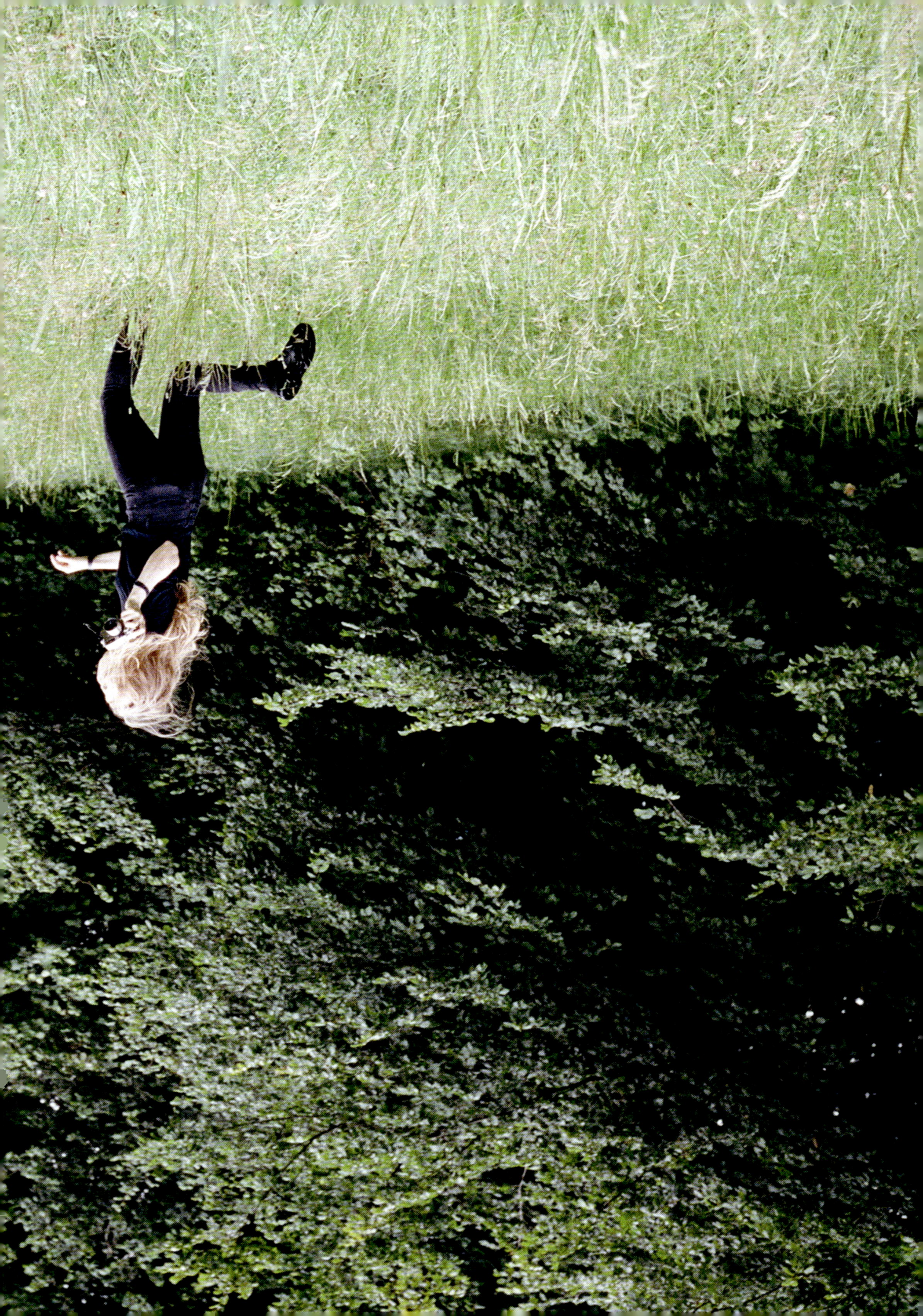

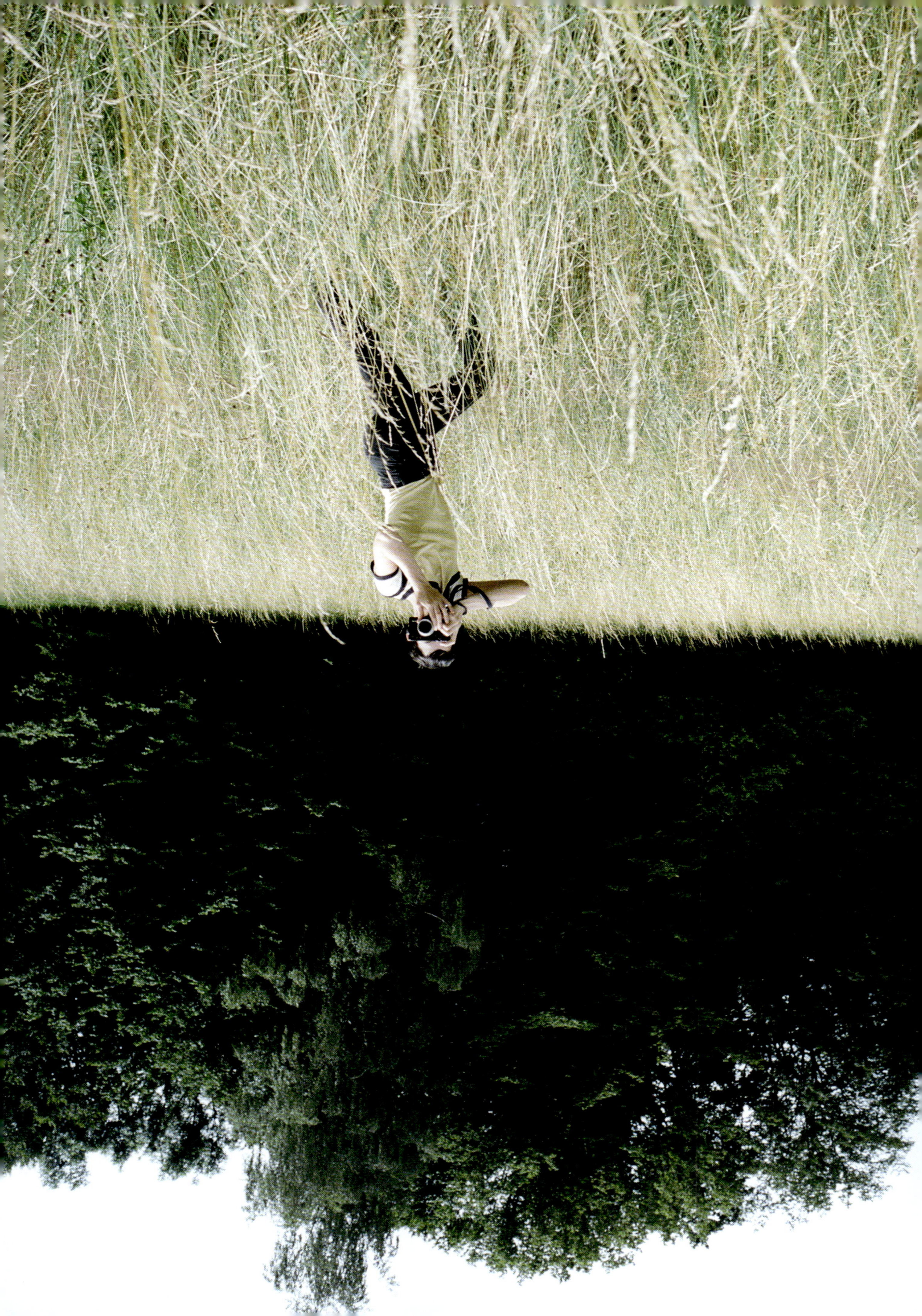

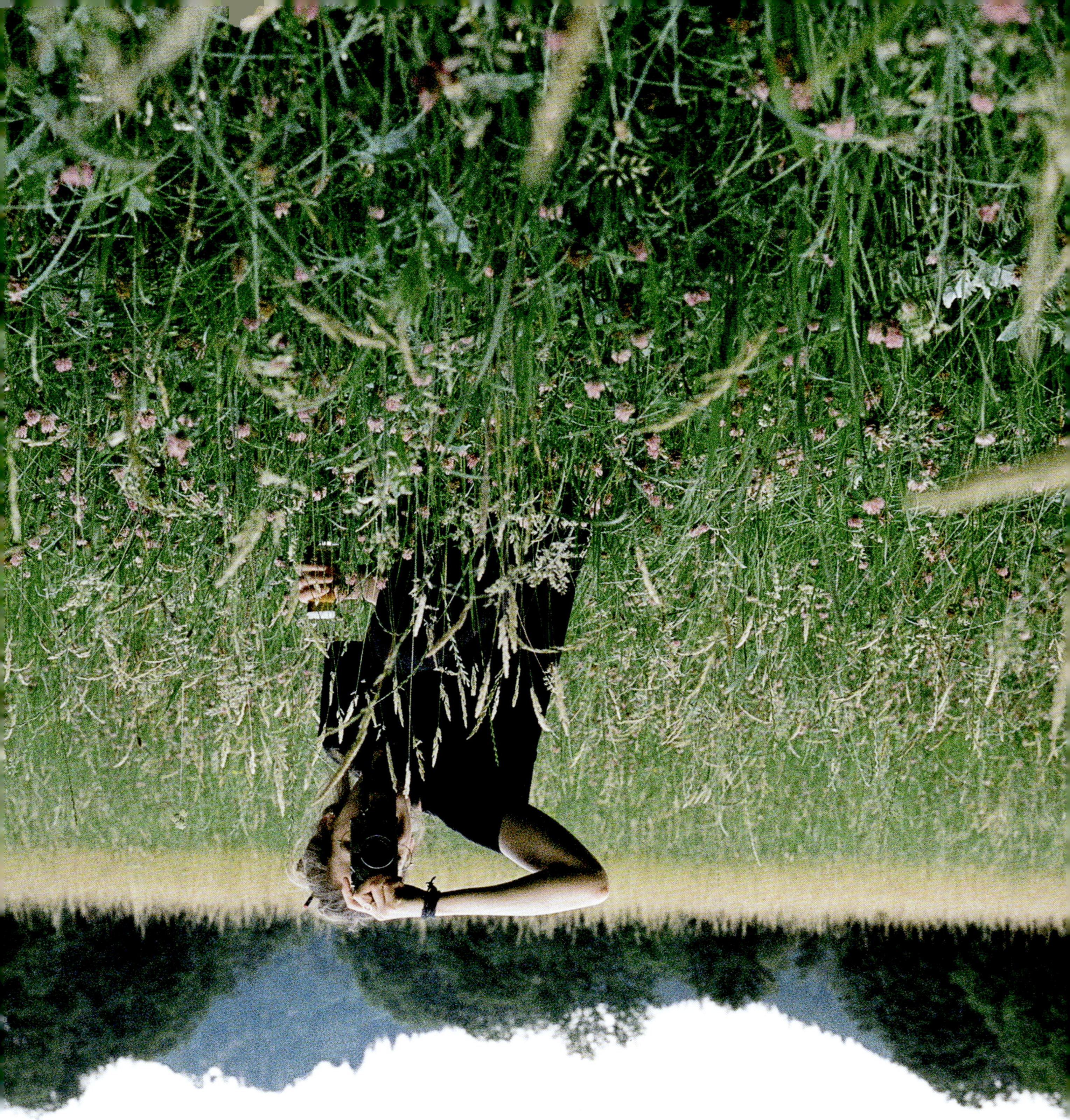

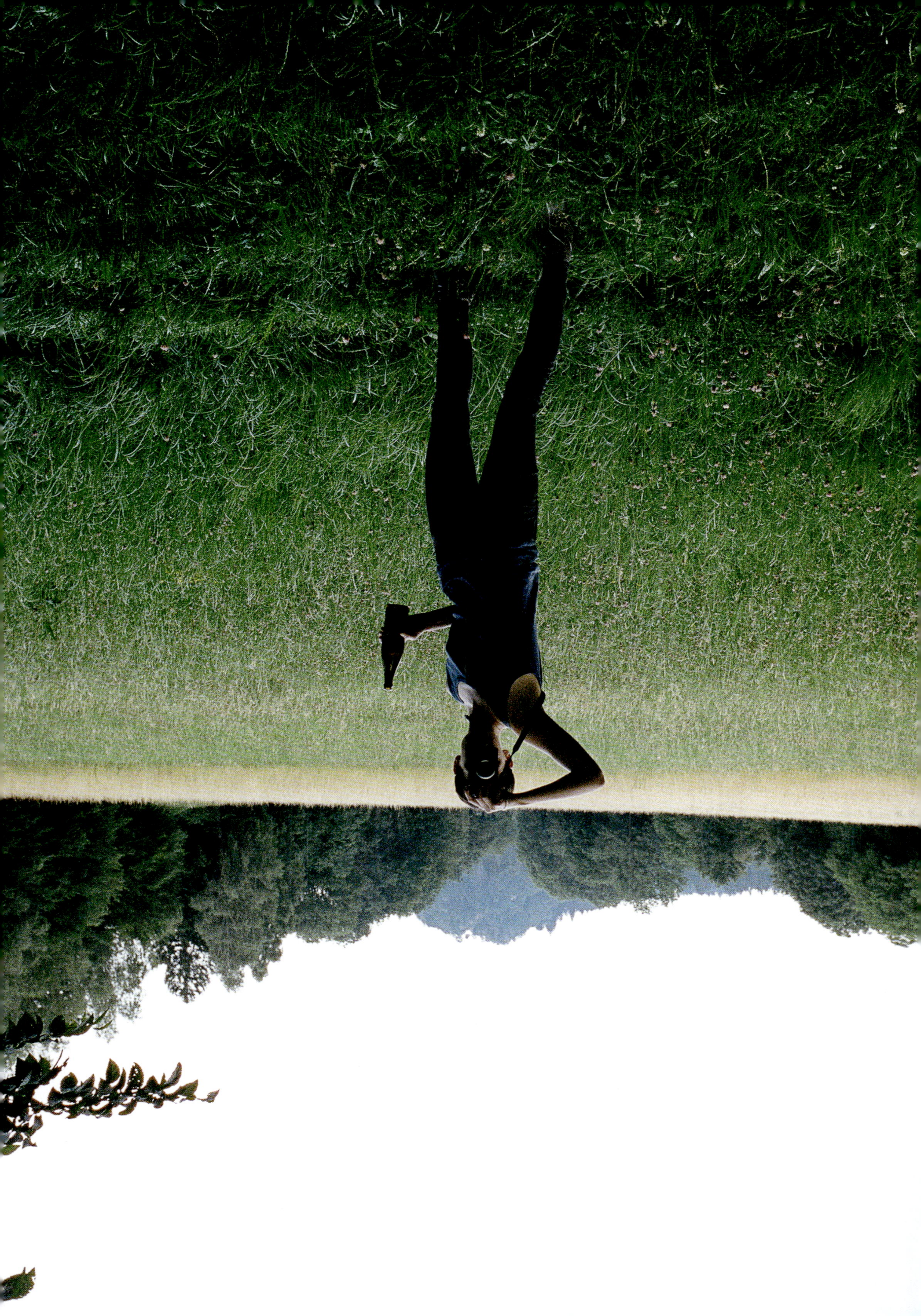

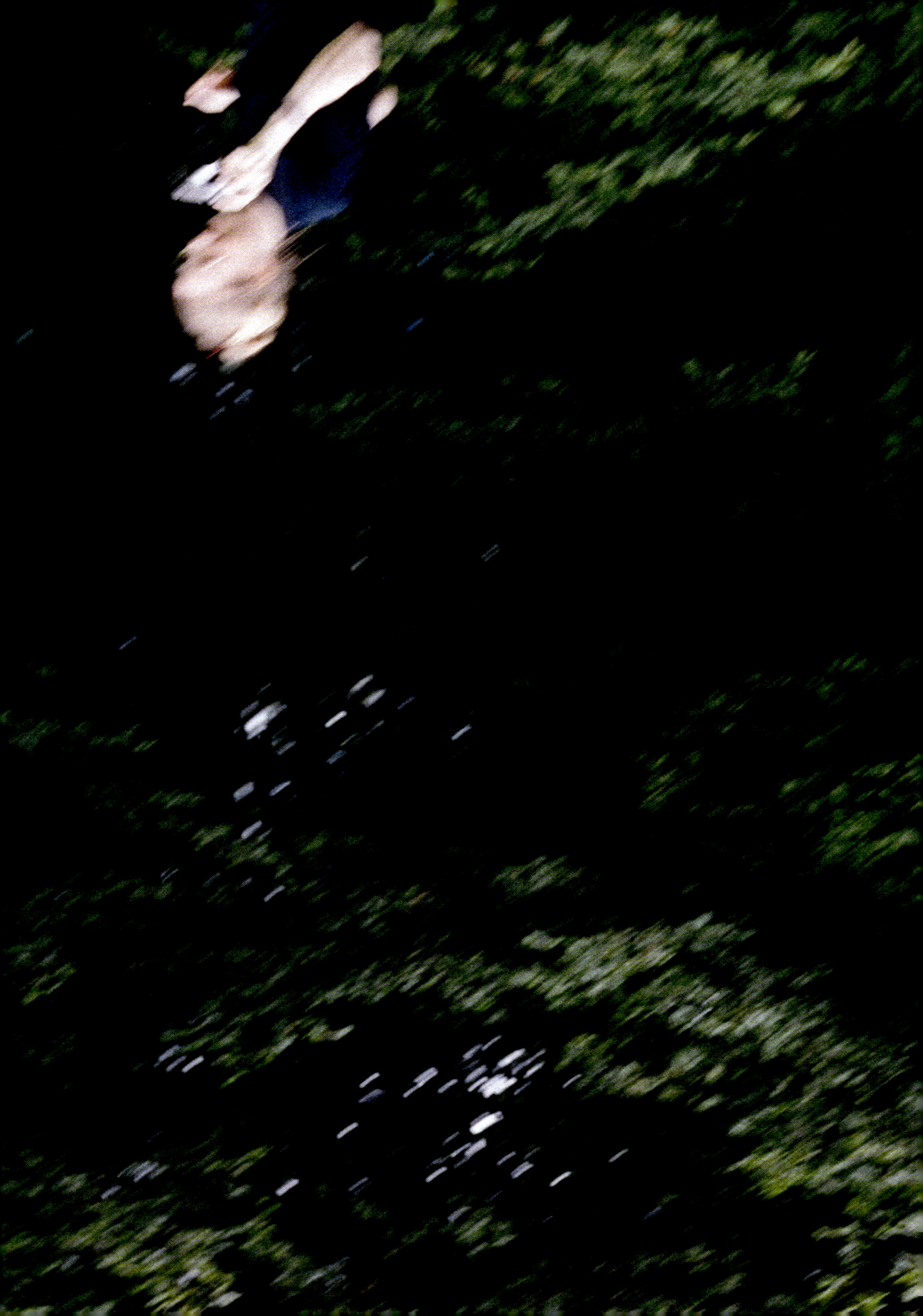

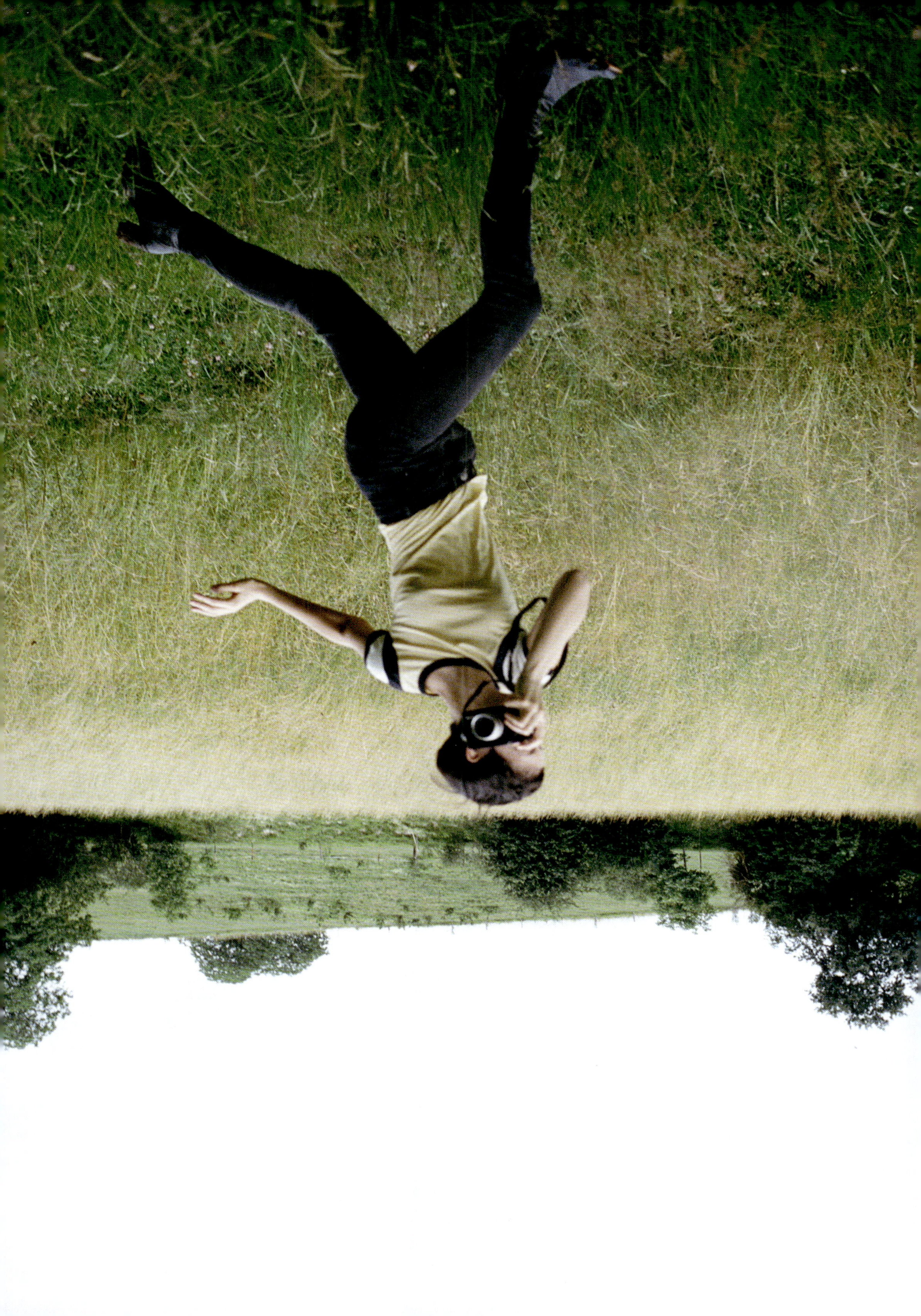

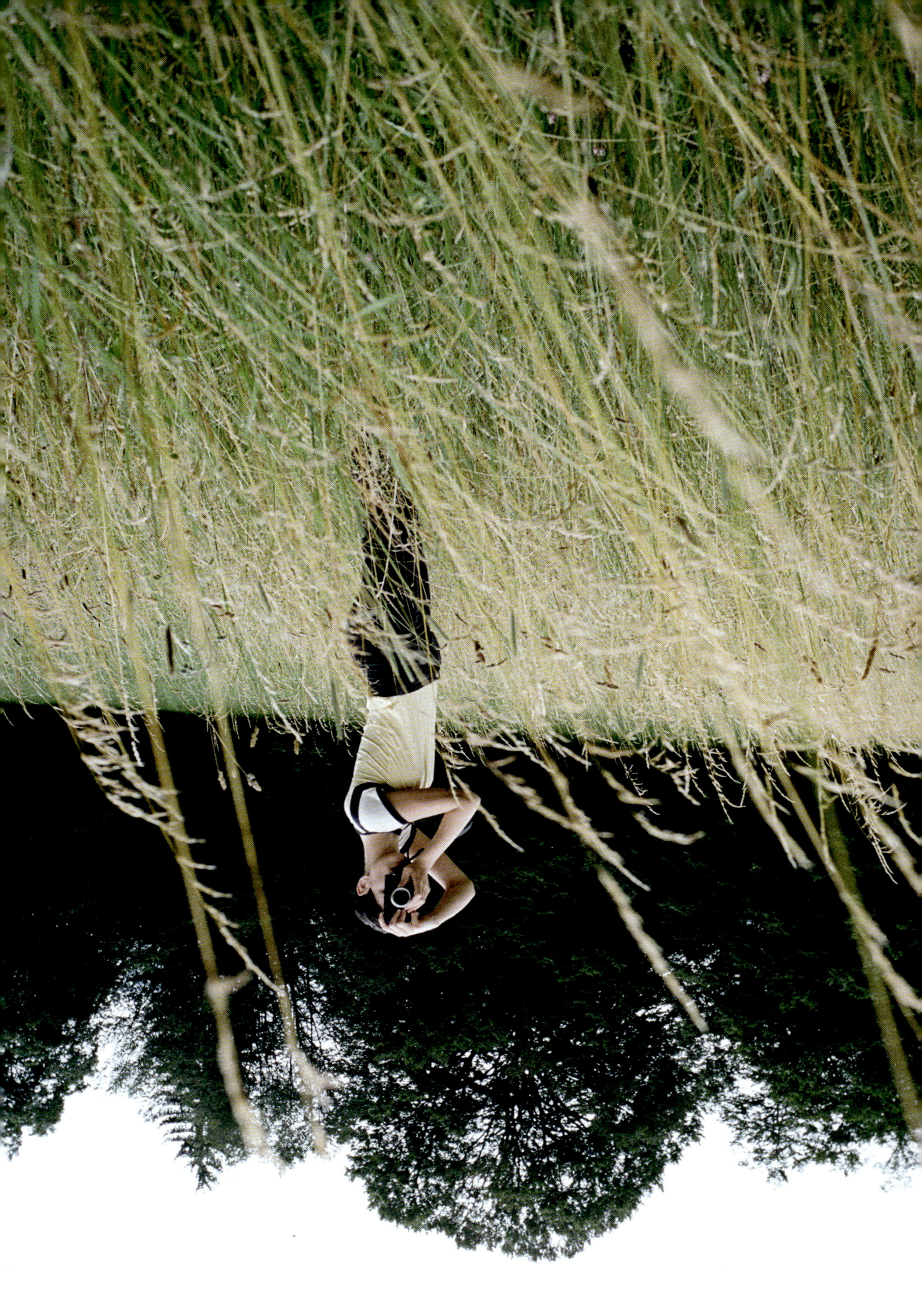

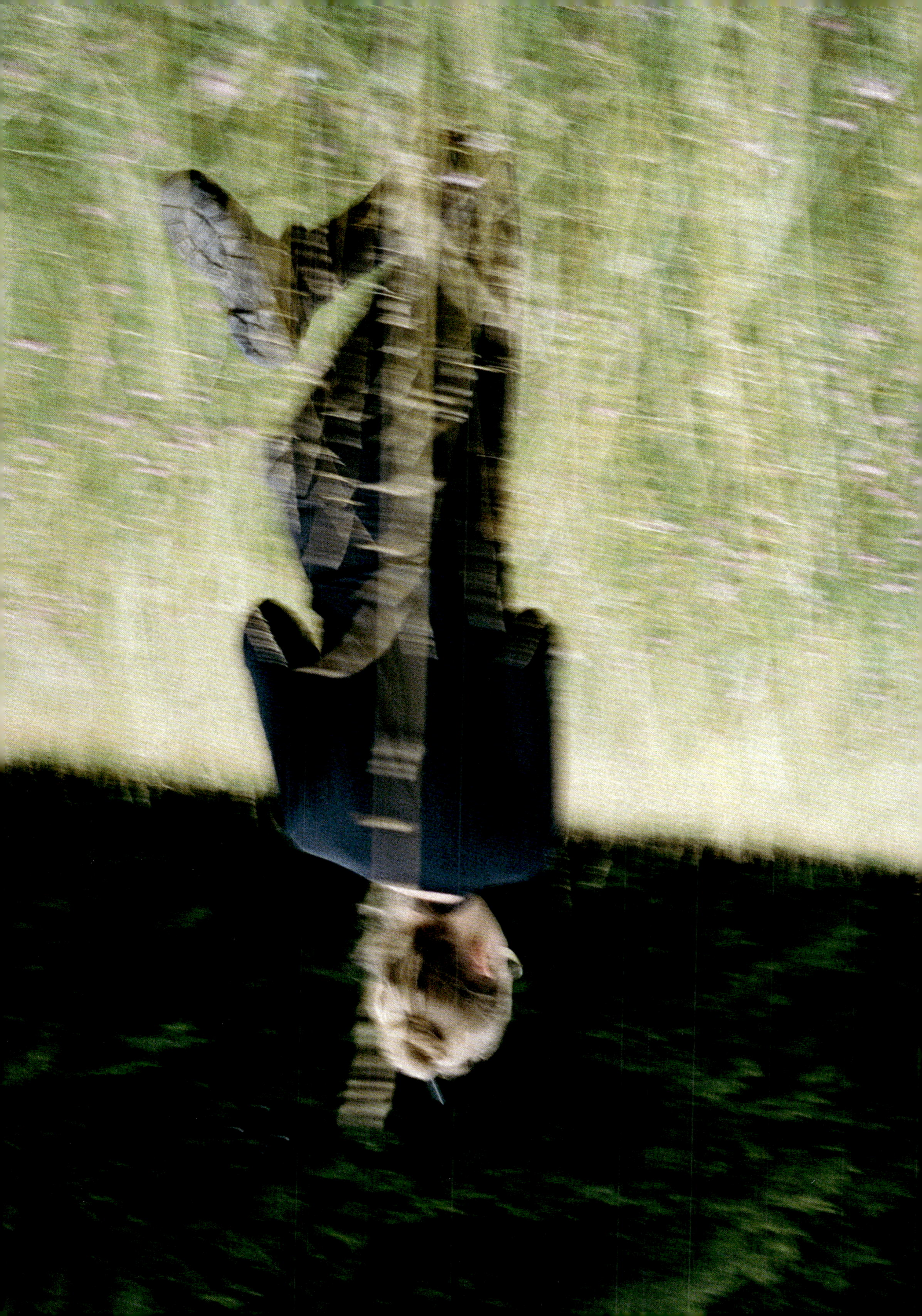

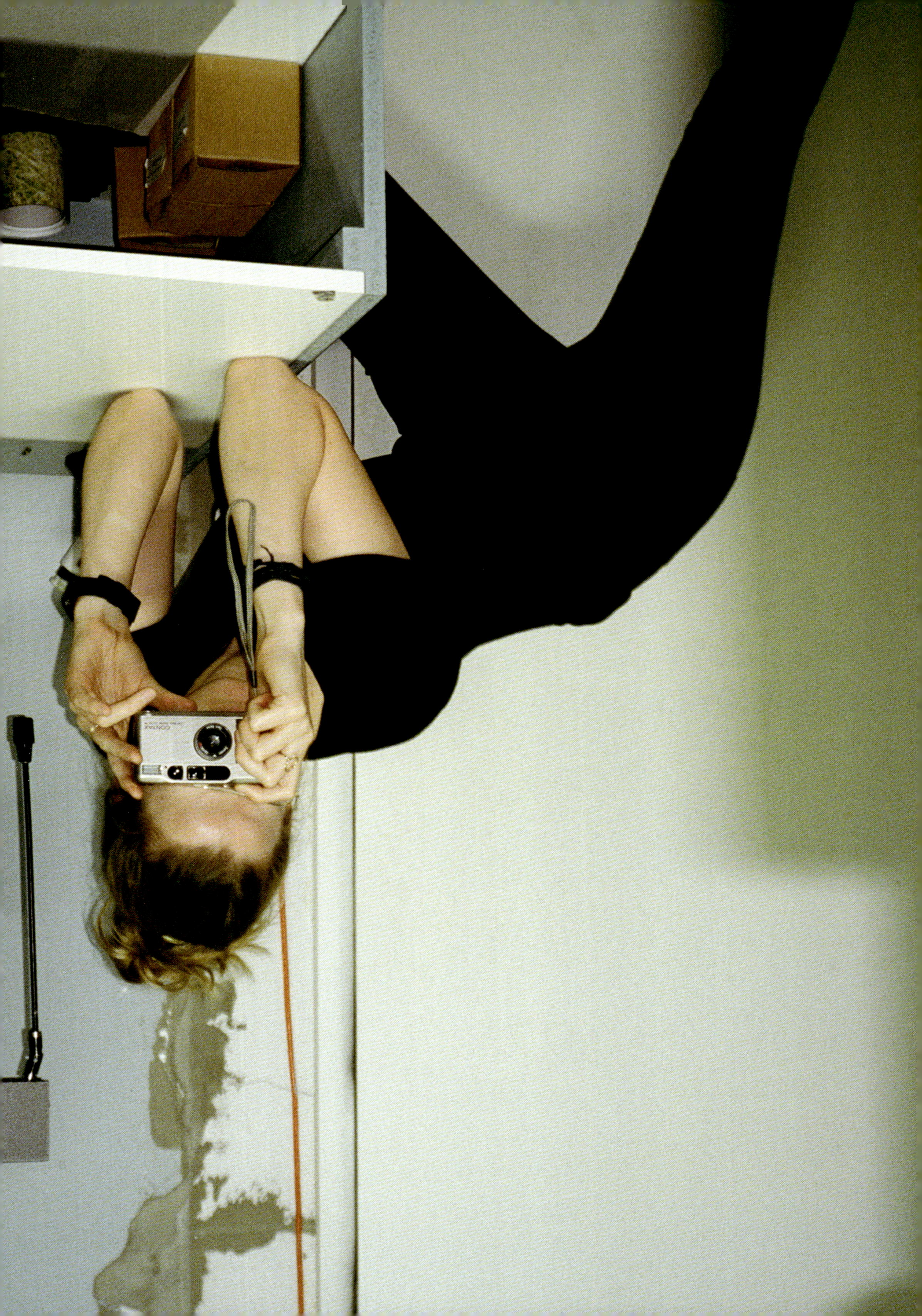

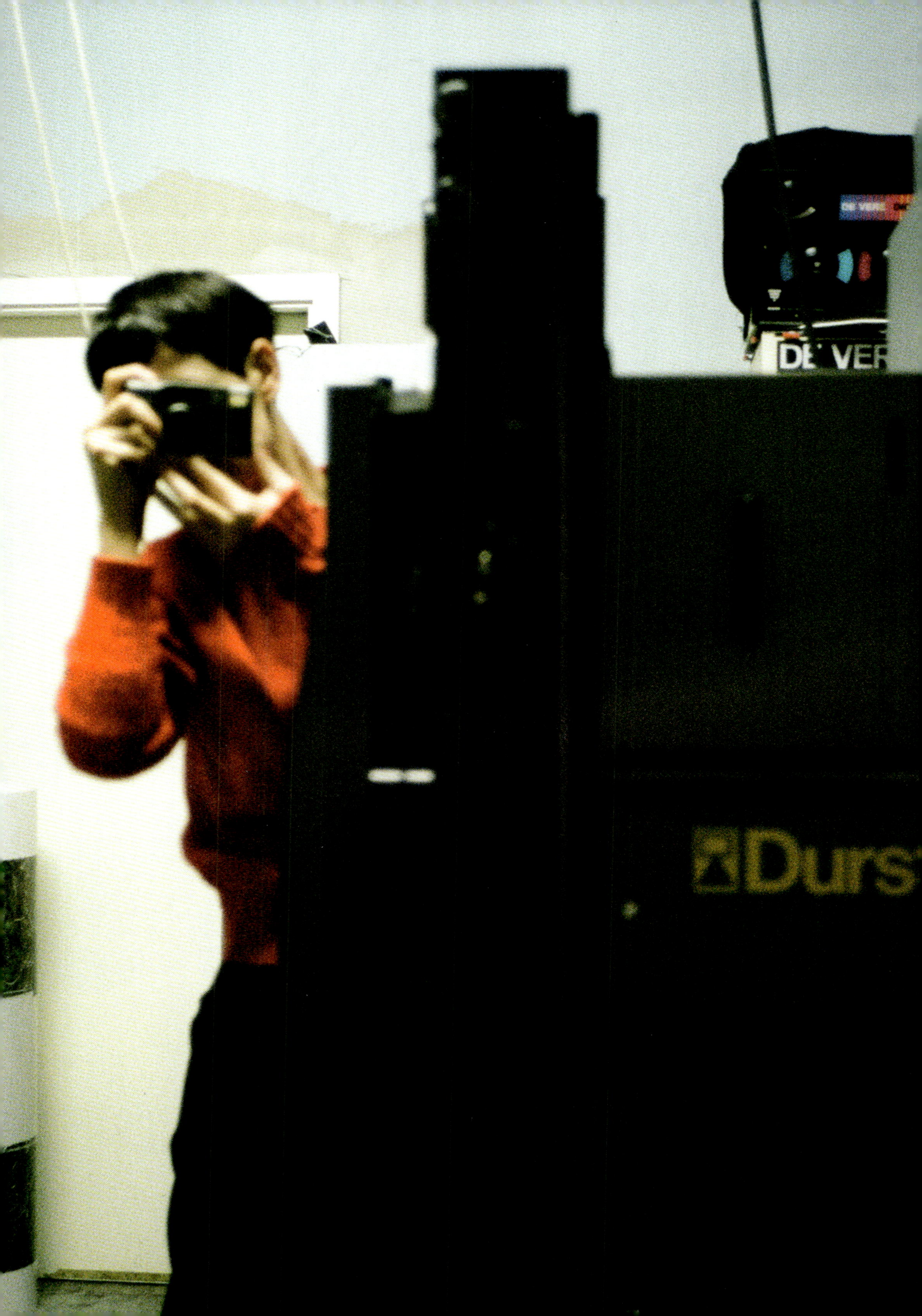

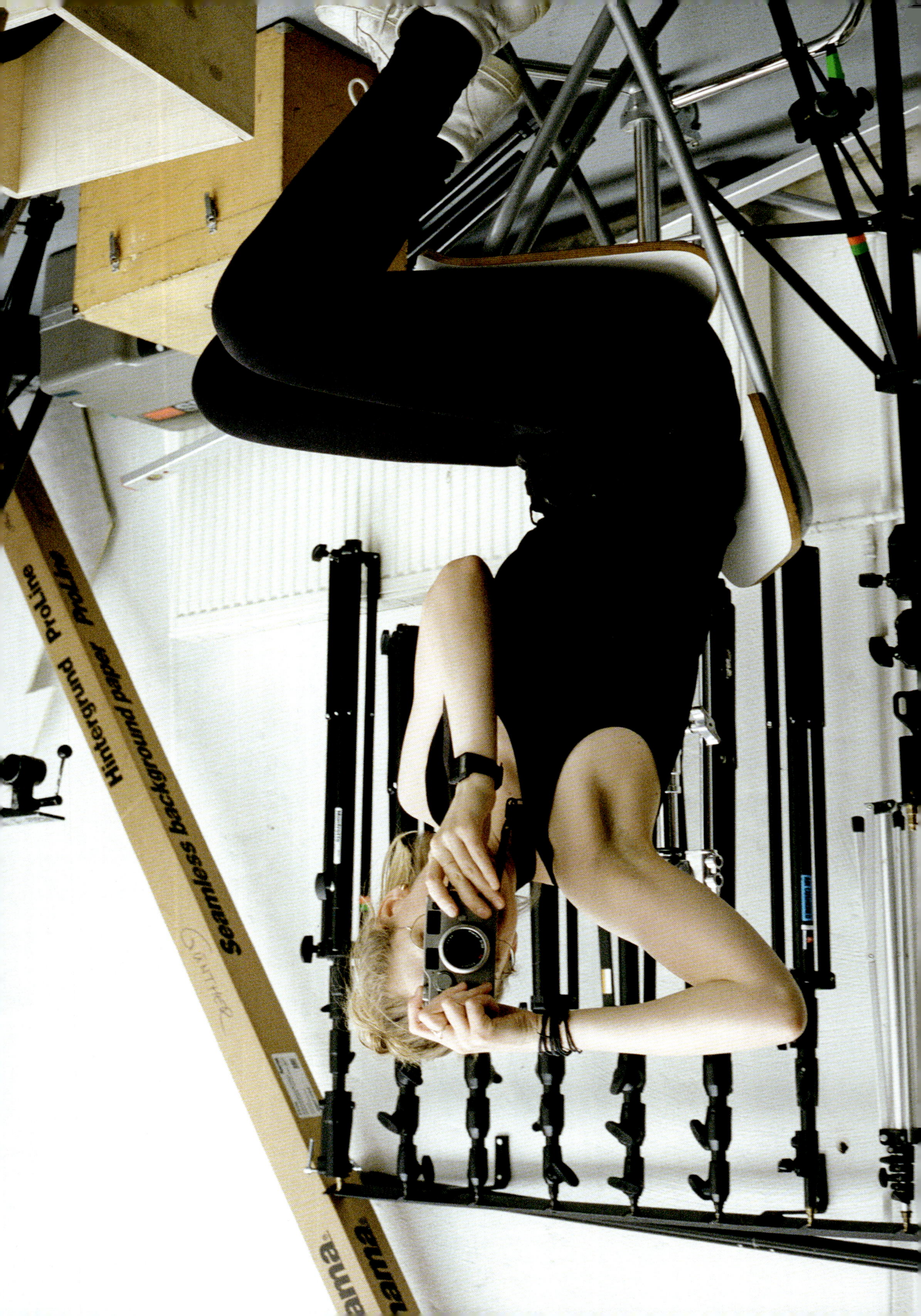
hama
Hintergrund ProLine
Seamless background paper ProLine

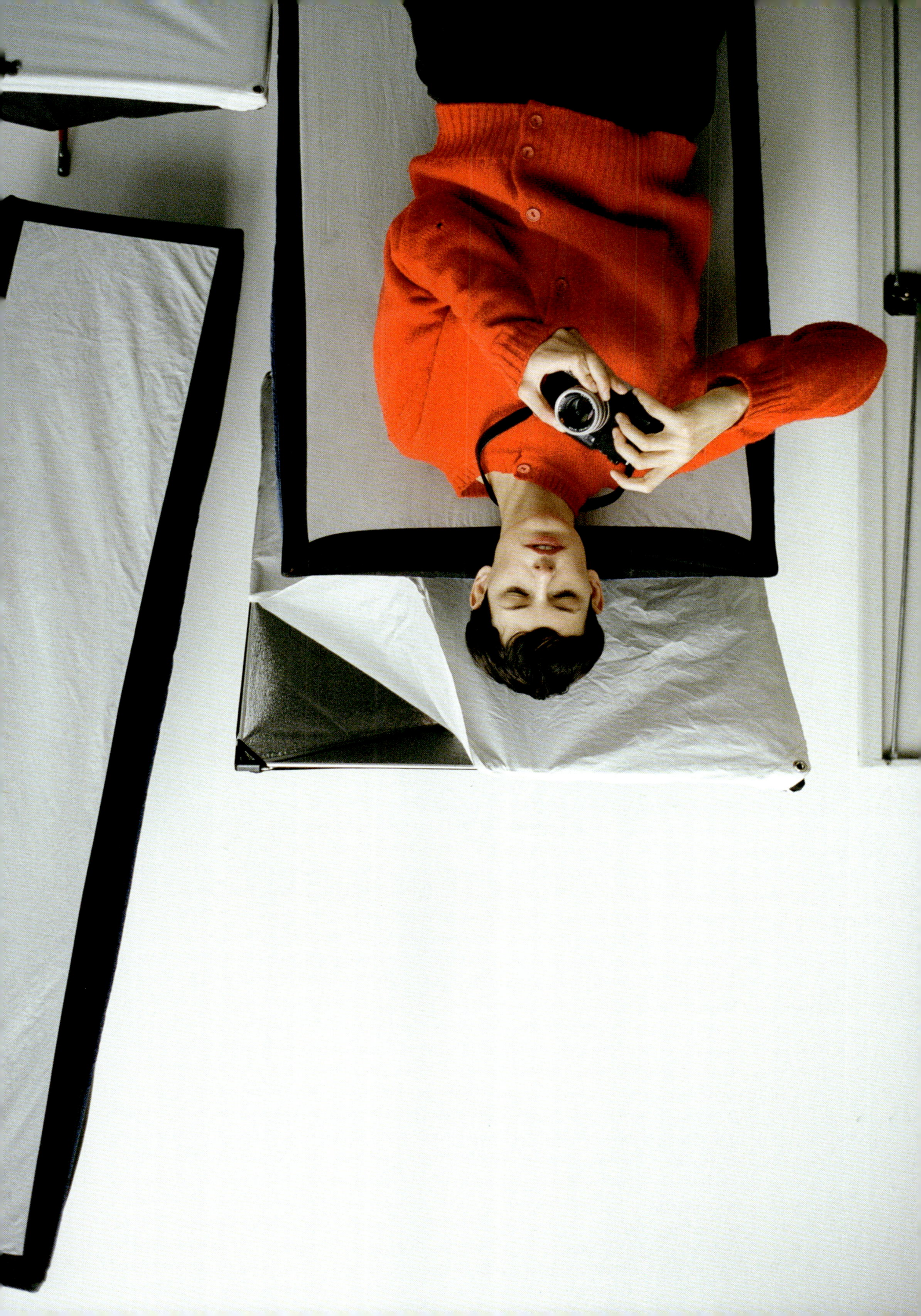

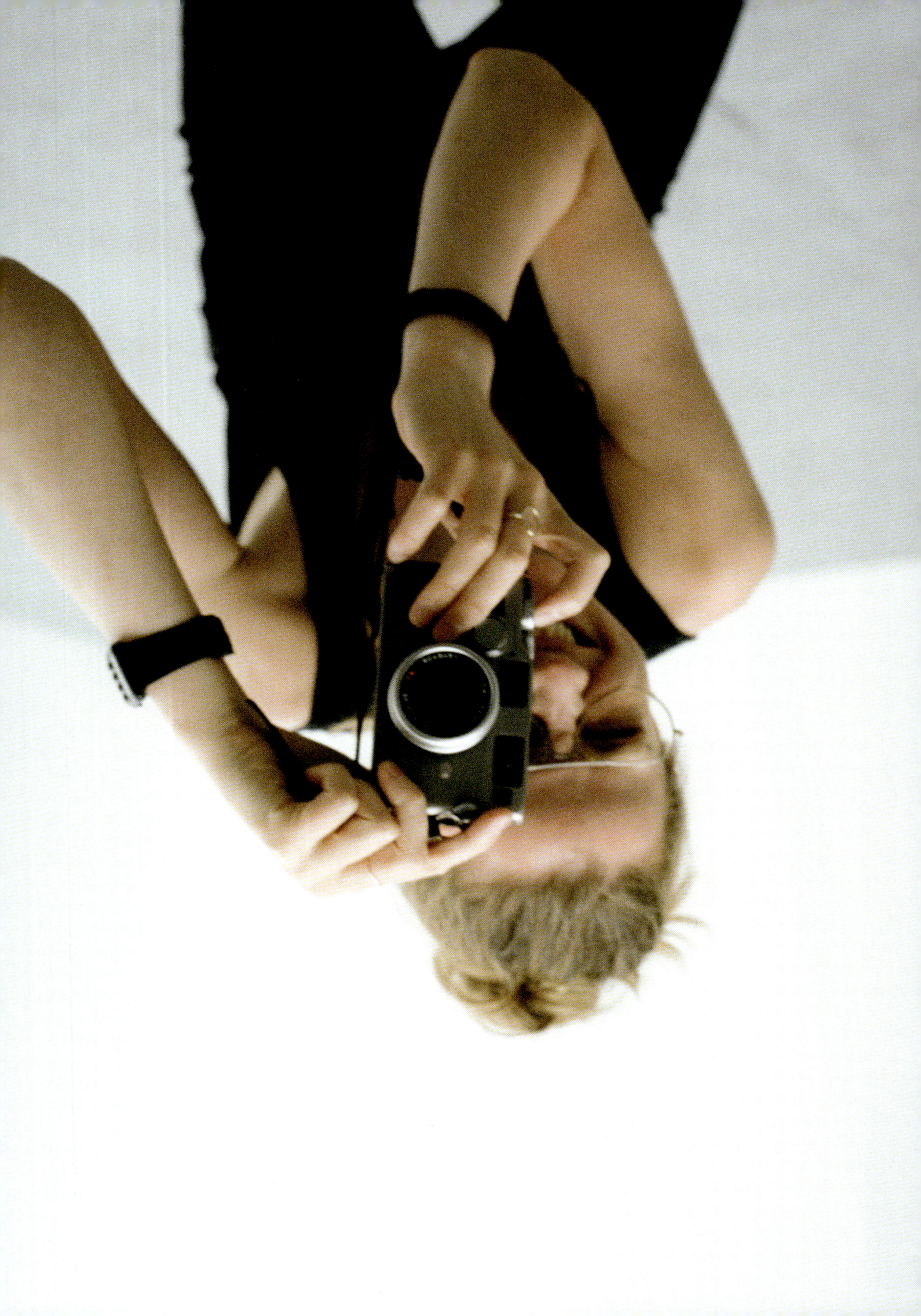

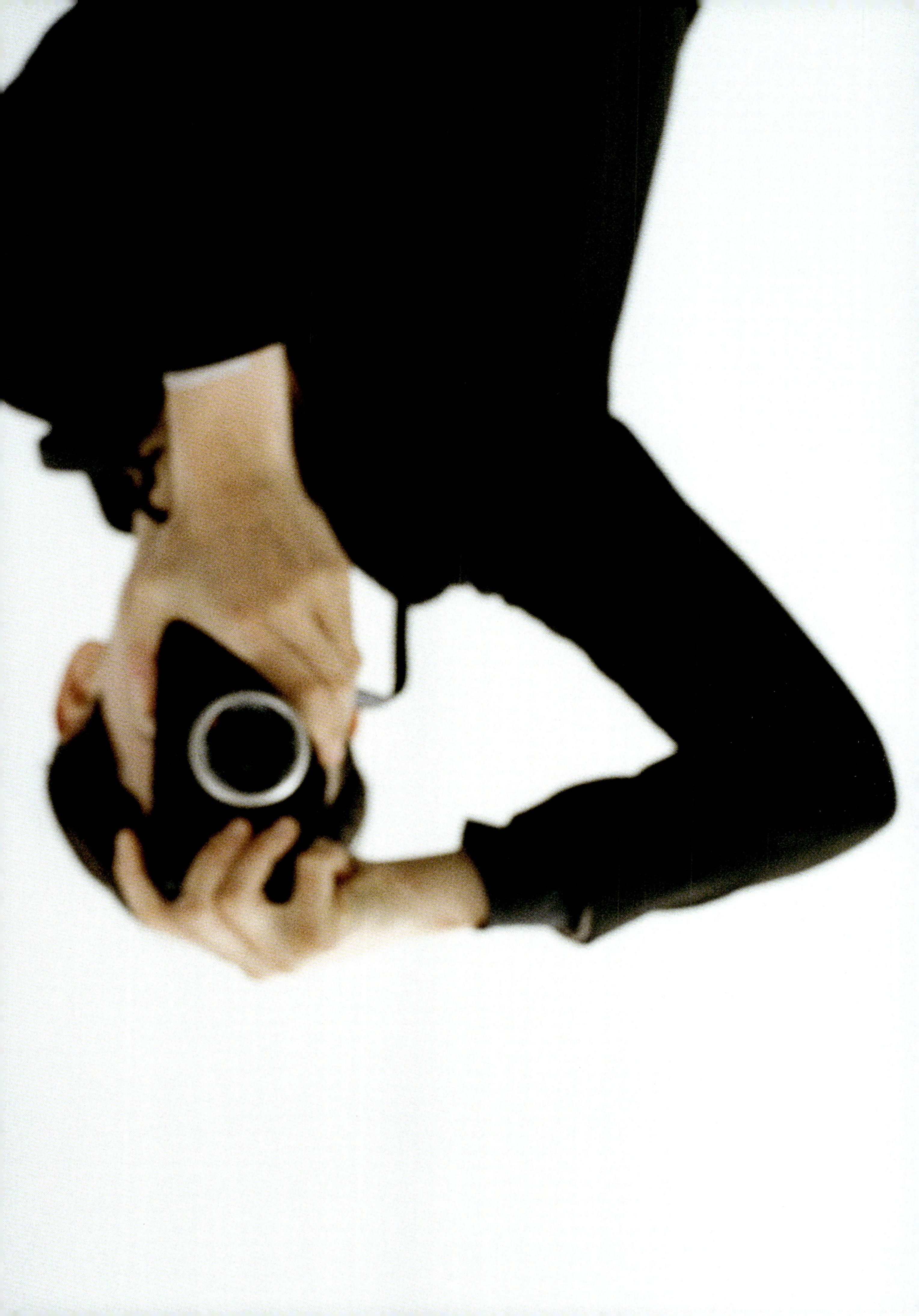

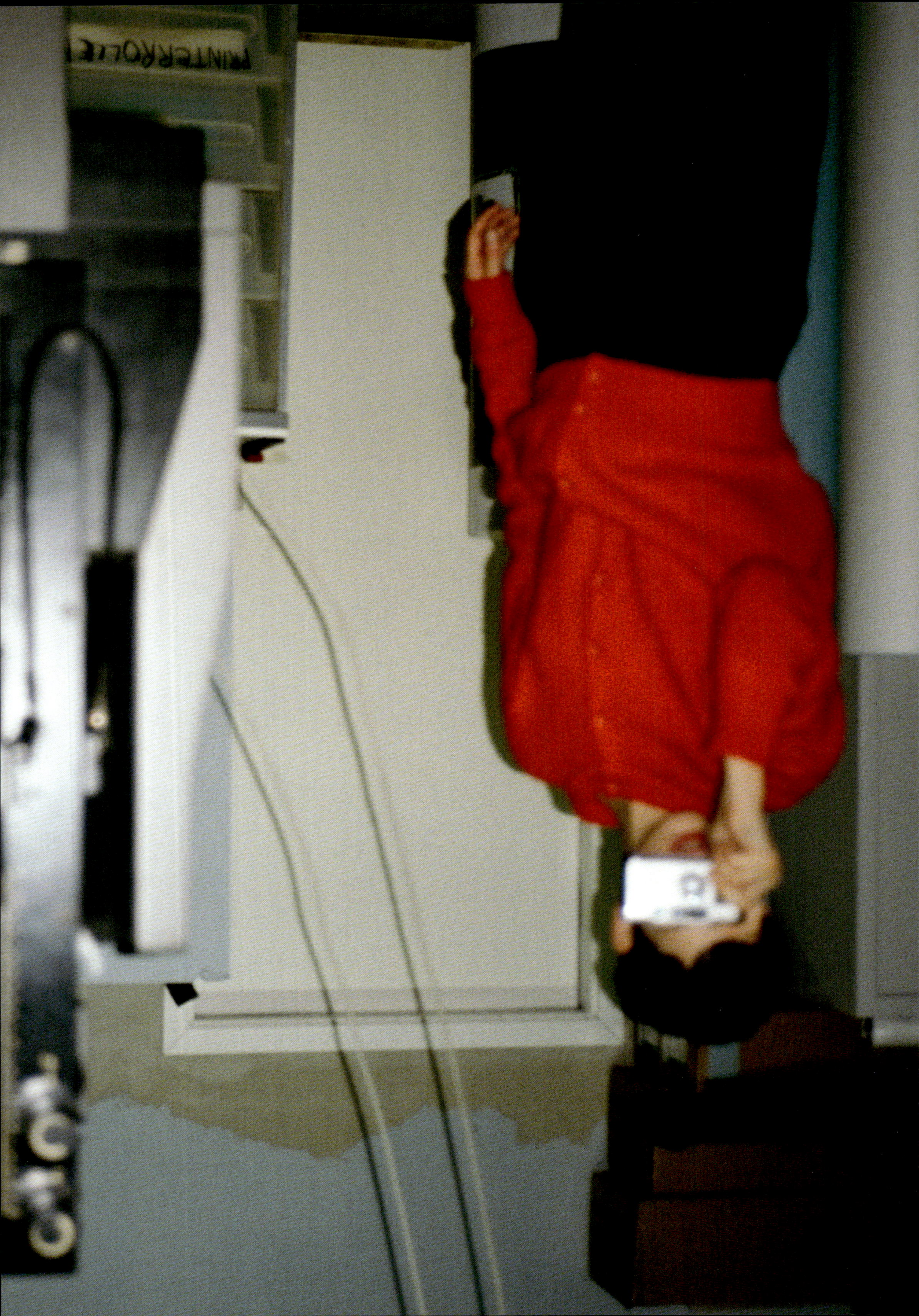

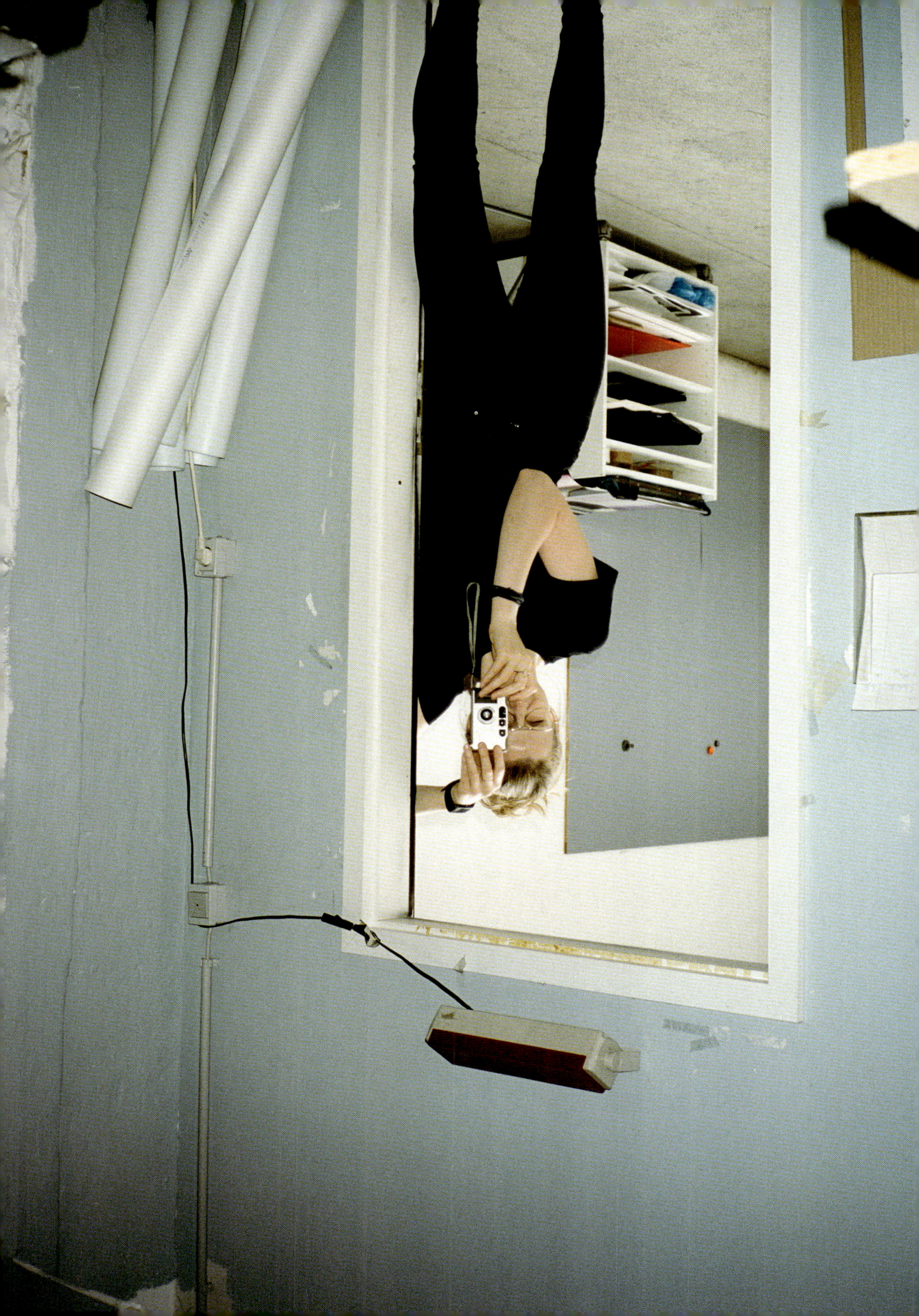

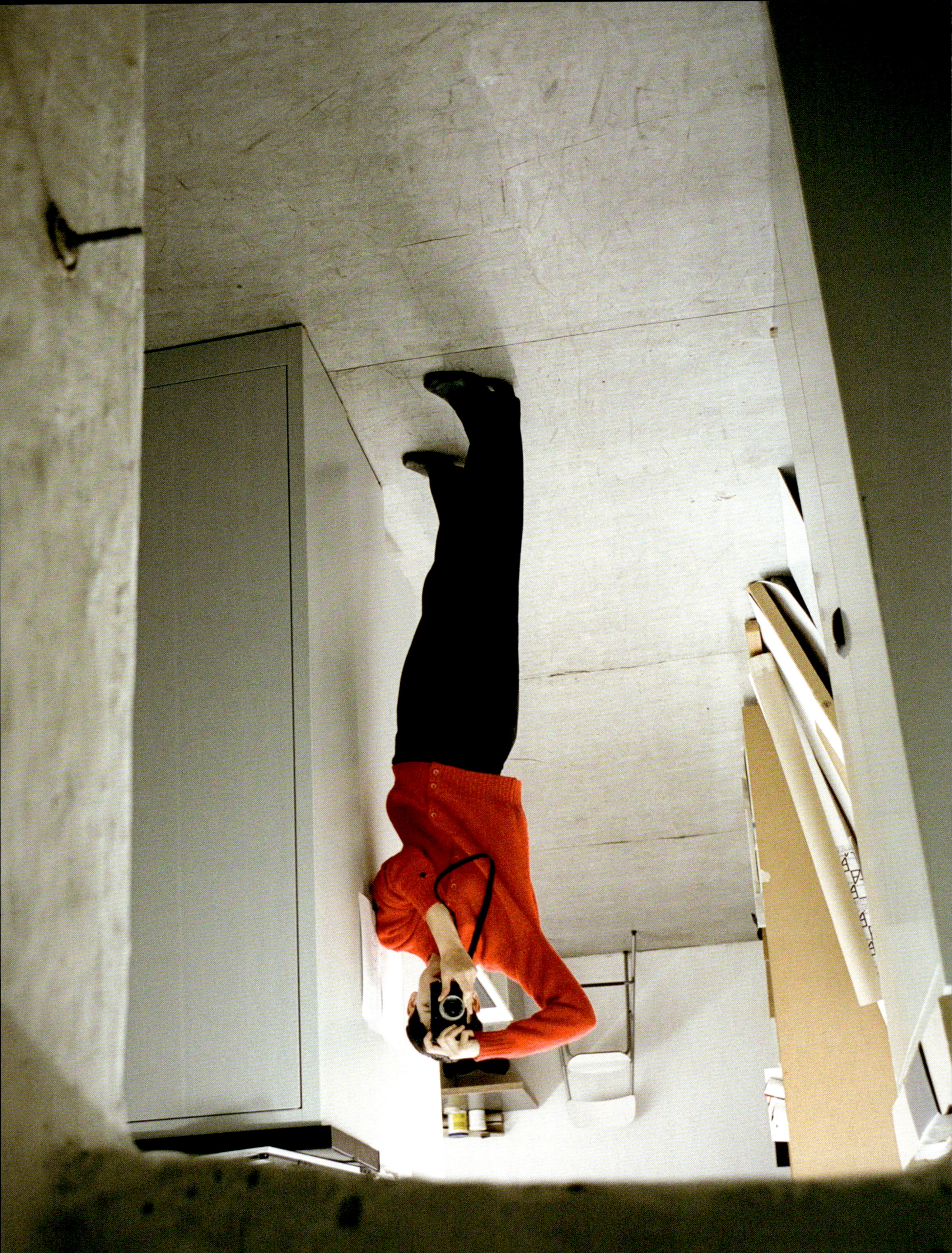

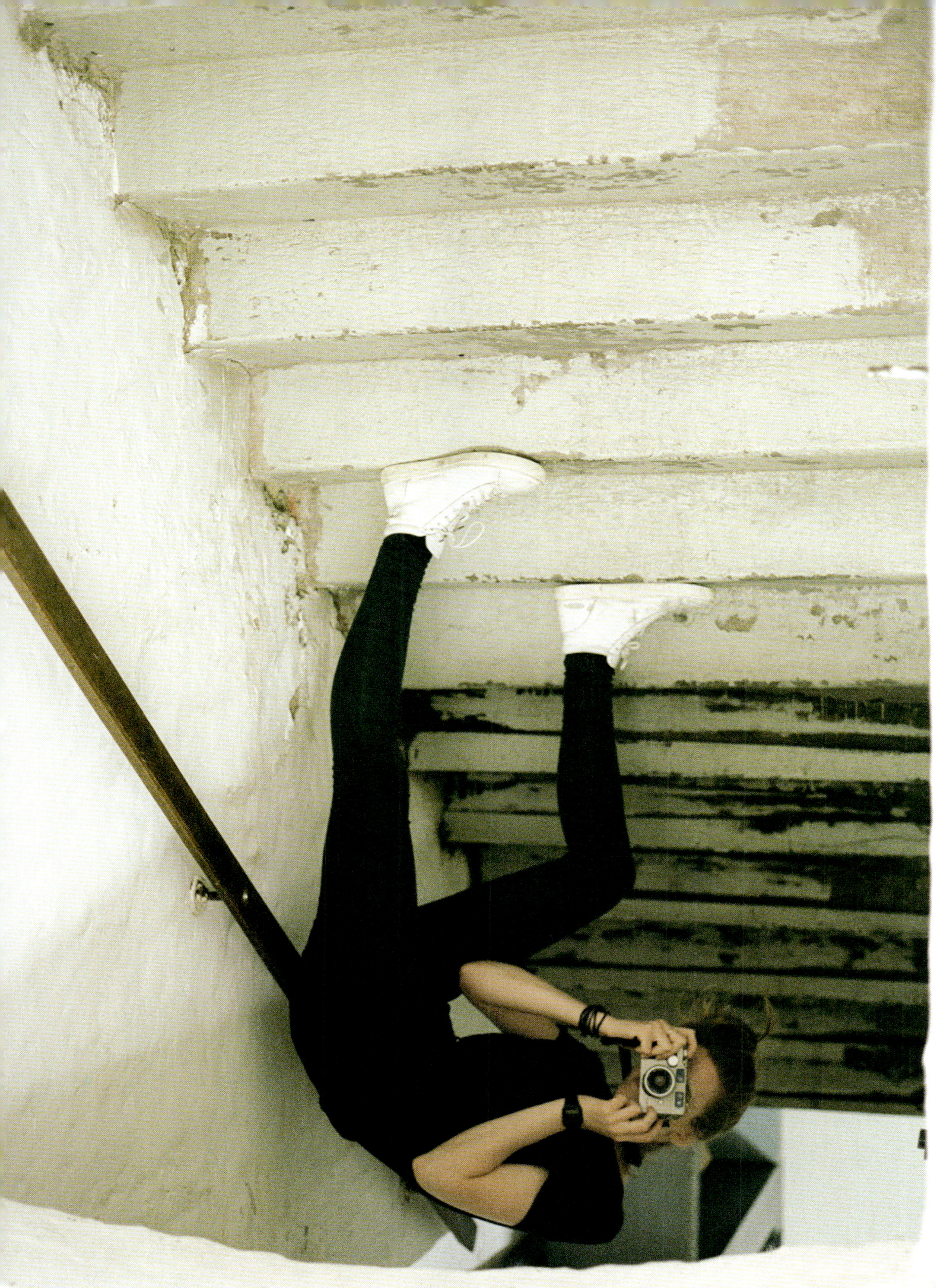

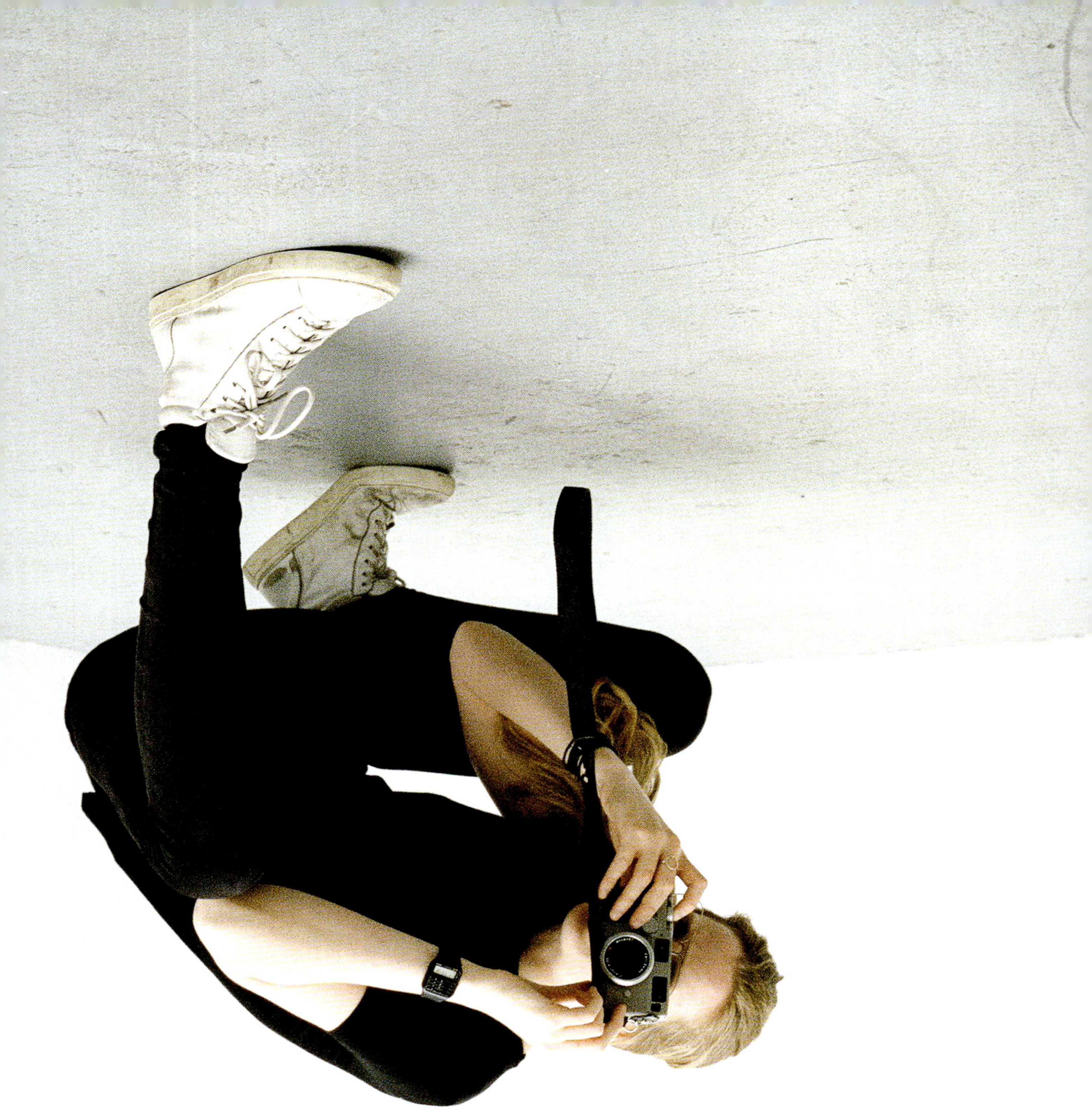

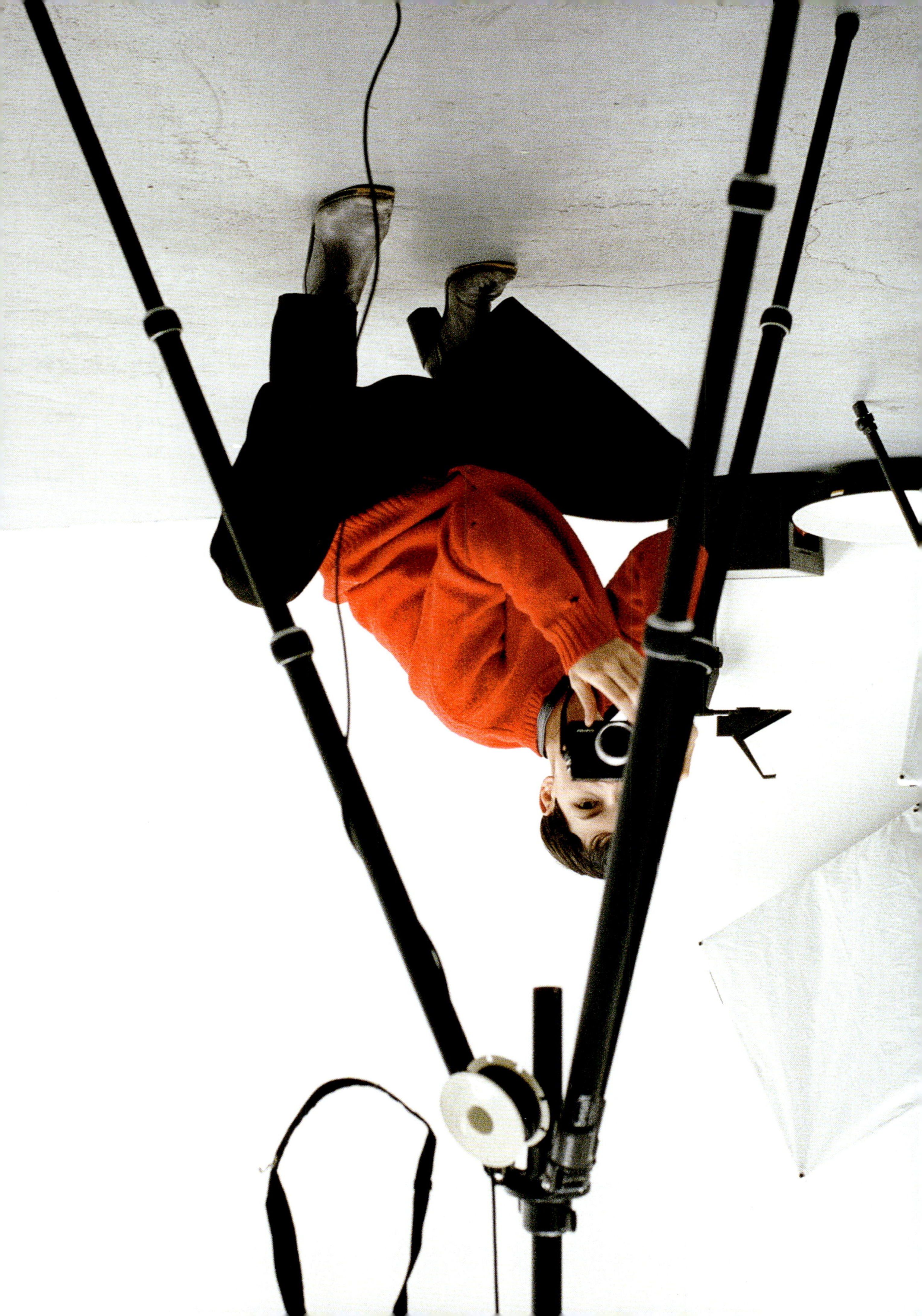

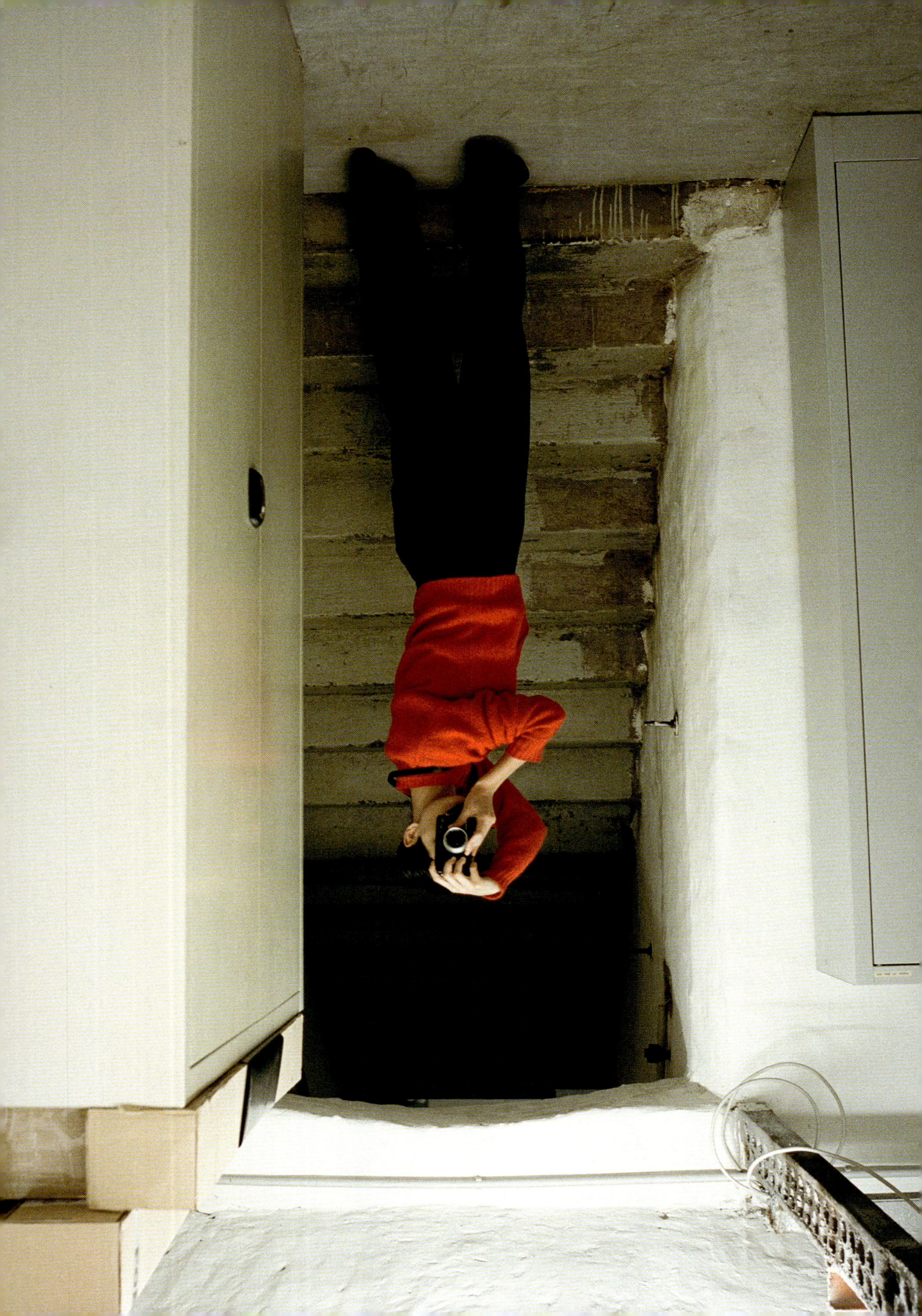

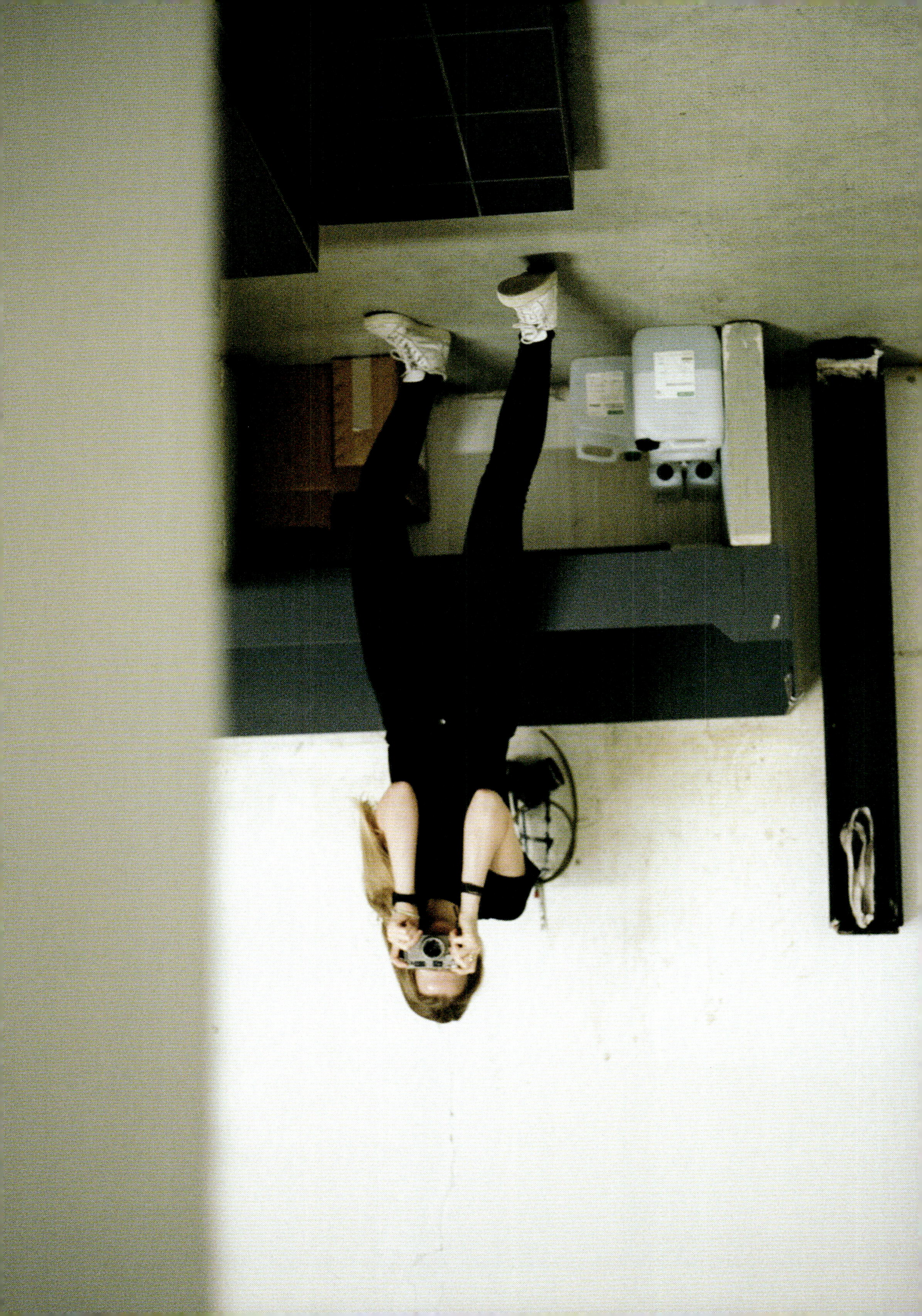

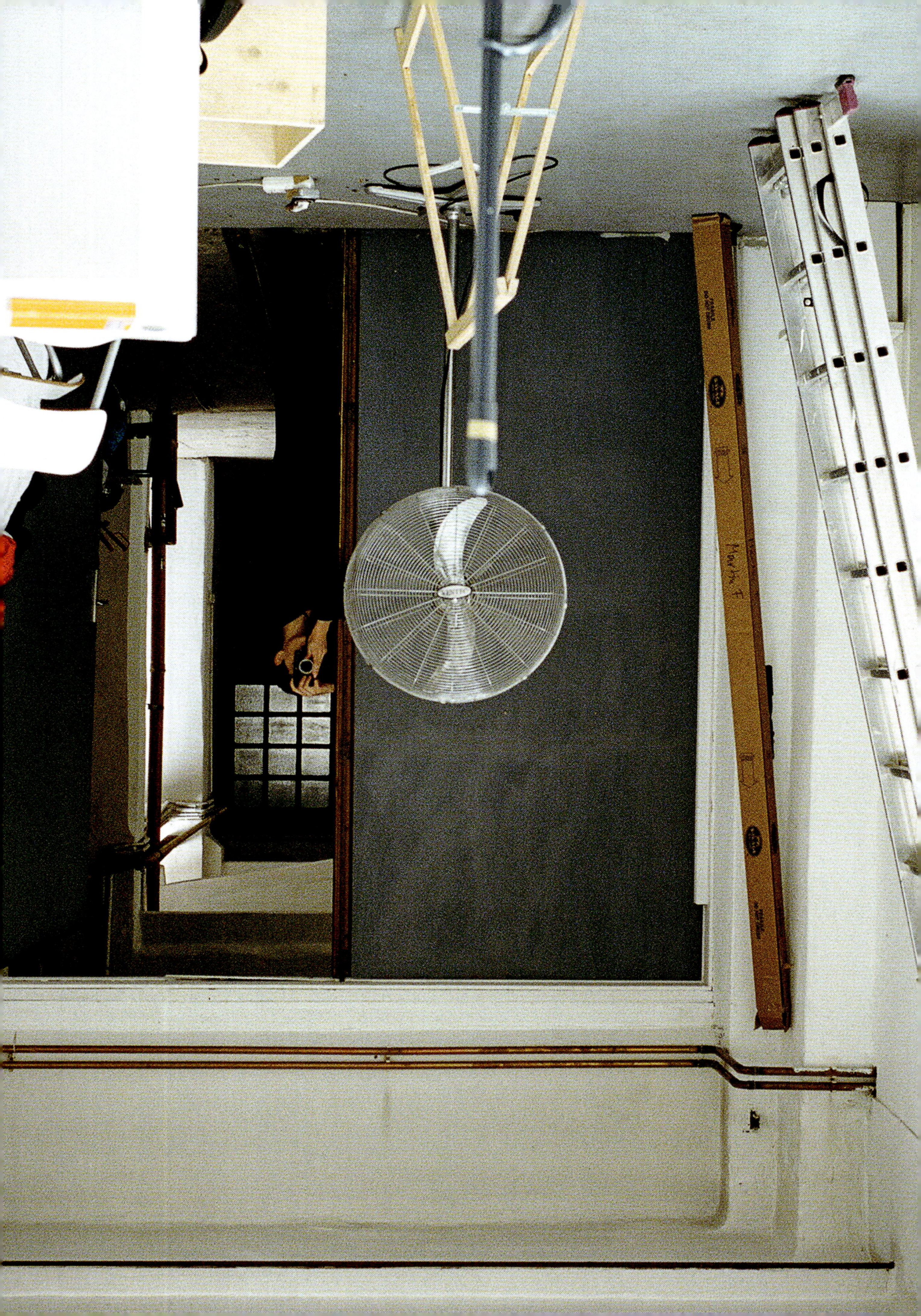

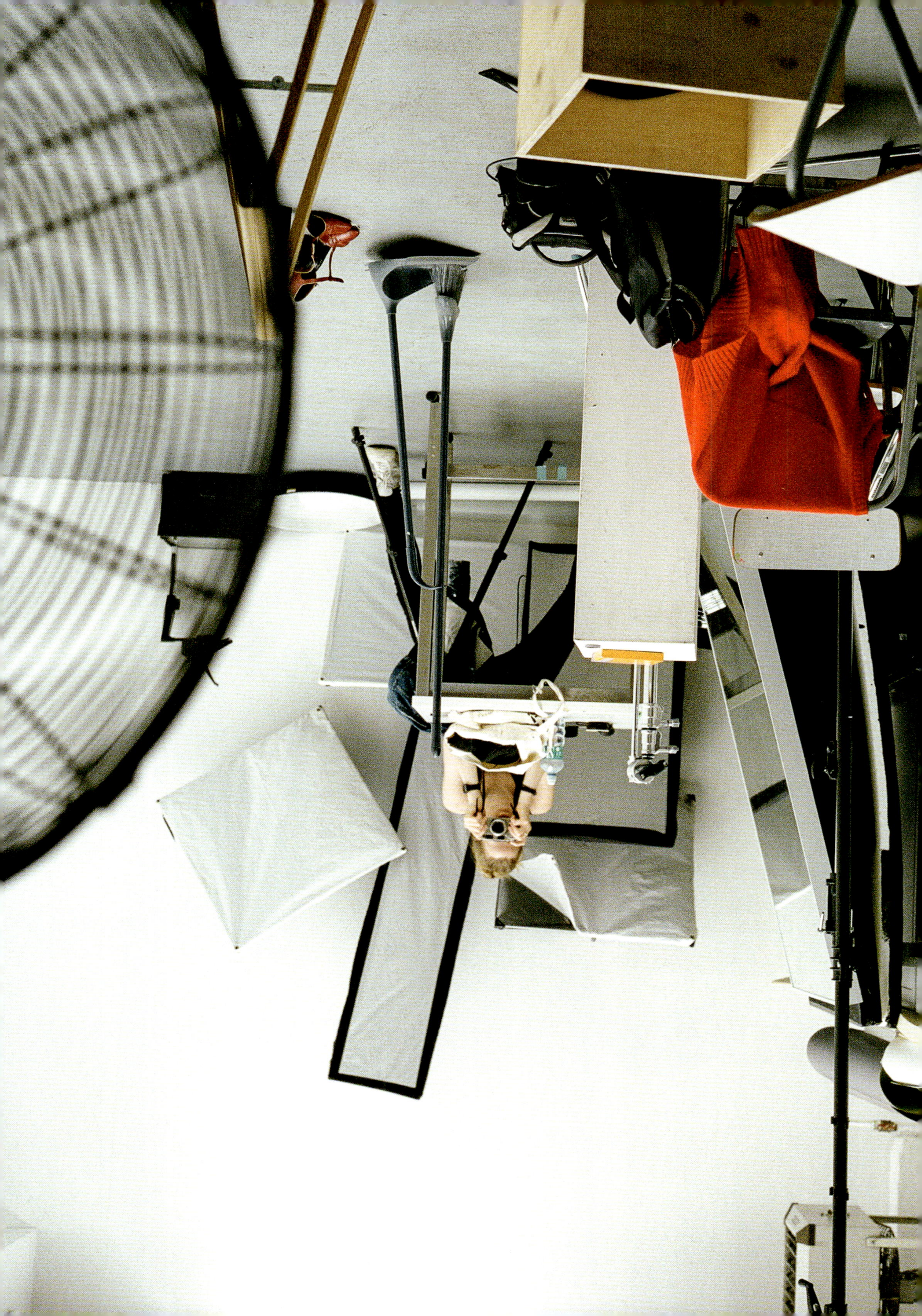

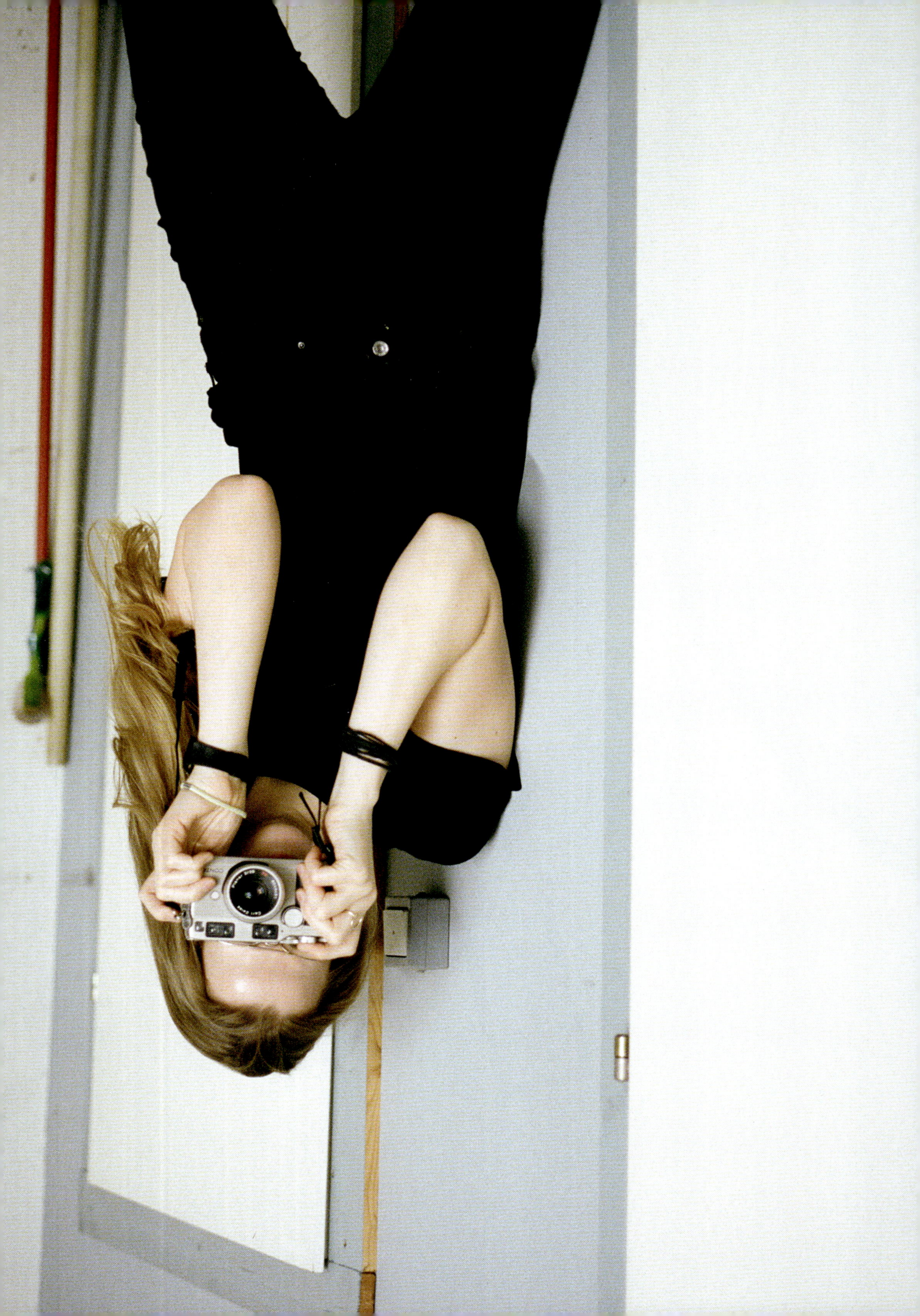

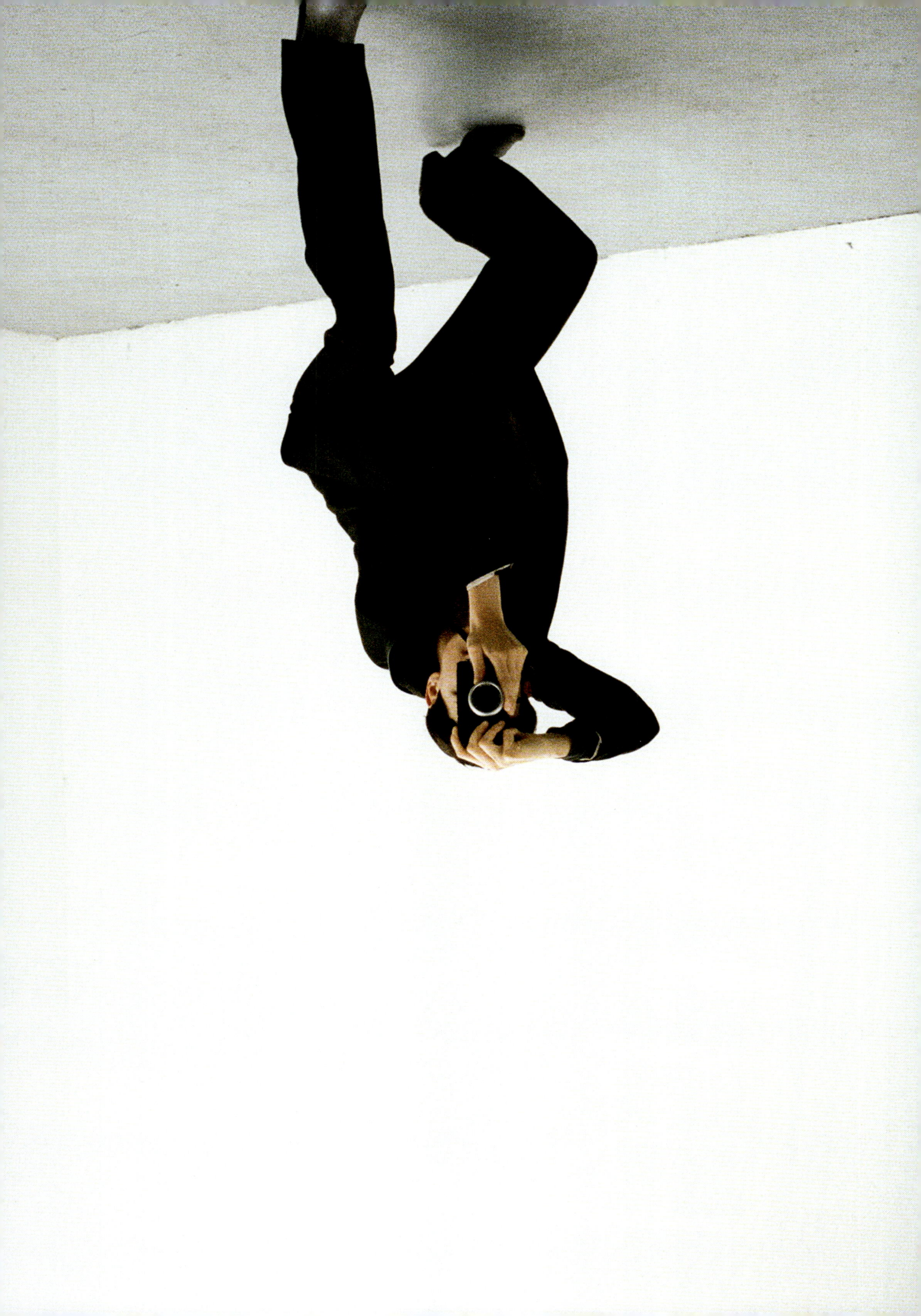

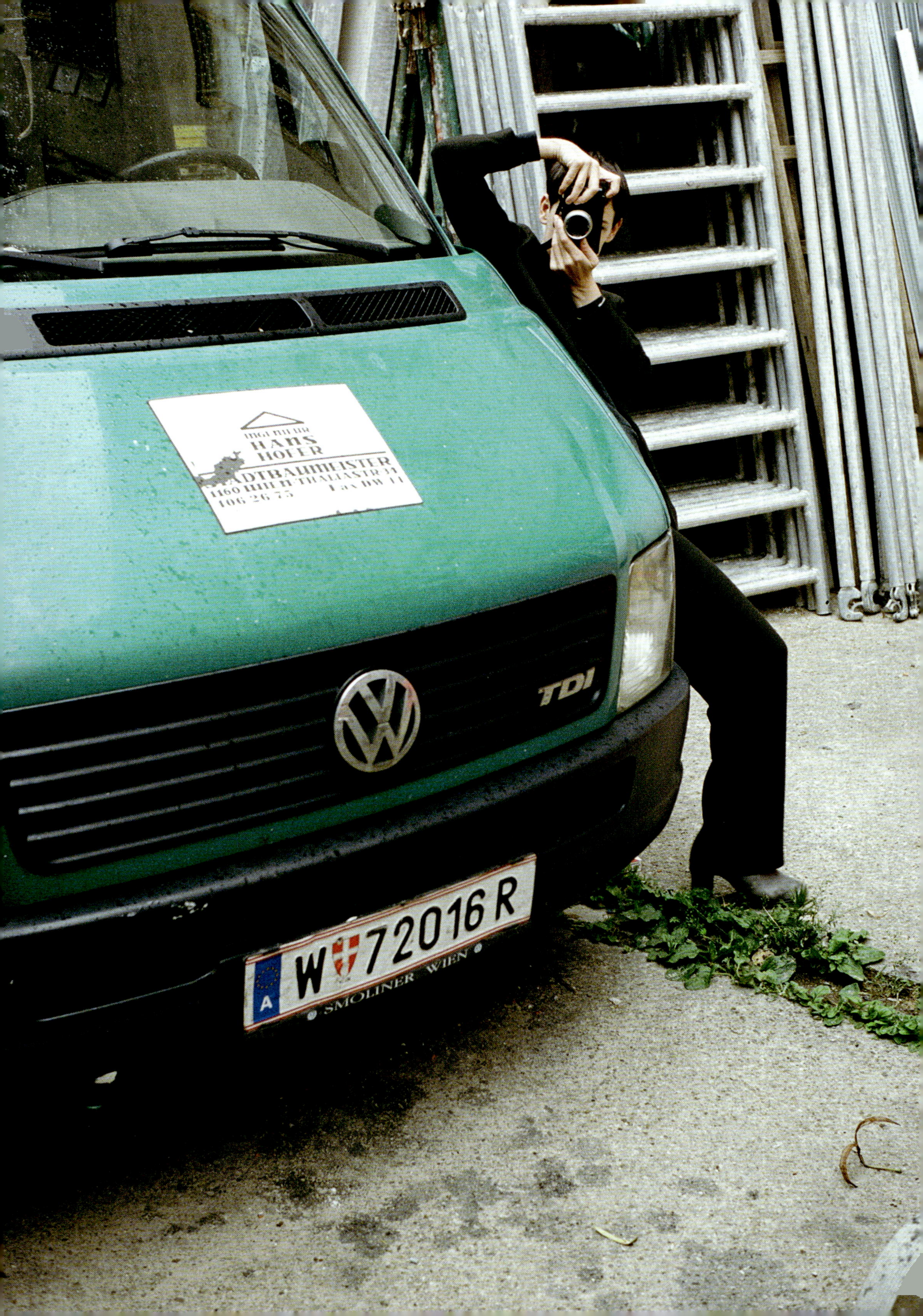
HANS
HOFER
106 26 75
TDI
W 72016 R
A
SMOLINER WIEN

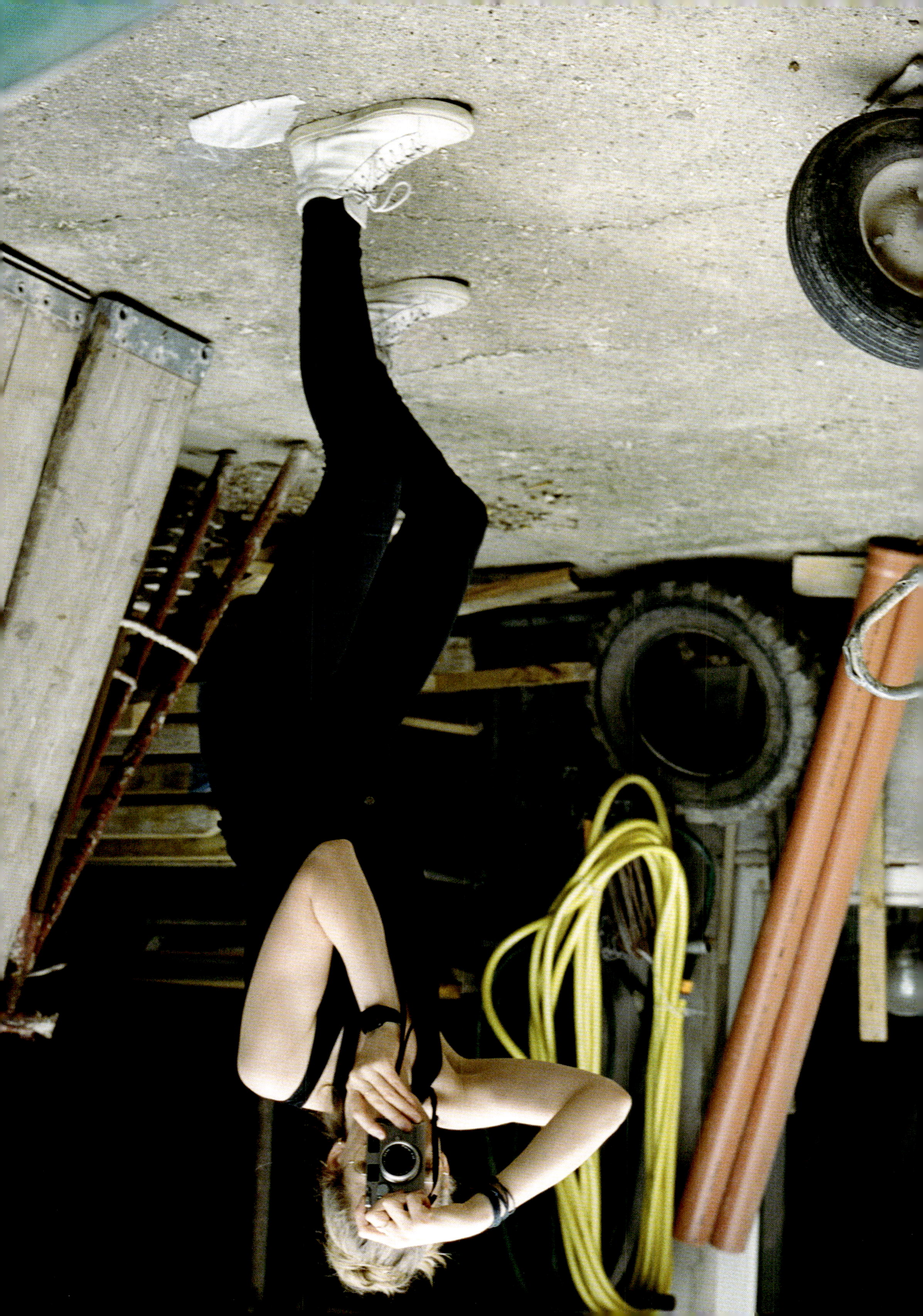

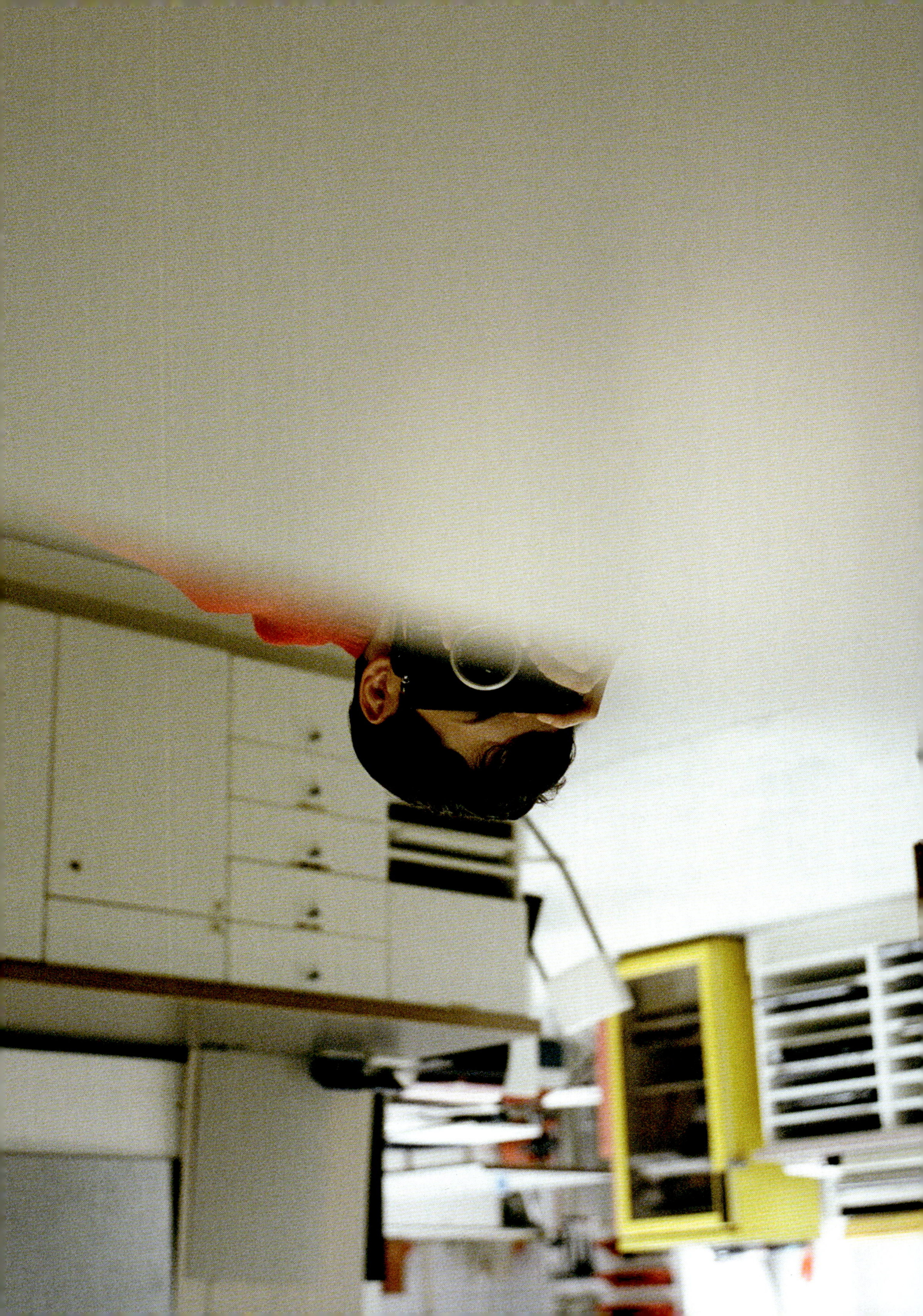

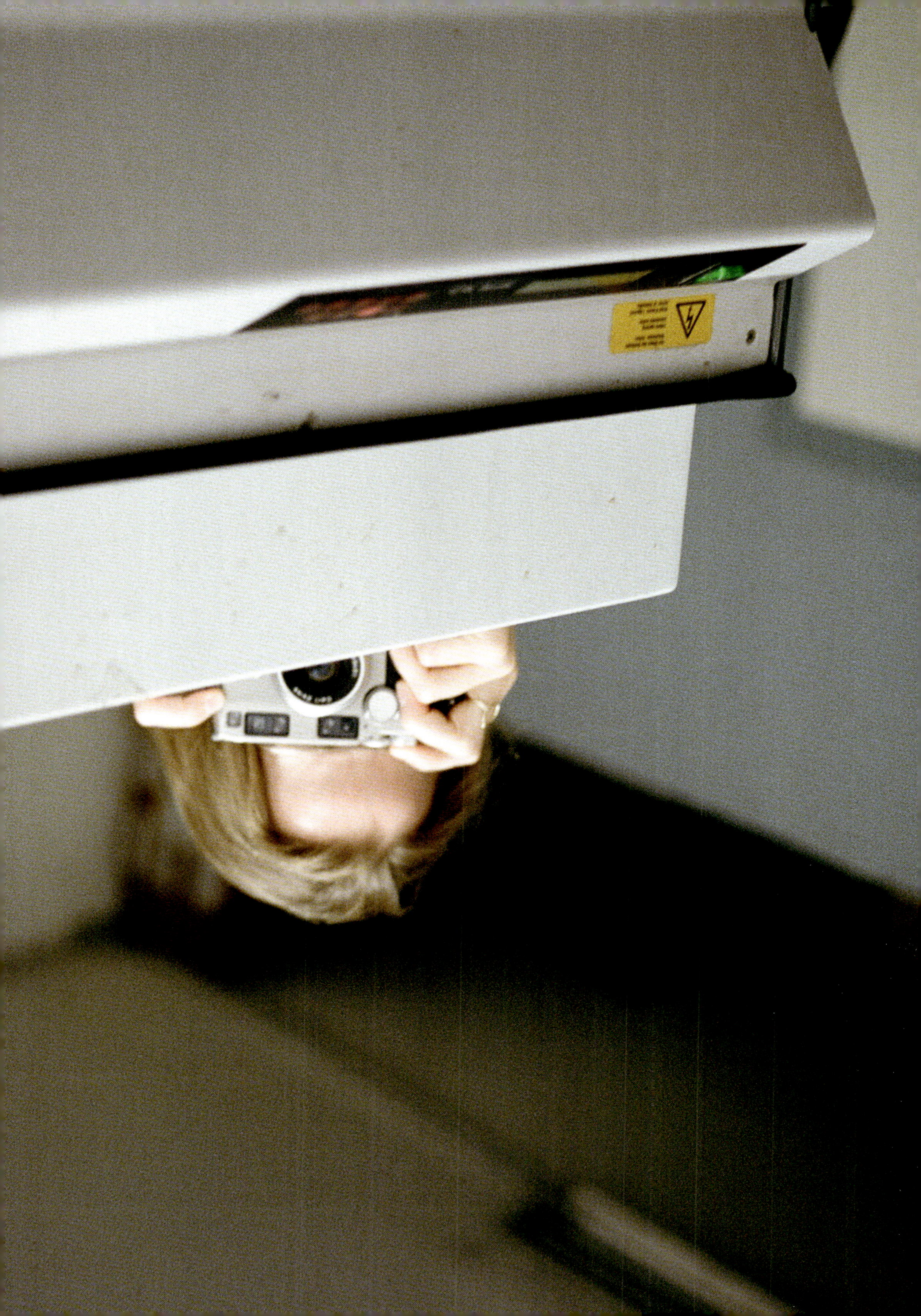

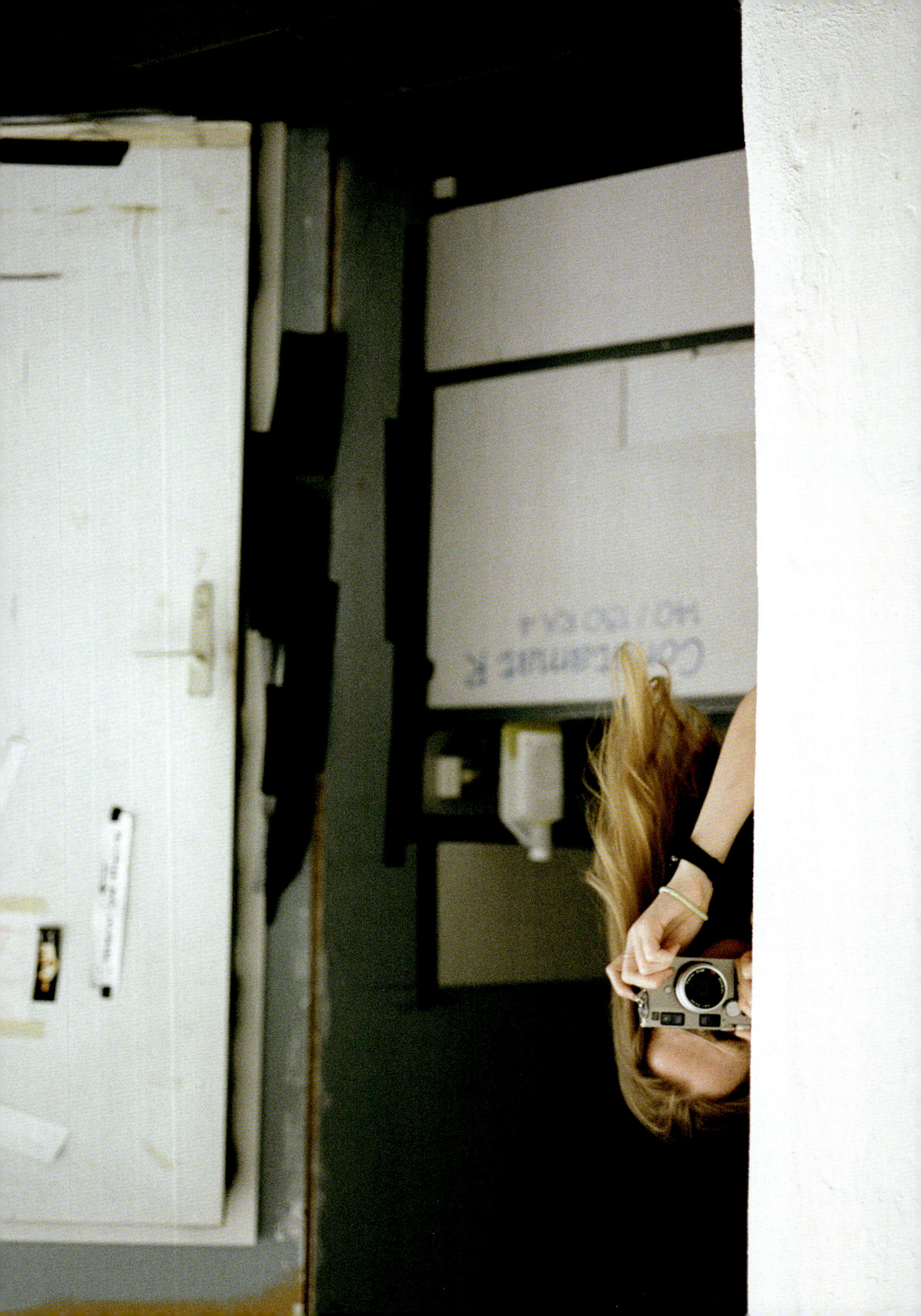

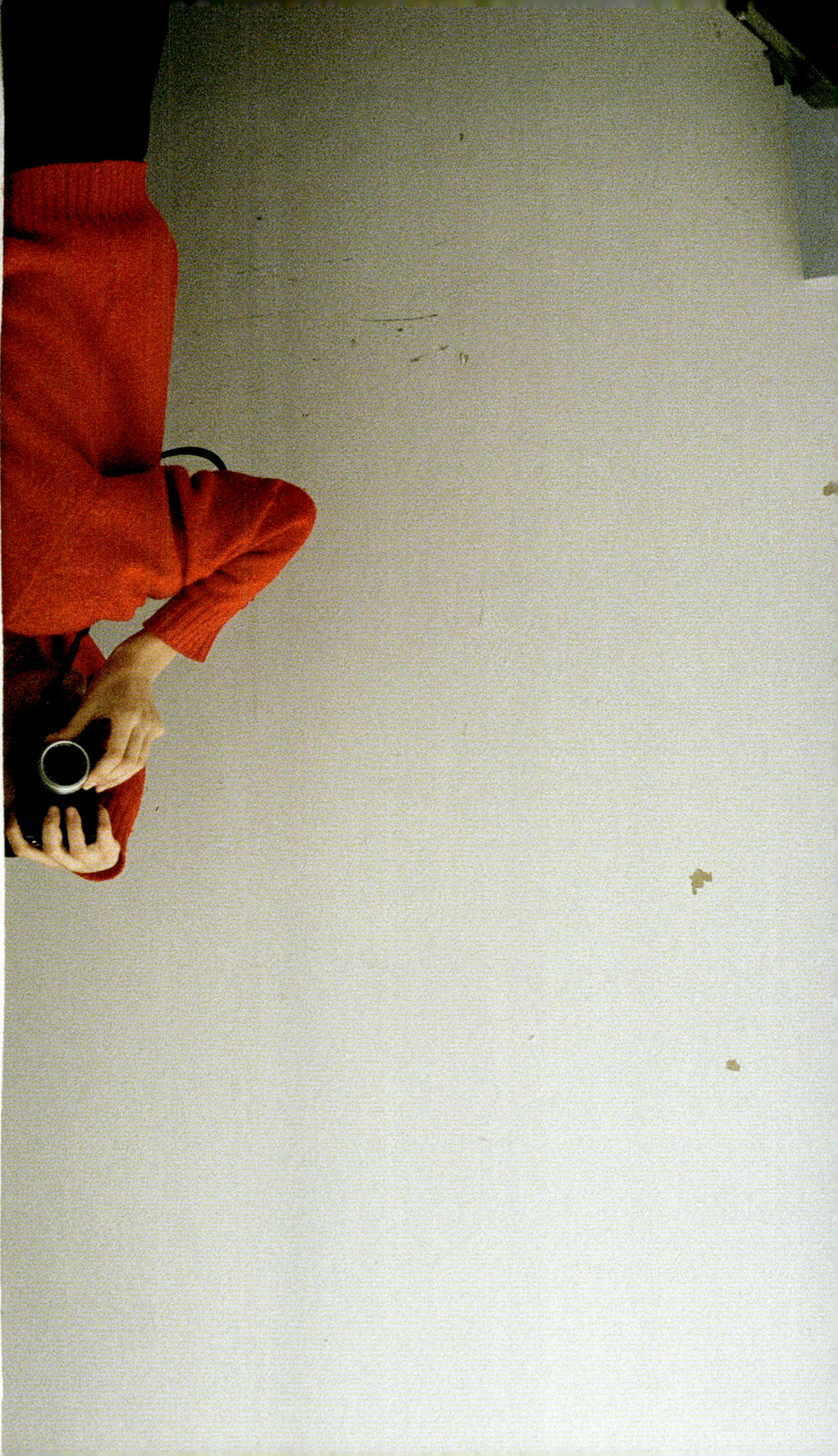

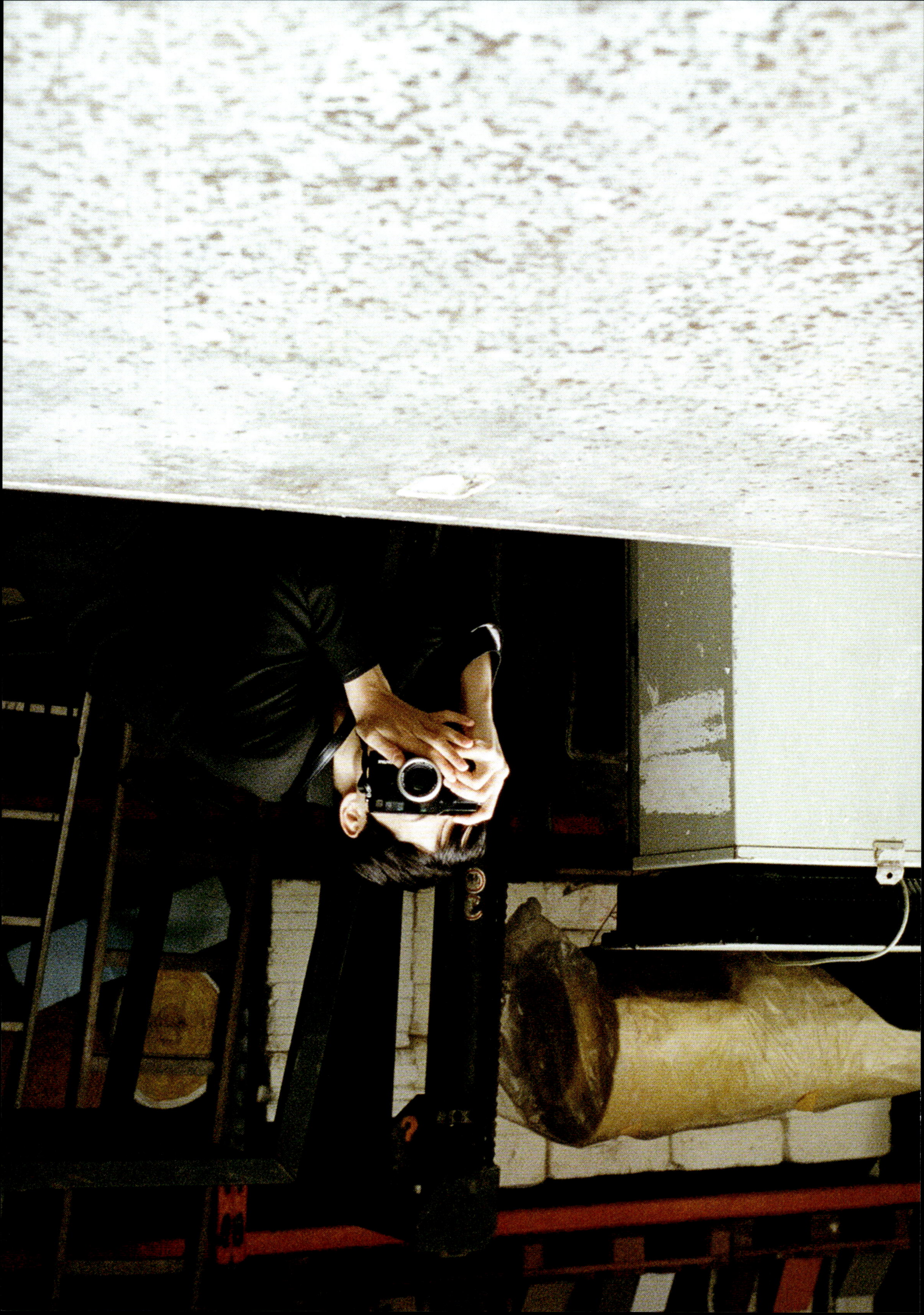

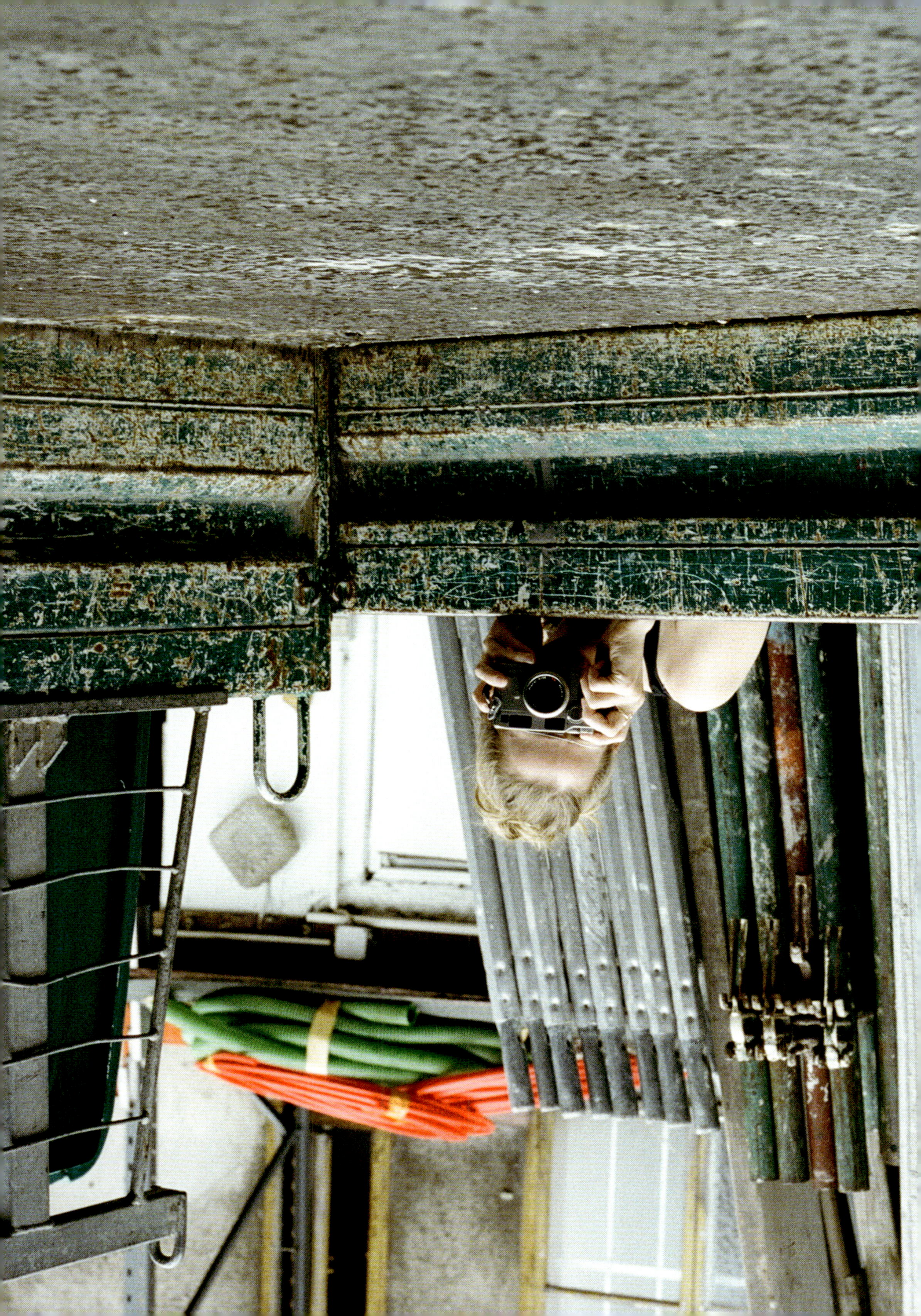

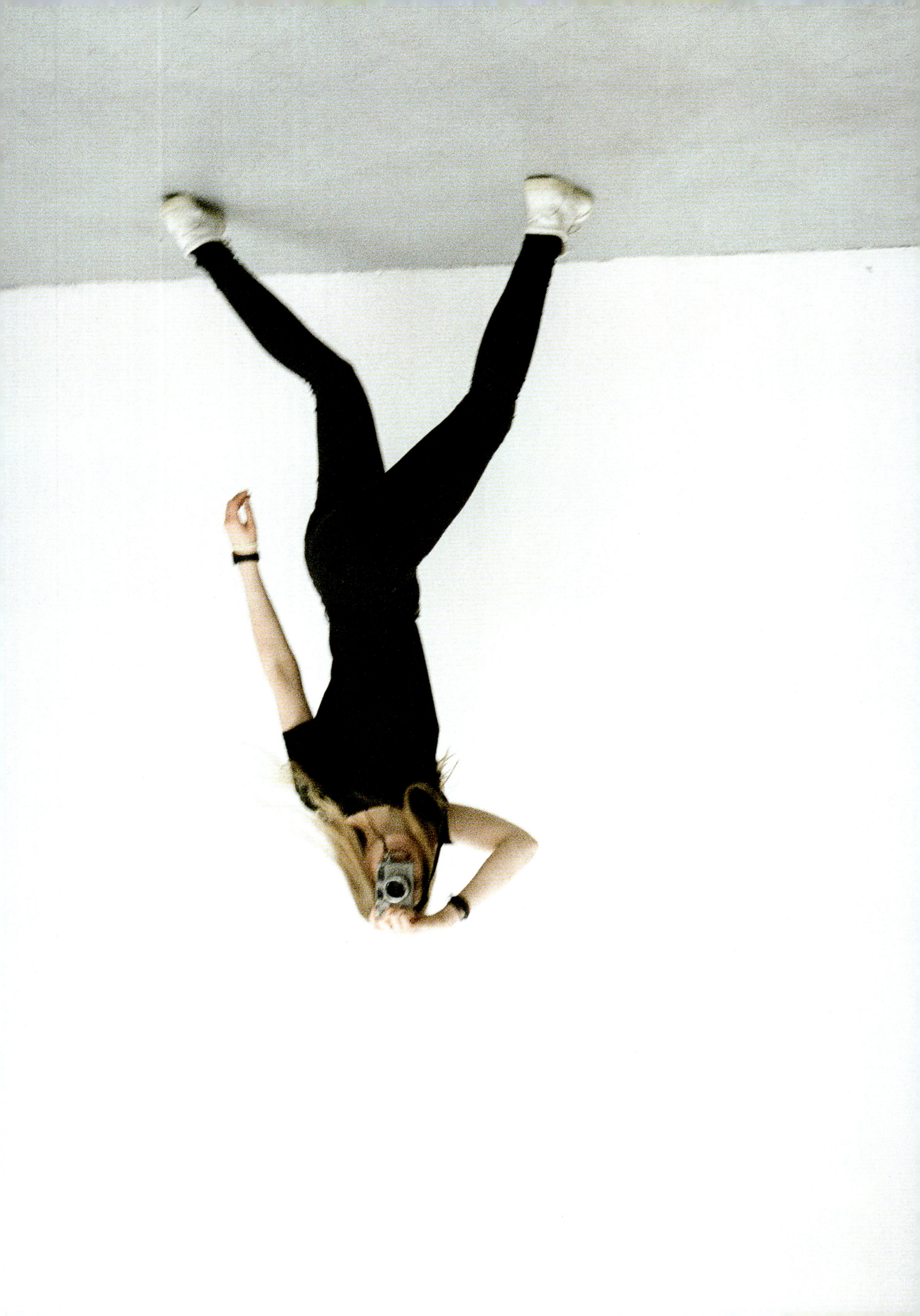

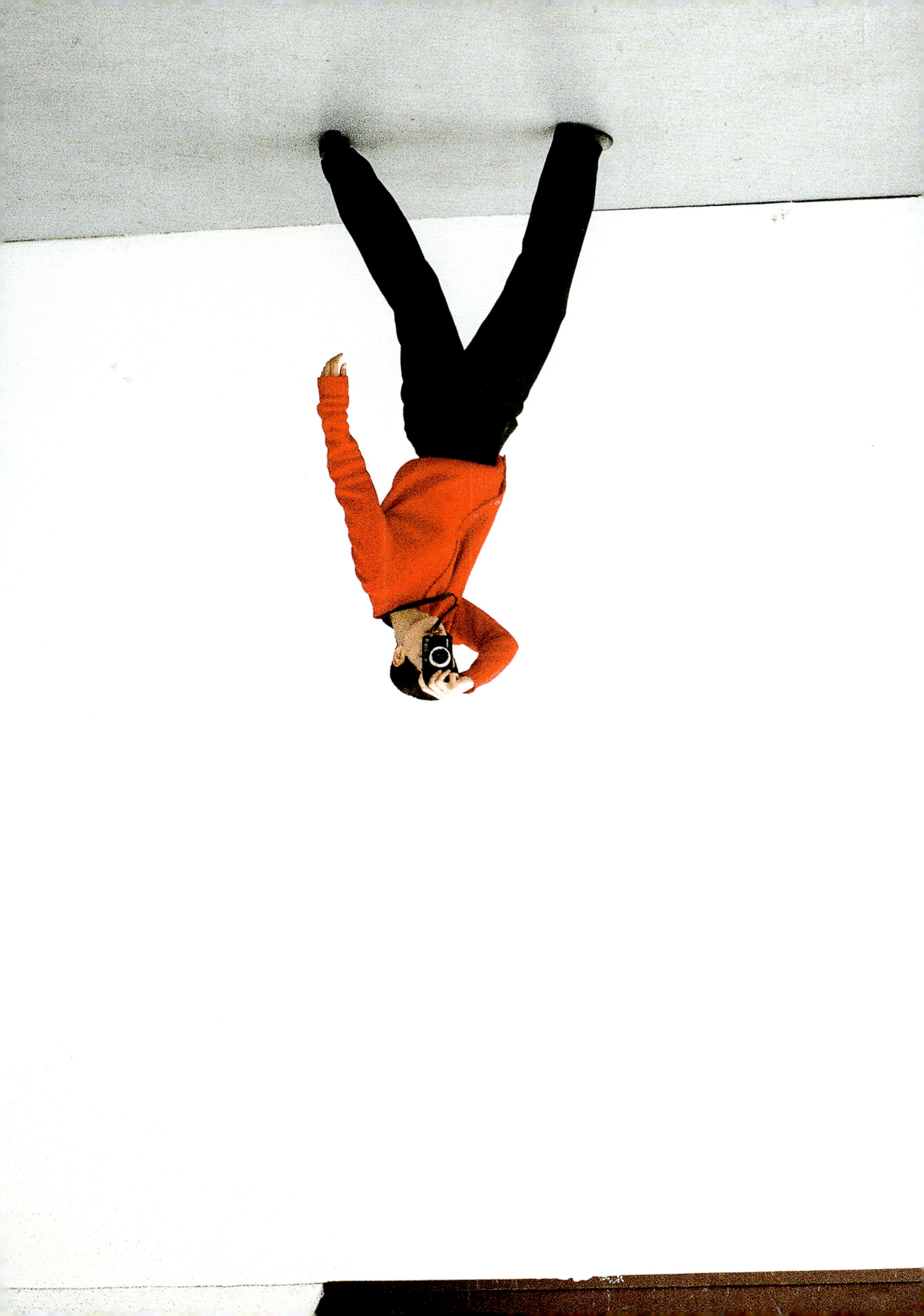

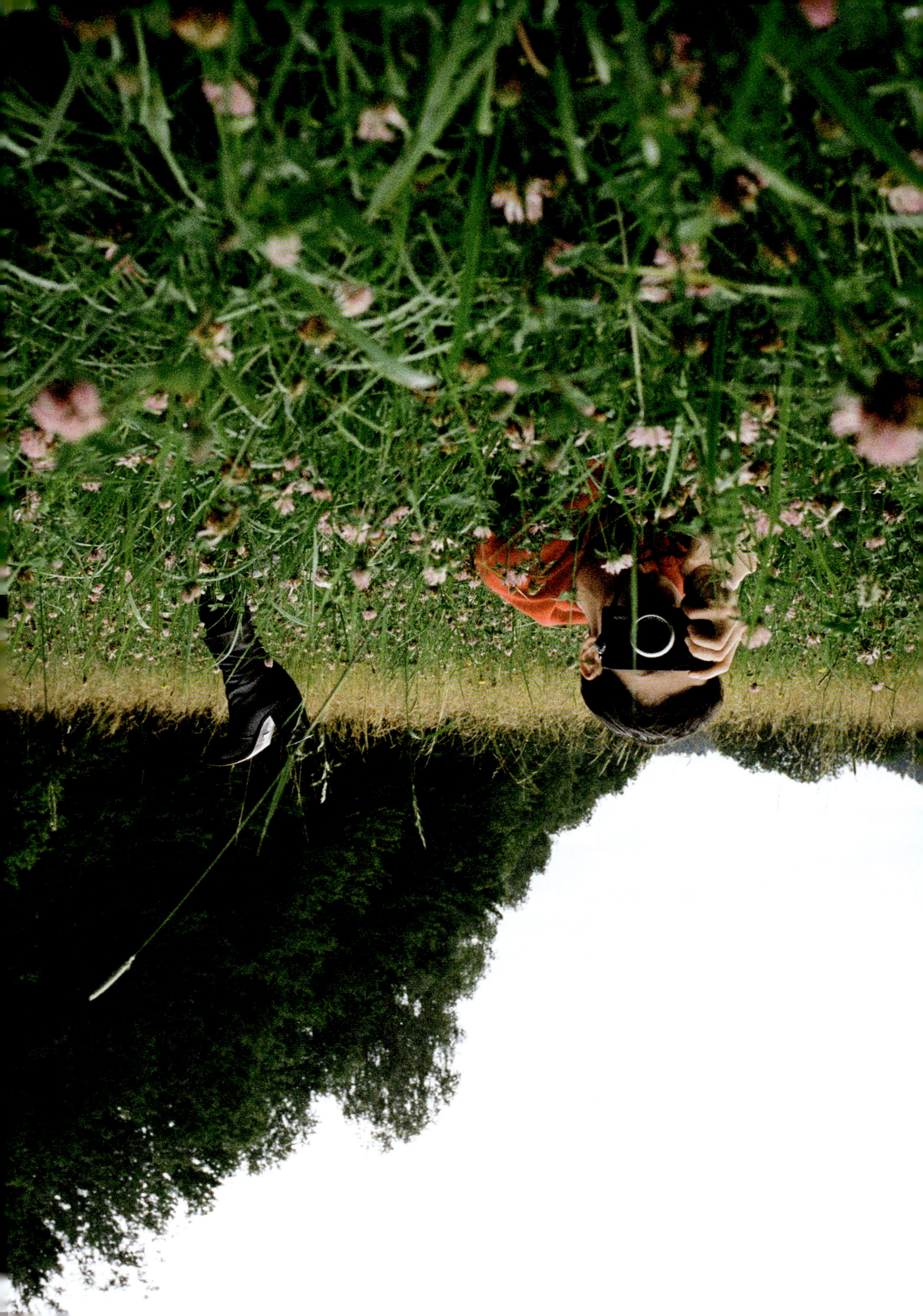

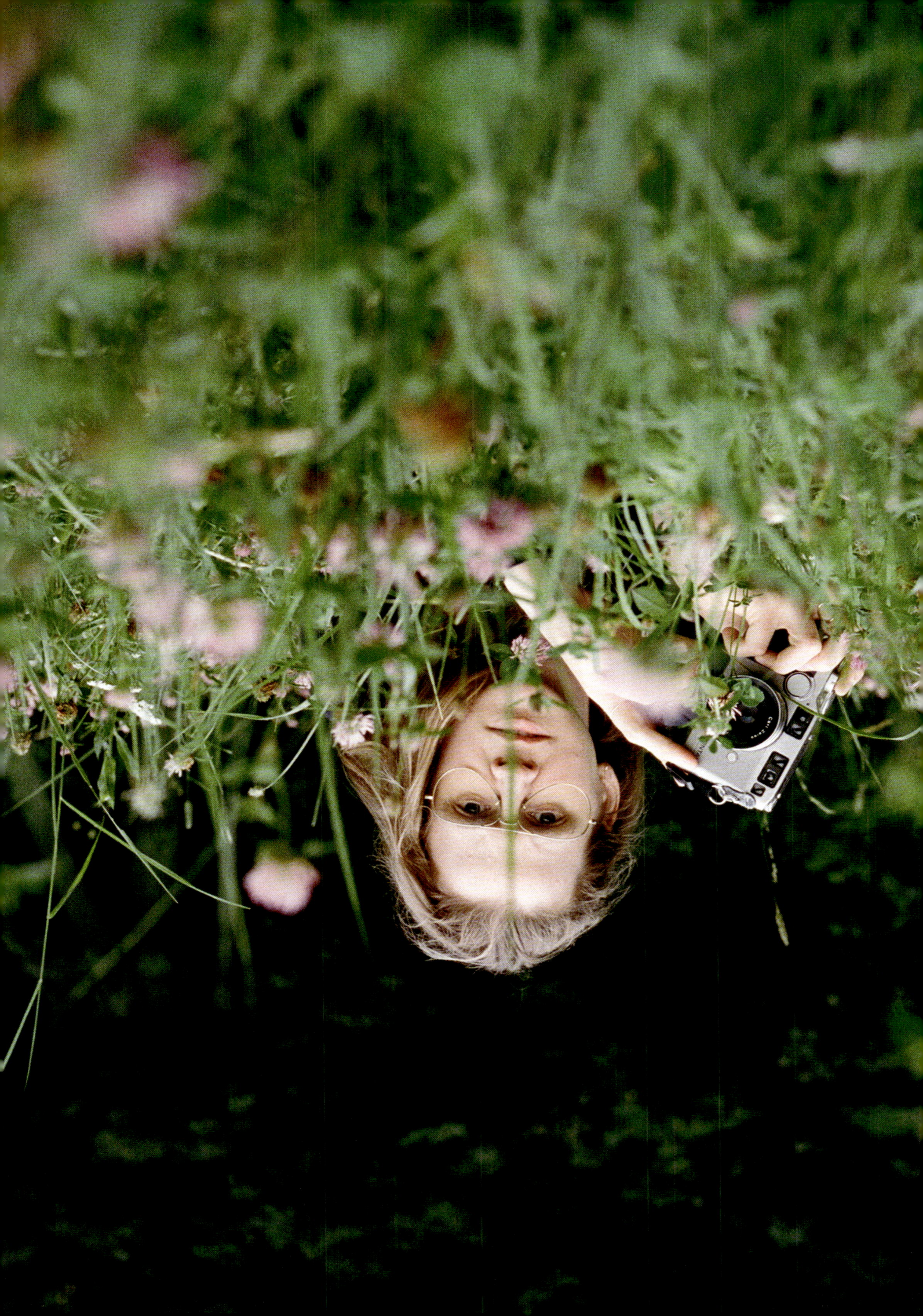

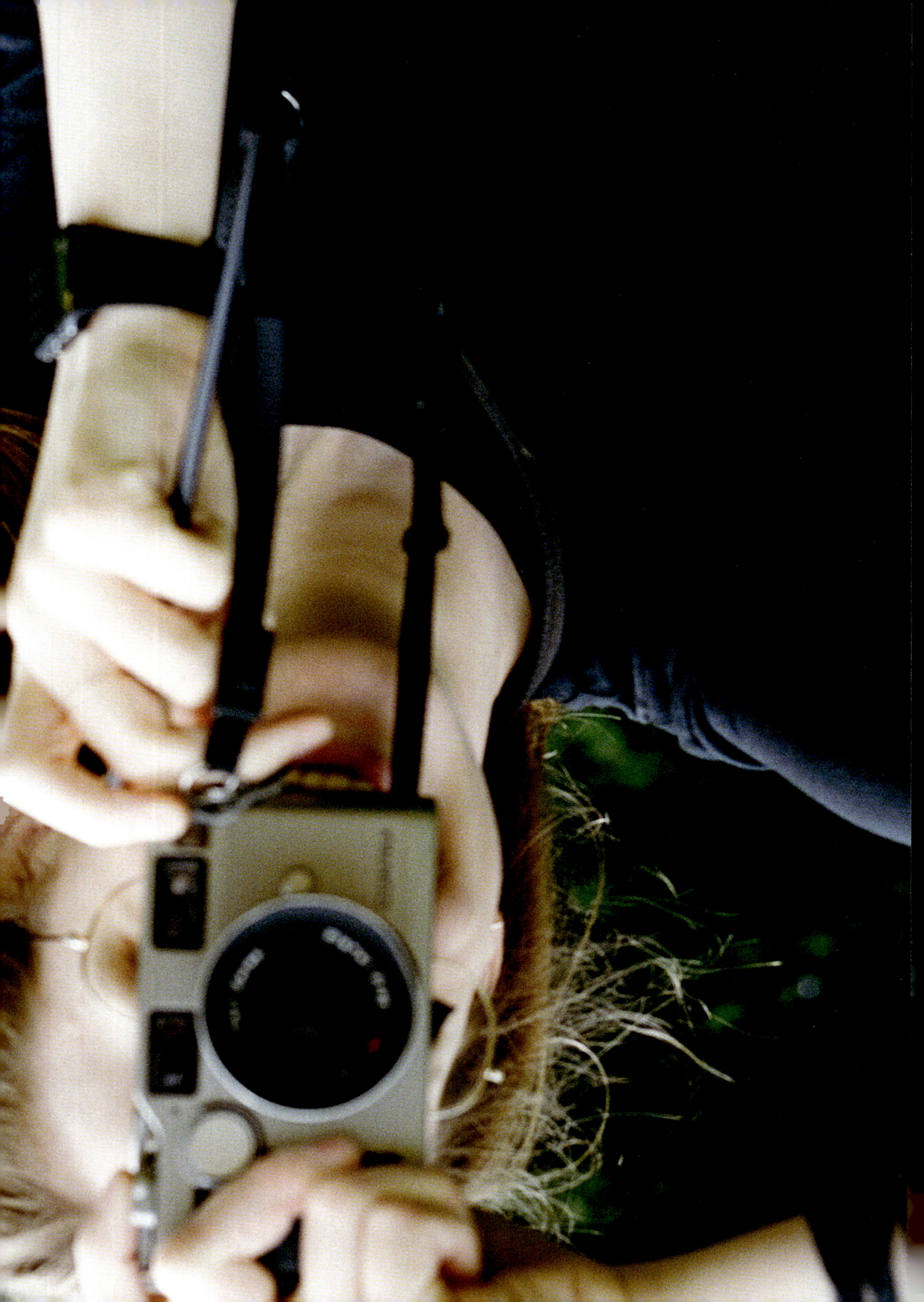

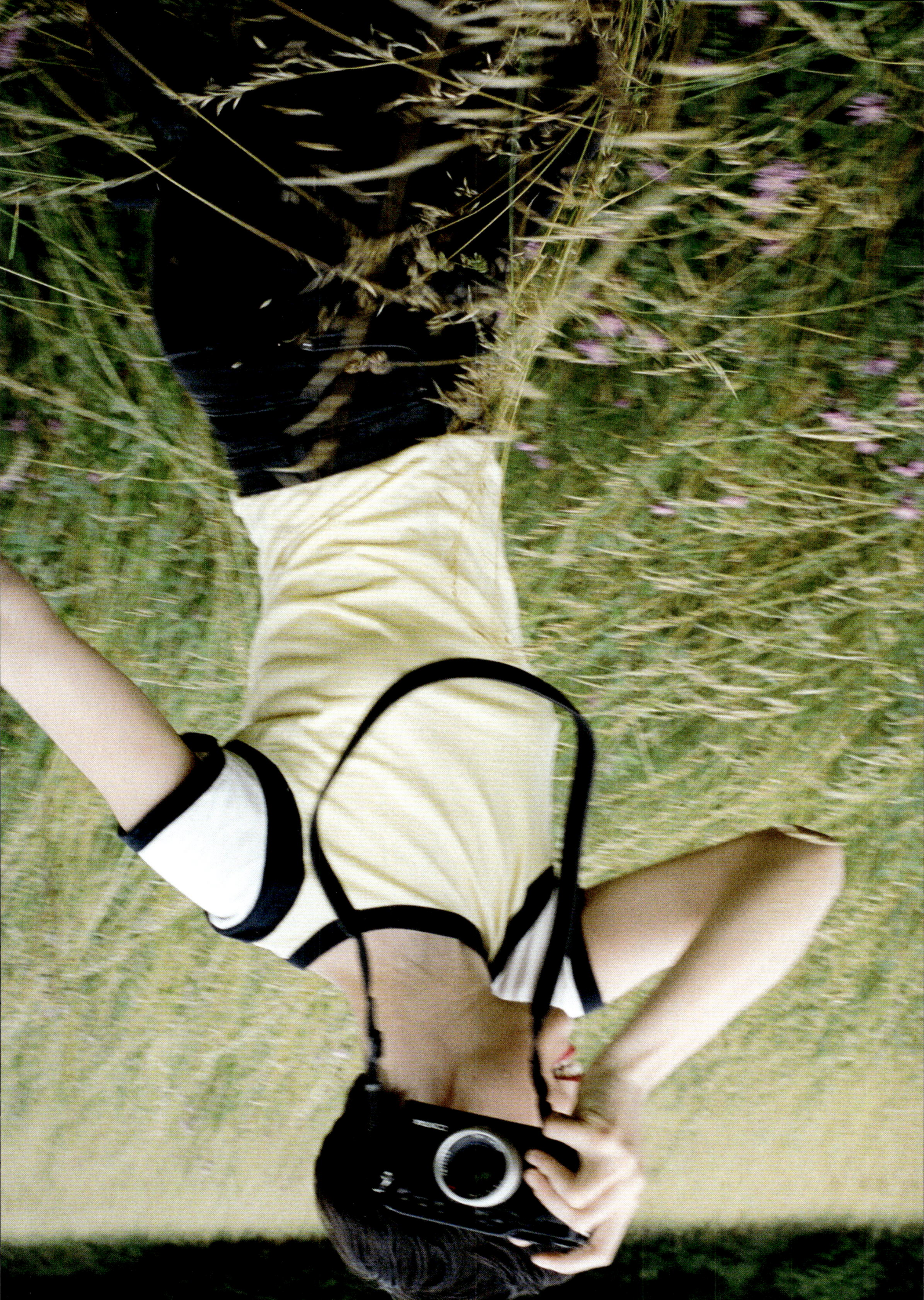

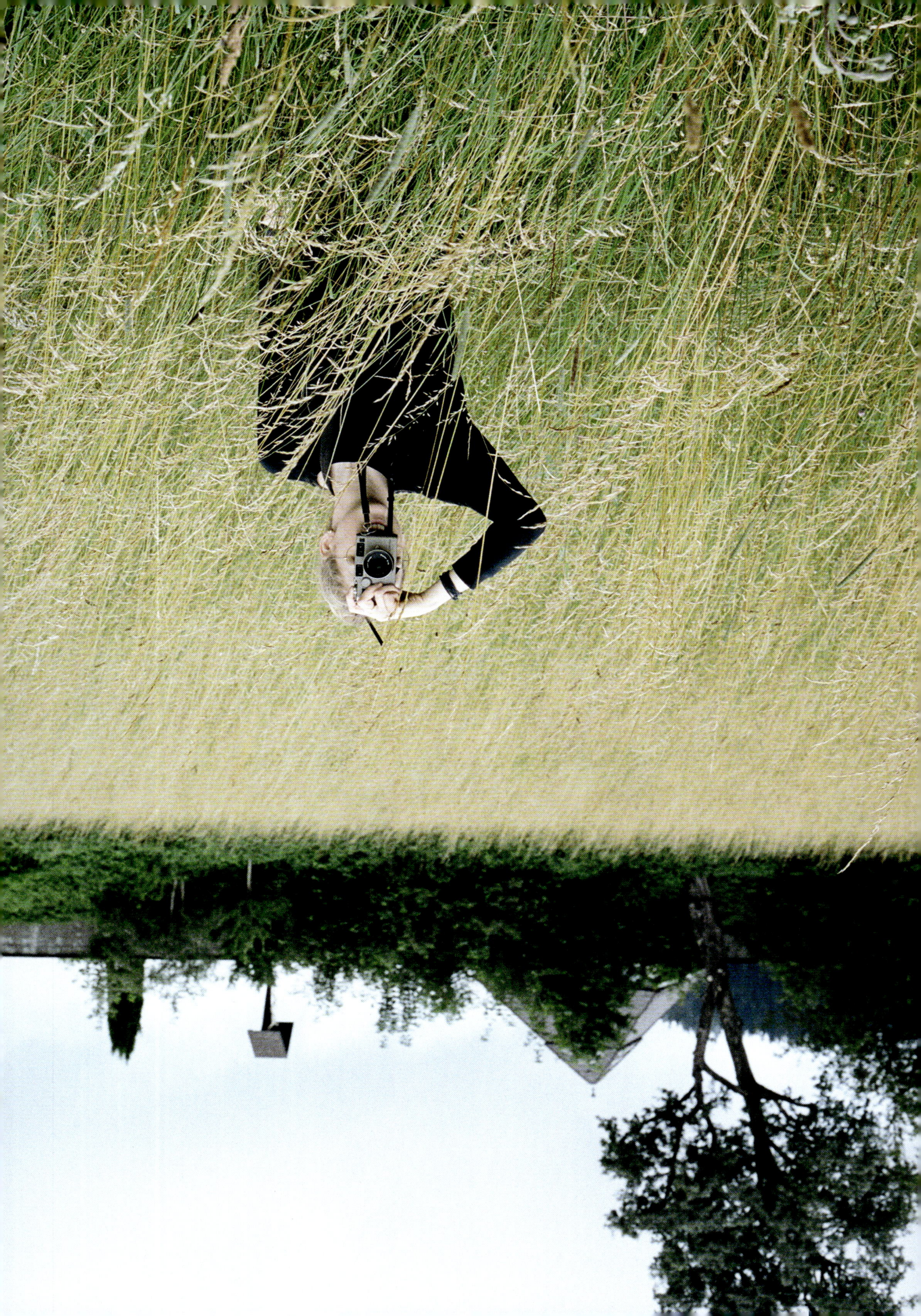

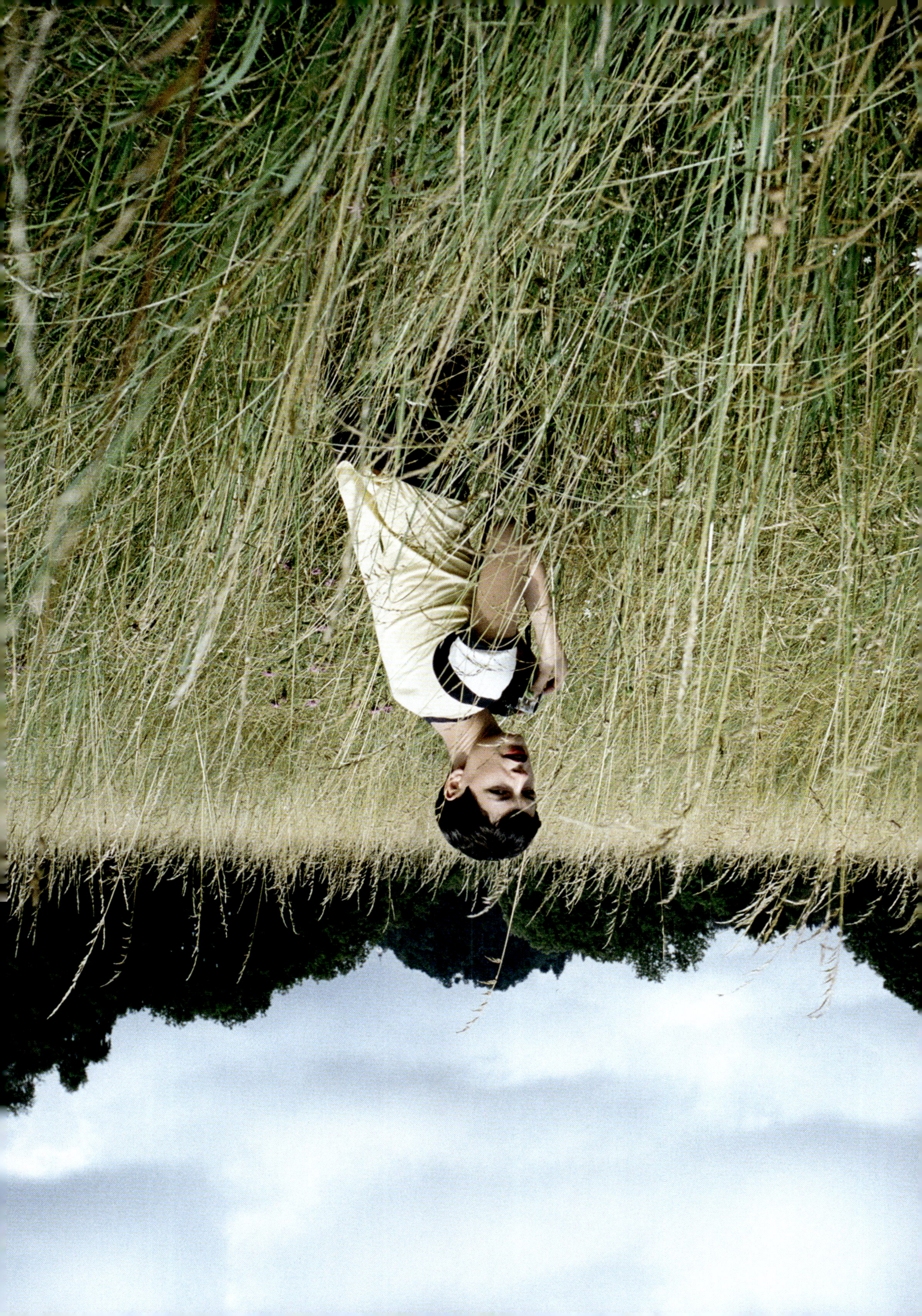

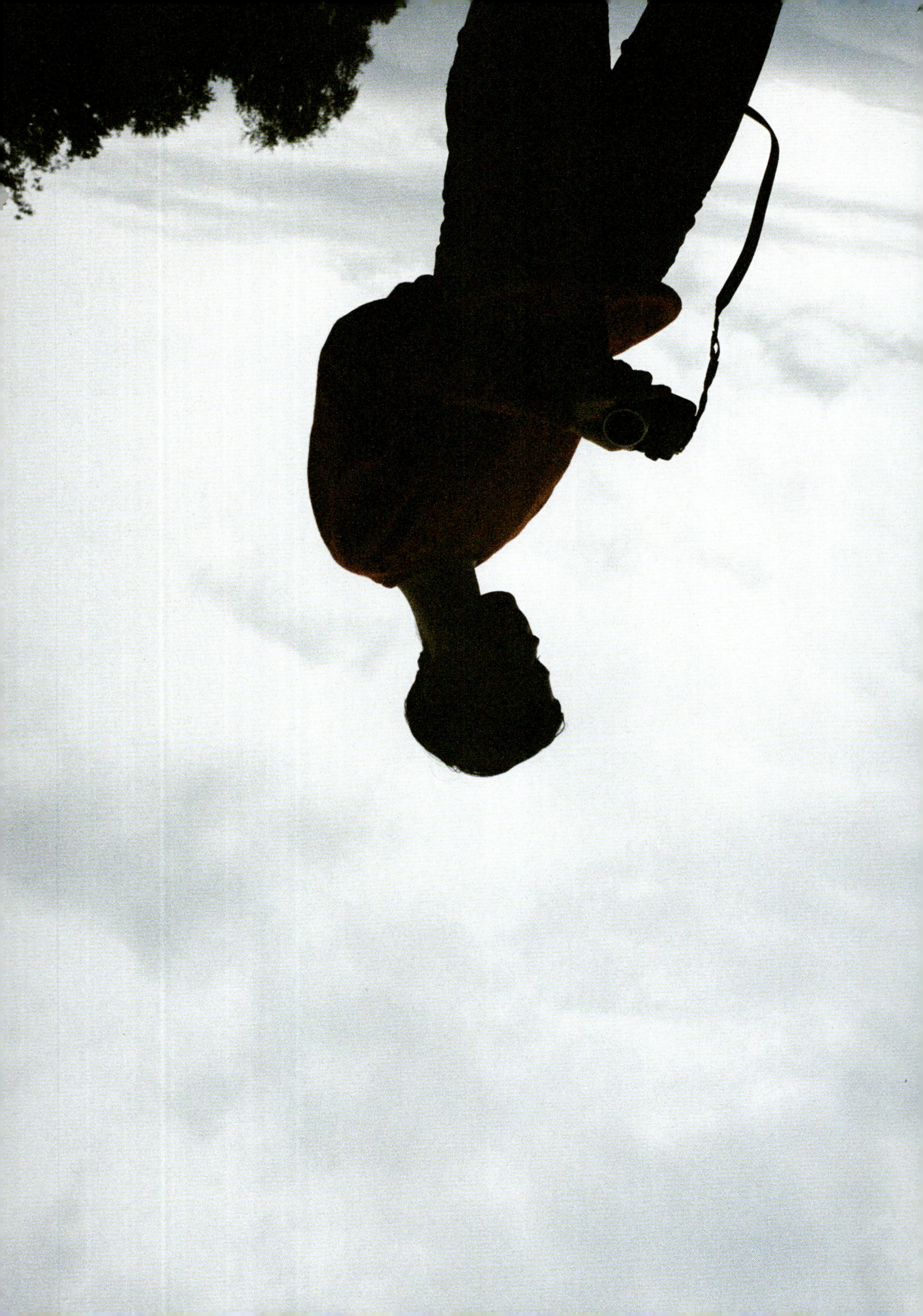

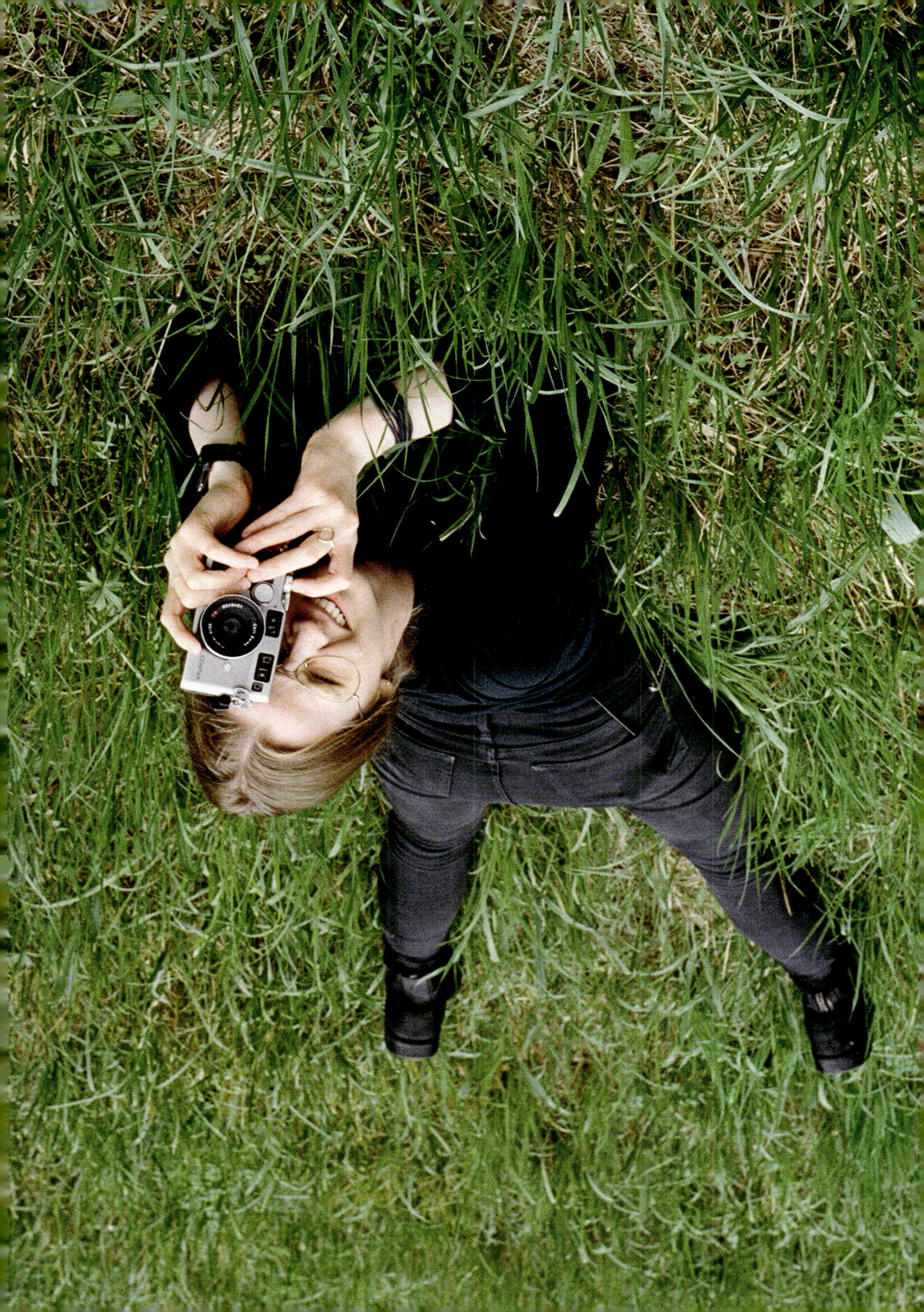

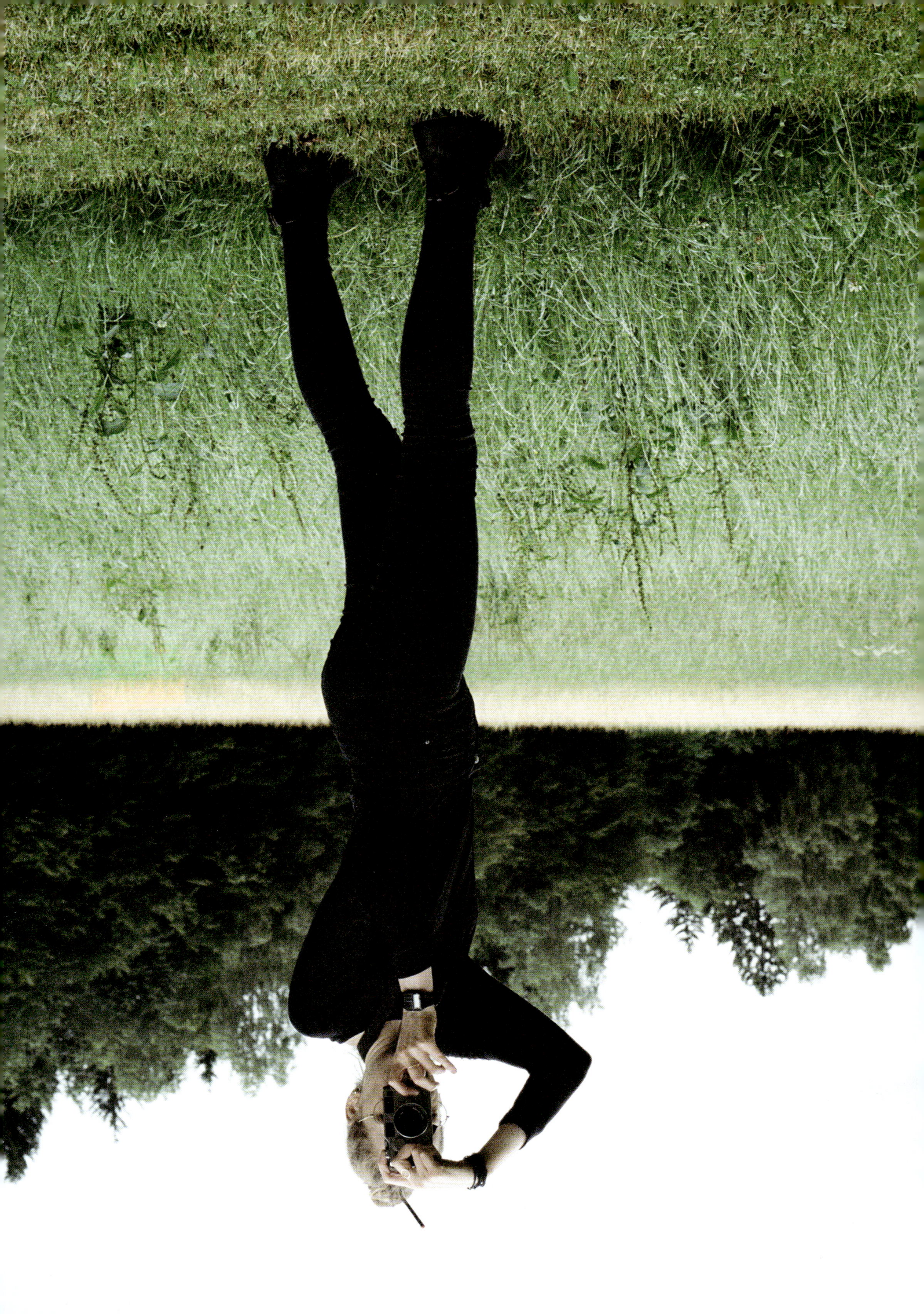

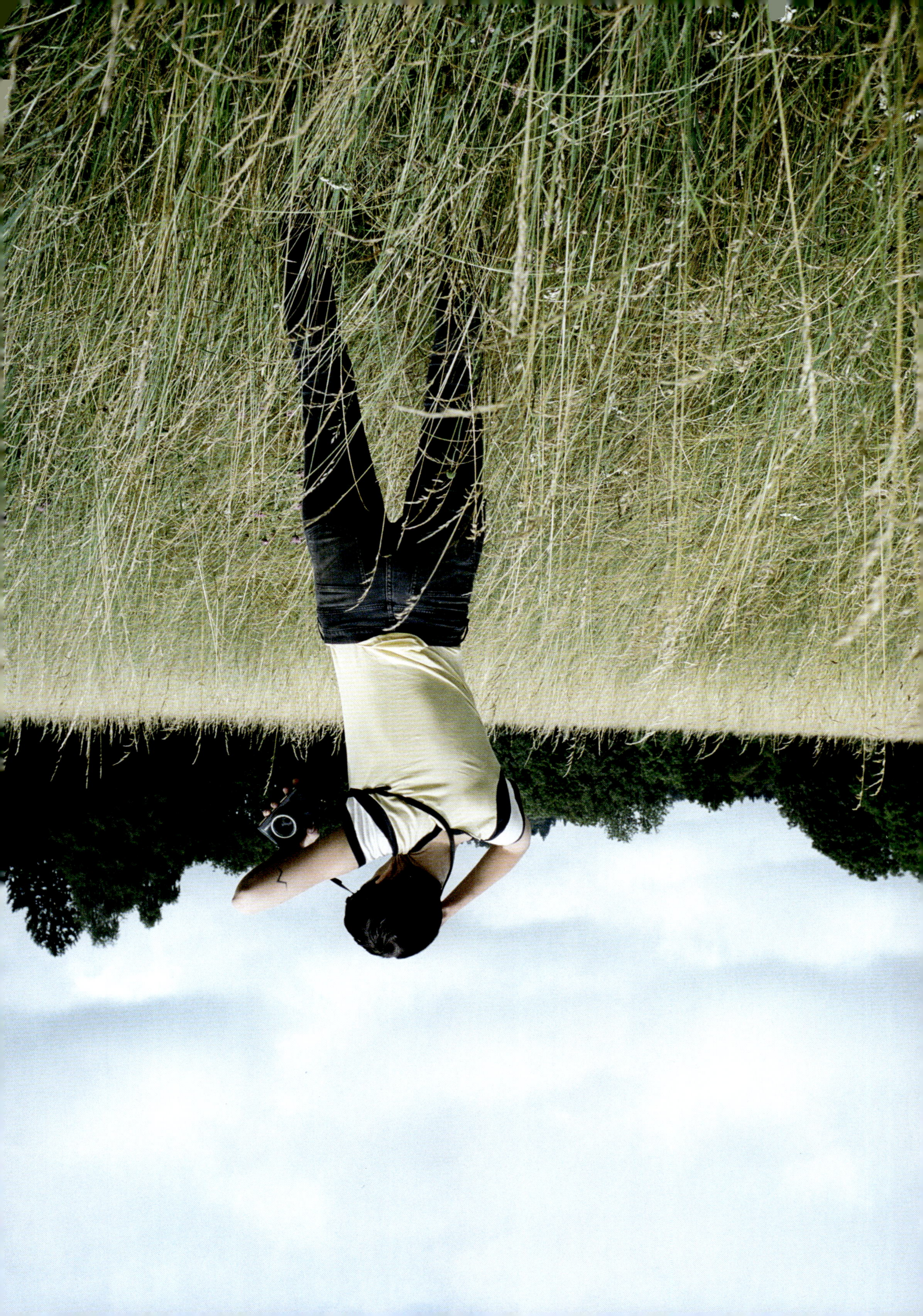

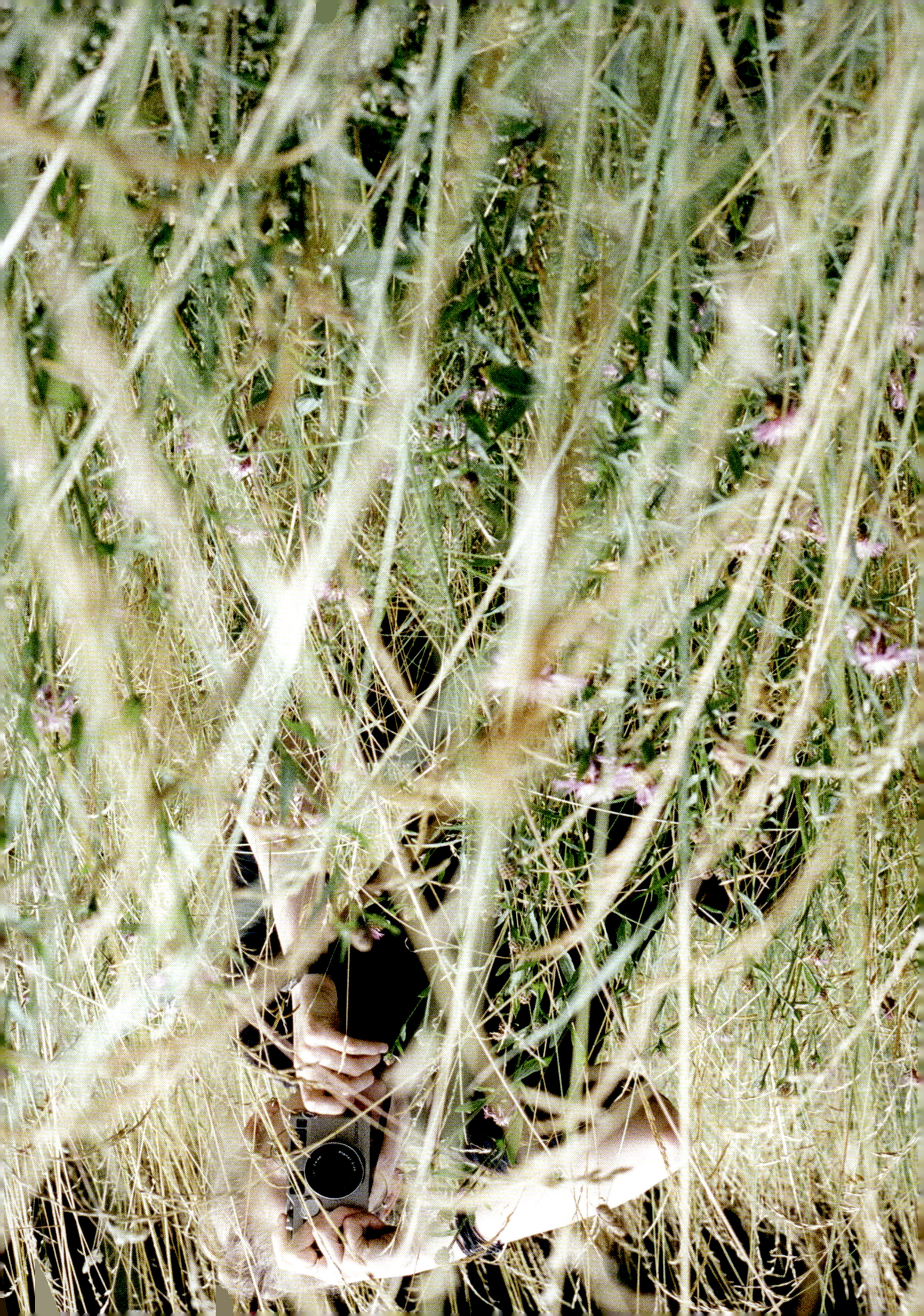

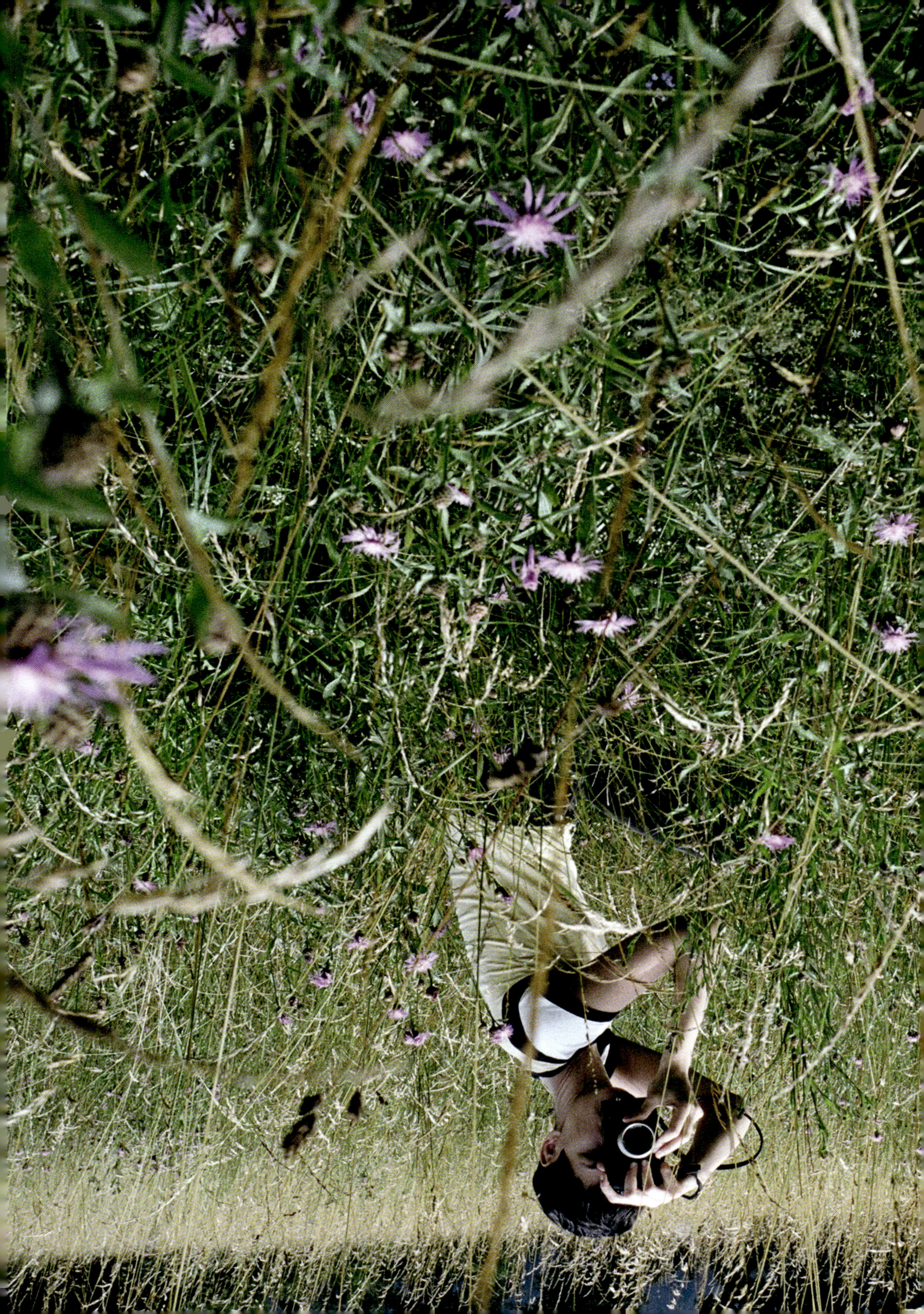

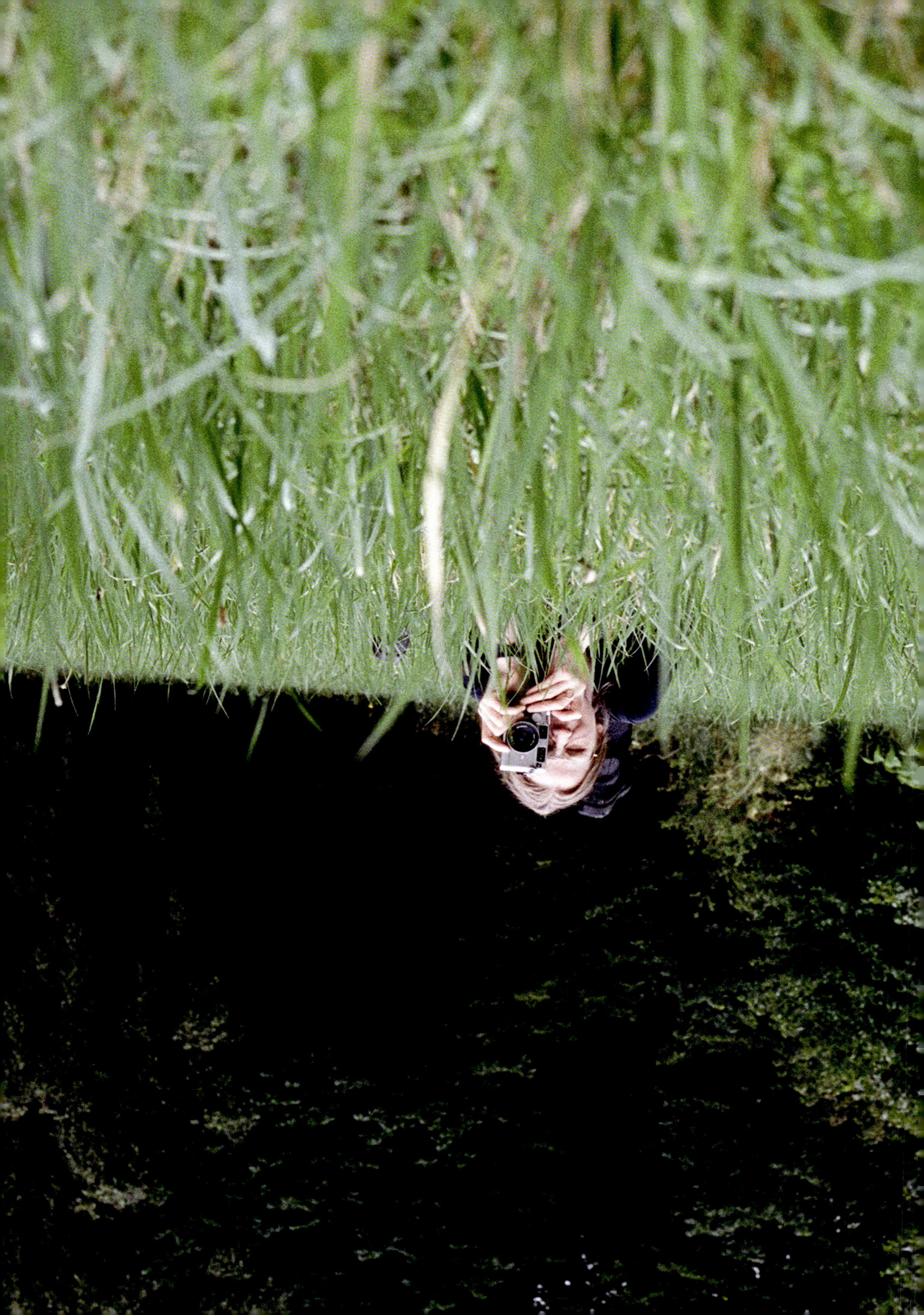

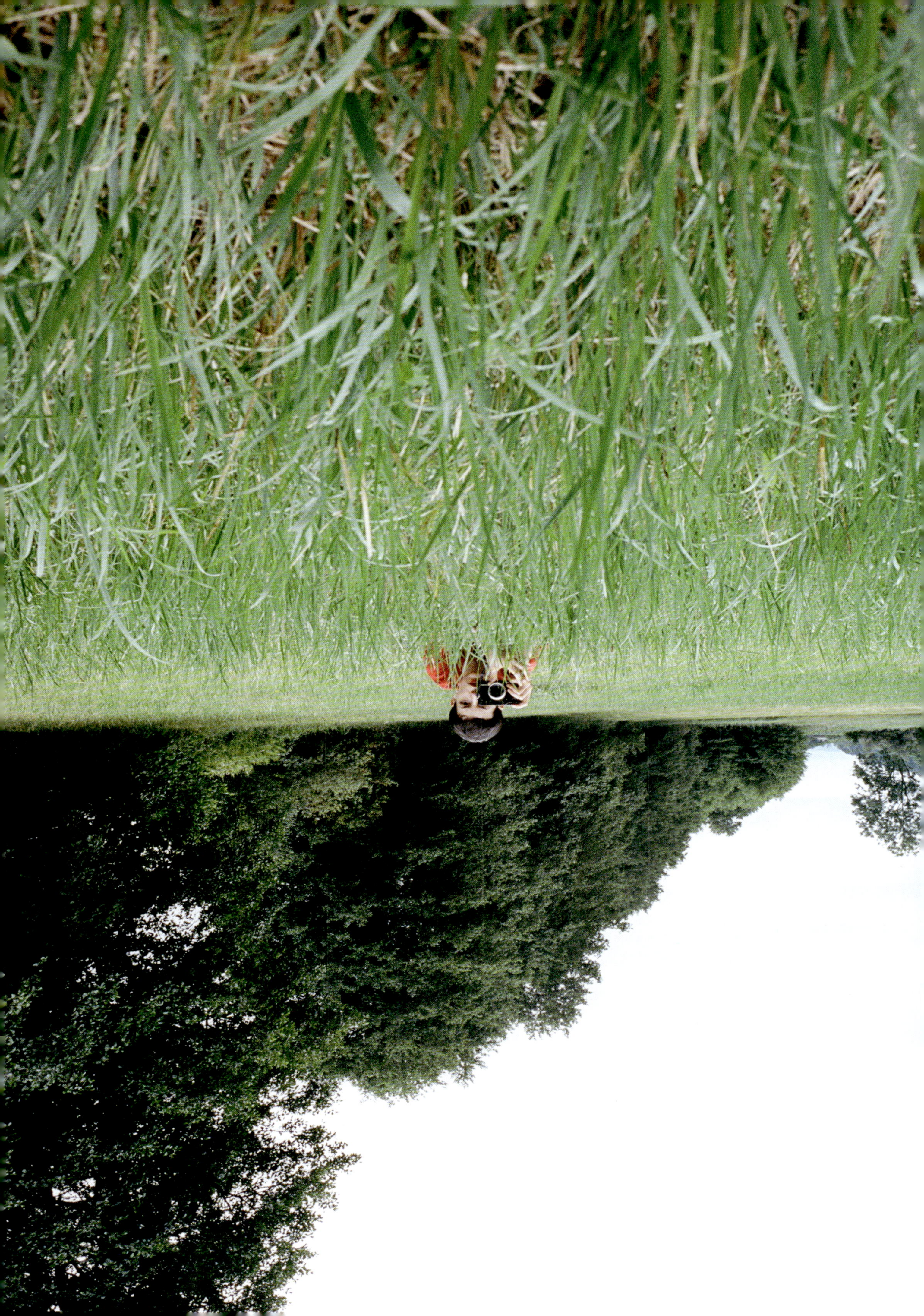

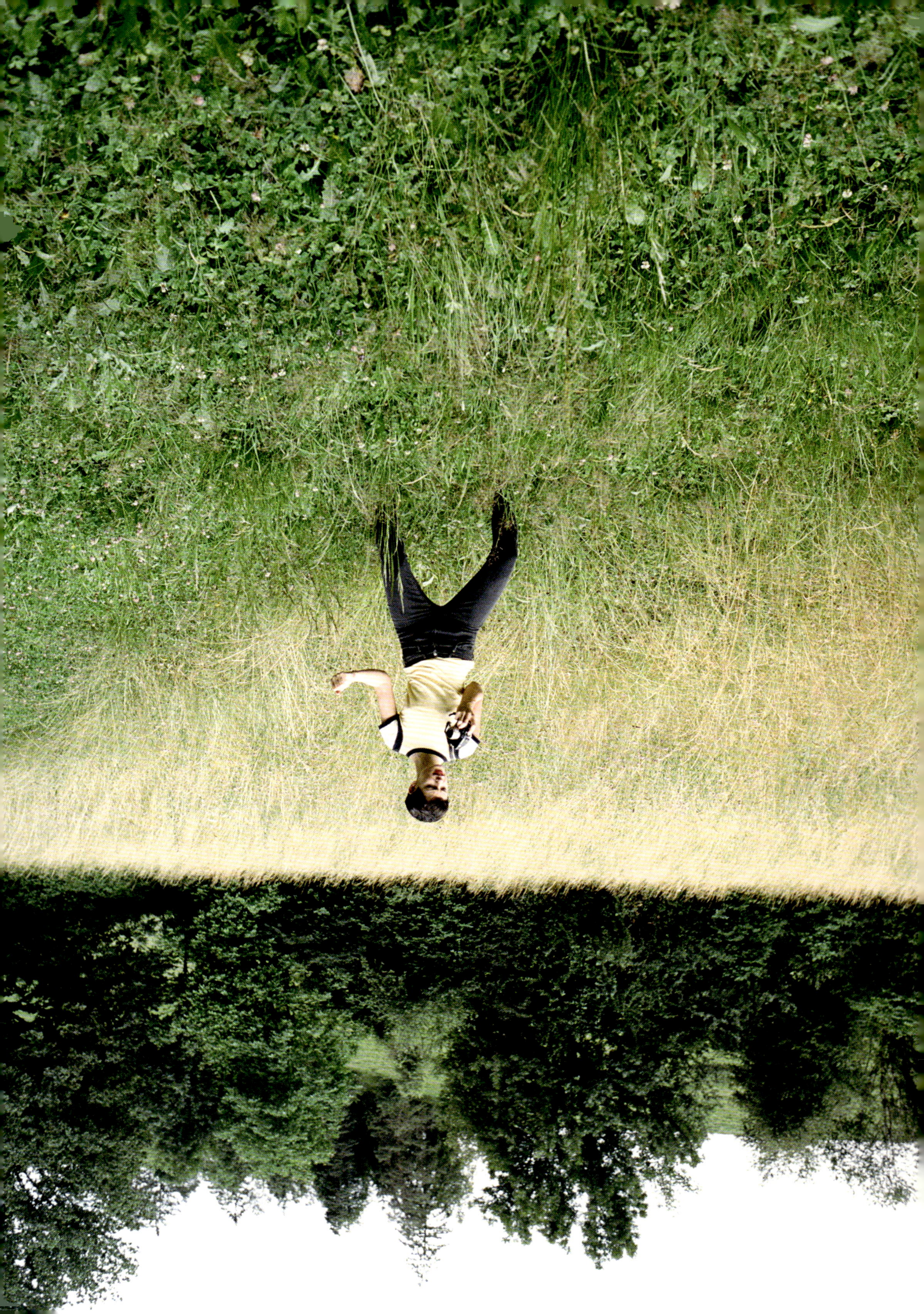

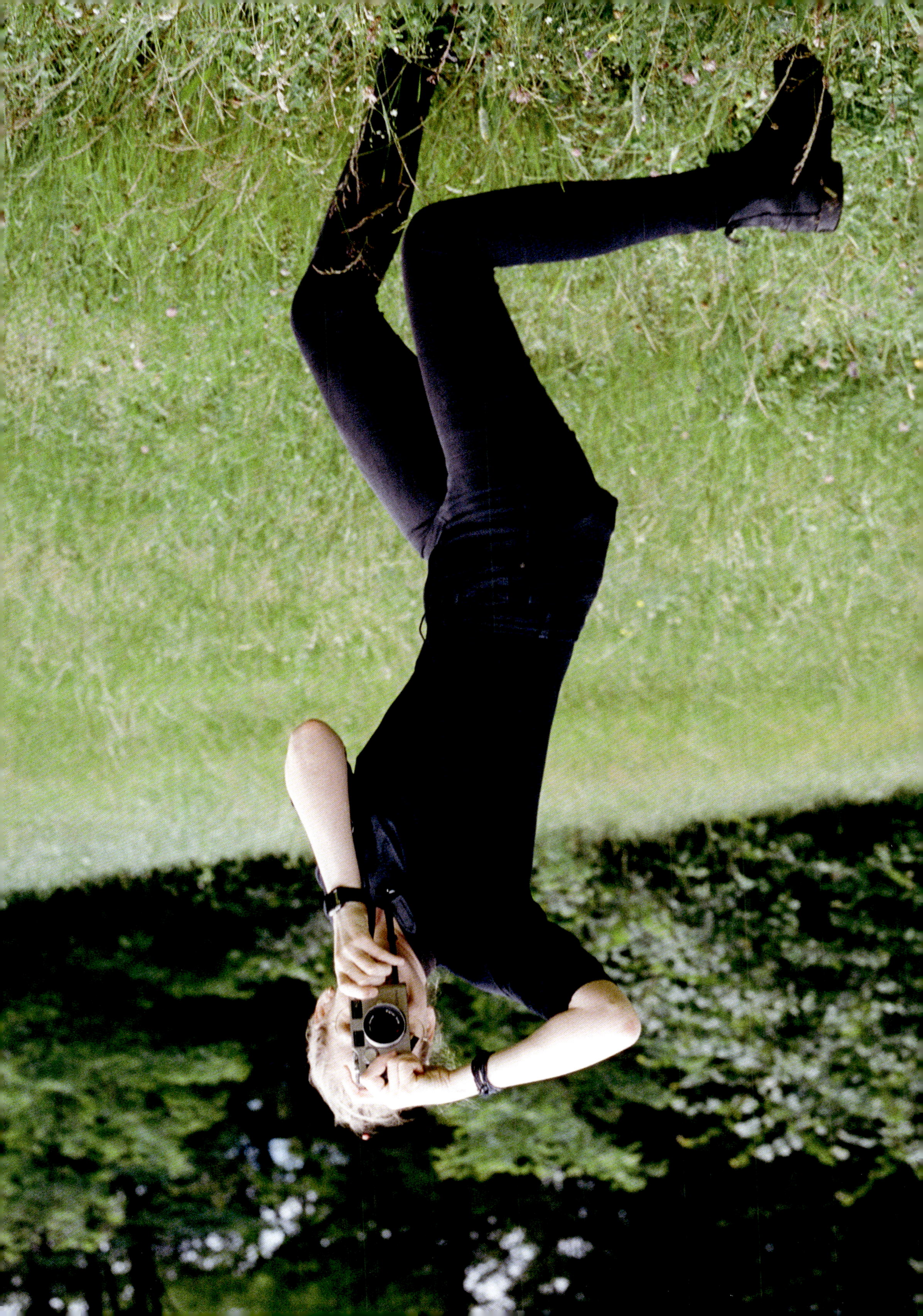

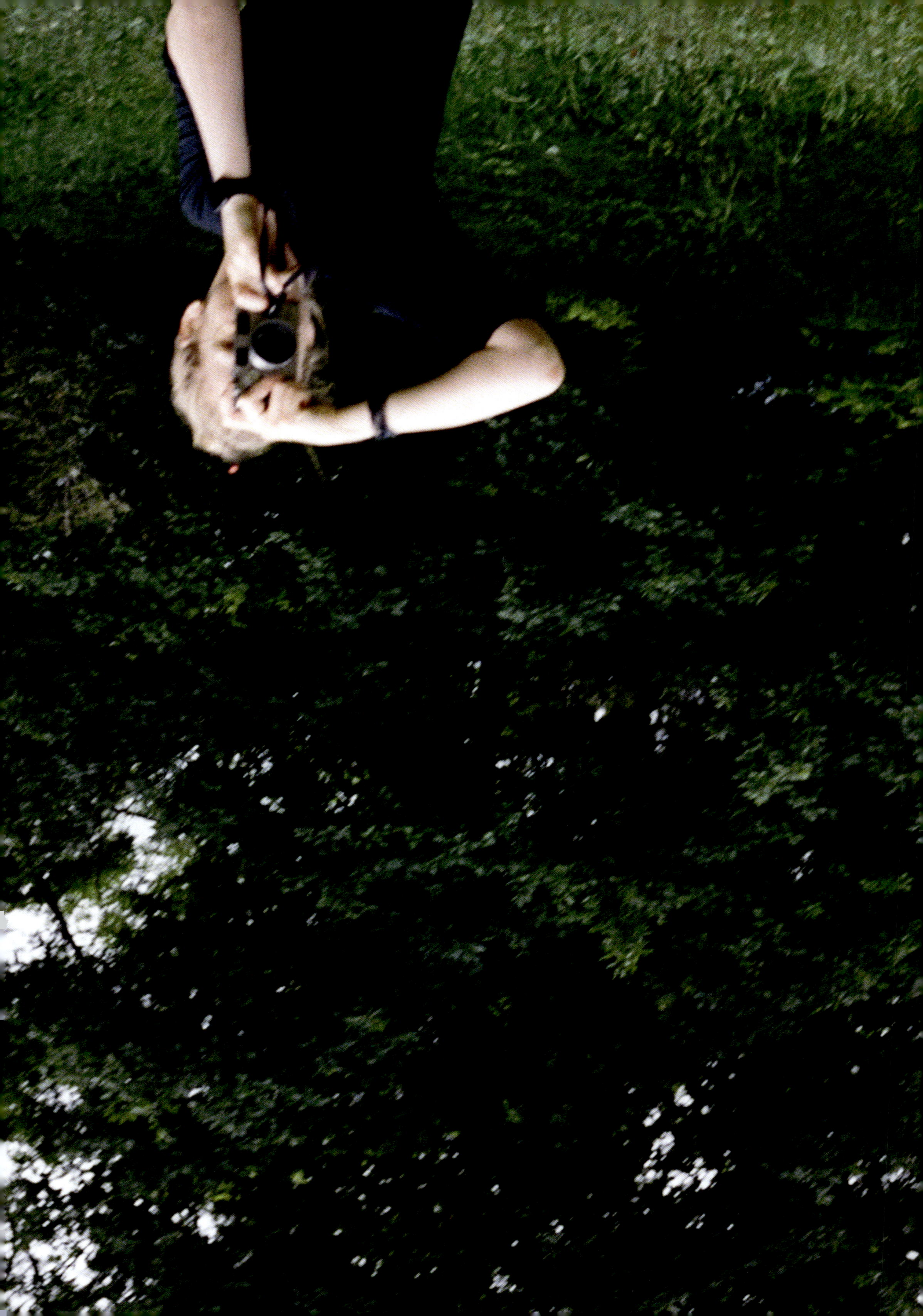

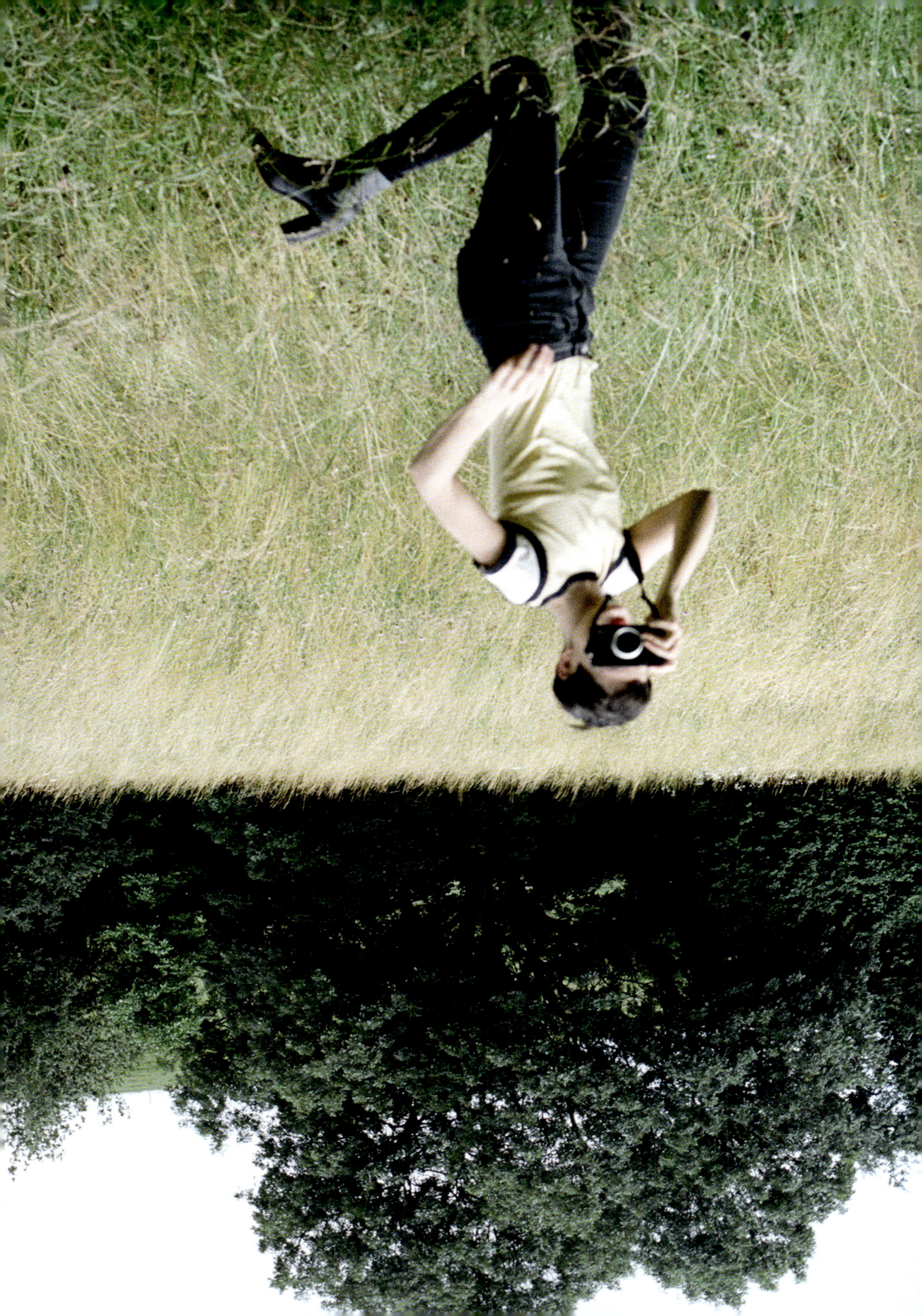

WHITE FLAG

Putz Thun

PAMPAM